CALENDAR OF THE COURT BOOKS OF THE BOROUGH OF NEW WOODSTOCK
1588-1595

Cover illustration: Oak chest, apparently medieval with later iron fittings, used to store the borough records. The records were accessible only in the presence of named keykeepers, who in 1588 were the mayor and town clerk. (WBM.82 Borough Council Orders 1580, clause 56, January 1558; *VCH Oxon*. xii. 391). The dimensions of the chest are 190cm x 45cm x 45cm.

The Oxfordshire Record Society

CALENDAR OF THE COURT BOOKS OF THE BOROUGH OF NEW WOODSTOCK 1588-1595

(WBM 78/1; including reference to Fair Copy versions in WBM 77/1 & Bodleian MS.Top.Oxon.d.47)

Edited by Royston F Taylor

VOLUME No. 63

2002

ISBN 0 902509 43 8

Produced for the Society by
Past Historic, Kings Stanley, Gloucestershire
Printed in Great Britain by MPG Books Ltd, Bodmin, Cornwall

TABLE OF CONTENTS

page

FOREWORD

This edition of the Woodstock Borough Court Book 1588-1595 is noteworthy for having its origins in weekly classes set up some years ago under the auspices of Oxford University Department for Continuing Education. Several participants decided to continue their work thereafter as the Woodstock Local History Group under the guidance of Miss Mary Hodges, who had been the classes' tutor.

The volume is the fruit of many years of dedicated labour by members of the History Group. The society is especially grateful to Mr Royston Taylor, who has undertaken the bulk of the editing work. Miss Hodges and Dr Paul Brand, FBA, have provided constant support and expert advice. The society would also like to thank Woodstock Borough Council for allowing access to its records, and the Marc Fitch Fund and West Oxfordshire District Council for generous financial support.

Oxford, June 2002

Christopher Day
General Editor, O.R.S.

EDITOR'S PREFACE

Work on this calendar started in 1996 as a follow-up to that carried out immediately before on the calendar of WBM 78/2, the Court Book of the Borough of New Woodstock 1607-14. It has therefore benefited from the studies and assistance provided on that volume.

I am deeply indebted to, and forever grateful for, the long-standing comradeship, discussions and advice unstintingly given me by my colleagues of the Woodstock Local History Group: Pat Crutch, Mary Hallissey, Mollie Moisley and Jack Shipp working together under the aegis of the Woodstock Society. Above all in this study I owe most to the inspiring tutorship and guidance of our mentor Miss Mary Hodges who has unfailingly sparked and nourished our individual interests in exploring the treasures of the Woodstock records. Grateful thanks are also due to Mary Hodges and Pat Crutch for their valiant efforts converting my typed texts and amending indexes into computer-generated typeset copy compatible with final-volume formats.

An exploratory calendaring of the first folios of WBM B77/1 had been made by Sarah Tolley in the early days of the History Group, and this gave valuable incentive to the later project.

By courtesy of the Mayor and Council, the honorary archivist for Woodstock, Madeleine Simms, made available the documents WBM B78/1 and B77/1 essential for undertaking this work. I am also grateful to the other archivists and librarians at Oxfordshire Archives, particularly to Rosemary Hamilton for help on watermarks; also to Ruby Reid Thompson, archivist of Clare Hall, Cambridge, for guidance on the recording of watermarks; and to the Bodleian Library for reference to the fair copy of Woodstock court minutes, Bodleian MS. Top. Oxon. d.47 and various text books.

I am much indebted to Dr. Paul Brand of All Souls College, Oxford, for refereeing this text and for the substantial improvements his advice has brought to it; also to Christopher Day for suggesting the work on this volume, for his overall supervision of the text, and for seeing it through the press.

LIST OF ABBREVIATIONS

Common abbreviations are used for months, towns, counties and personal names.

B	Box within Woodstock Borough Muniments
B78/2	Woodstock Borough Court Book 1607-14.
B78/2 Cal.	Ditto. Calendar. ed. RF Taylor (1996)
Baker	JH Baker, *Introduction to English Legal History,* 3rd edn. (Butterworth 1990)
Bellamy	JG Bellamy, *Criminal Law & Society in Late Medieval & Tudor England* (Gloucester, 1986)
Beresford	MW Beresford, *Economic History Review*, 2nd series, 10 (1957/8), 221-238.
Briquet	CM Briquet, *Les Filigranes, Dictionnaire Historique des Marques du Papier*, 4 vols. 1968 Jubilee Edn. (Bodl. 25837 c.19)
Brooks	CW Brooks, *Pettyfoggers & Vipers of the Commonwealth: Lower Branch of Legal Profession in Early Modern England* (Cambridge, 1986)
Chambers	*Chambers's 20th Century Dictionary* (Edinburgh,1958)
Cheney	CR Cheney, *Handbook of Dates* (Royal Historical Society, 1991)
Connor	RD Connor, *The Weights & Measures of England* (HMSO,1987)
Dalton	Michael Dalton, *The Countrey Justice* (London, 1622)
Dance	EM Dance, *Guildford Borough Records 1514-1546*, Surrey Record Society, vol.XXIV (1958)
Elton	GR Elton, *Cambridge Historical Journal,* 11 (1954), 149-167.
Emery	Frank Emery, *Oxfordshire Landscape* (London, 1974)
Everitt	A Everitt, *Agrarian History of England & Wales,* IV, *1500-1640* (Cambridge, 1967)
Gaskell	P Gaskell, *A new Introduction to Bibliography* (Winchester, 1995)
Gelling	M Gelling, *The Place-Names of Oxfordshire* (Cambridge, 1954)
Gilmore	GD Gilmore, unpublished commentaries on the Bedford Court of Pleas, Bedford Borough Records (1984)

Gleason	JH Gleason, *The JPs in England 1588-1640* (Oxford, 1969)
Gretton	M Gretton, *Oxfordshire JPs in the 17th Century*, *O.R.S.* 16 (1934)
Hallissey & Shipp	M Hallissey & J Shipp, *O.L.H.* 3 (No. 6), 1991
Harris	CG Harris, *Oxfordshire Parish Registers & Bishop's Transcripts*, 3rd edn., O.F.H.S. (Oxford 1988)
Havinden	MA Havinden, *Household & Farm Inventories in Oxfordshire 1550-1590* (HMSO,1965)
Herrup	CB Herrup, *The Common Peace* (Cambridge, 1987)
Hodges	Mary Hodges, unpublished commentary; Oxford 1998 National Illegitimacy Rates
Holderness	BA Holderness, *Agricultural History Review*, 24, pt.II (1976)
Holdsworth	WS Holdsworth, *A History of English Law*, IV (London, 1924)
Hoskins	WG Hoskins, *Agricultural History Review*, 12 (1964)
Ivamy	ERH Ivamy, *Law Dictionary*, 10th edn. (London, 1988)
Jacob	G Jacob, *A New Law Dictionary*, 10th edn. (London, 1782)
Jones	N Jones, *God and the Moneylenders* (Oxford, 1989)
Lambarde	W Lambarde, *Eirenarcha* (London, 1591)
Langbein	JH Langbein, *Prosecuting Crime in the Renaissance* (Cambridge, Mass., 1974)
Latham	RE Latham, *Revised Medieval Latin Word-list*, (London 1979)
Maitland	FW Maitland, *The forms of Action at Common Law* (Cambridge, 1968)
Milward	R Milward, *Glossary of Household, Farming & Trade Terms from Probate Inventories*, 3rd edn. (Derbyshire Record Society, 1986)
MSS. Wills	Oxon.Wills & Inventories of the Oxford Diocese (in O.R.O.)
Muldrew	C Muldrew, *The Economy of Obligation* (Basingstoke, 1998)
O.E.D.	*Oxford English Dictionary*, 2nd edn. (Oxford 1933)
O.F.H.S.	Oxfordshire Family History Society
O.L.H.	*Oxfordshire Local History*
O.R.O.	Oxfordshire Record Office

O.R.S.	*Oxfordshire Record Society*
Rogers	JE Thorold Rogers, *A History of Agriculture & Prices in England, VI, 1583-1702* (Oxford 1887)
Rodwell	Rodwell (ed.), *Historic Towns in Oxfordshire a Survey of the new County* (Oxford, 1975)
Sharpe	JA Sharpe, *Early Modern England 1550-1760* (London, 1987)
Sheppard	R Sheppard & E Newton, *The Story of Bread* (London, 1957)
Slack	P Slack, 'Books of Orders', *Trans. Royal Historical Society*, 5th series, 30 (1980)
Speed	J Speed, *The Counties of Britain – a Tudor Atlas* (London, 1988)
Stevenson	Allen Stevenson, *Briquet vol. I The Pots of Normandy*, (1966/7)
Taylor 1991	RF Taylor, *O.L.H.,* 3 (6), 1991
Taylor 1992	RF Taylor, *O.L.H.*, 3 (8), 1992
Trice-Martin	C Trice-Martin, *The Record Interpreter* (Chichester, 1982)
Underwood	D Underwood, *Revel, Riot and Rebellion 1603-1670* (London, 1985)
V.C.H.	*Victoria County History, Oxon.* xii (Oxford 1990)
Walter	J Walter, 'The Oxfordshire Rising', *Past and Present,* No.107 (1985)
WBM	Woodstock Borough Muniments
WBM B78/2	Woodstock Borough Court Book 1607-14
WBM B78/2 Cal.	Calendar of WBM B78/2 (in O.R.O. and Oxford Central Library, Westgate)
WBM B78/3	Woodstock Borough Court Book 1614-21 (in preparation)
WBM B82	Woodstock Borough Council Orders & Constitution, (1580)
WCA	M Maslen (ed.), *Woodstock Chamberlains' Accounts 1609-50;* O.R.S. 58 (1993)
Witney Courts	JL Bolton & M Maslen, *Calendar of Witney Court Books 1538-1610;* O.R.S. 54 (1985)
Wood	ES Wood, *Historical Britain* (London, 1997)
Woodstock Baptisms	Woodstock Parish Registers, Baptisms 1662-1682
Woodstock Burials	Woodstock Parish Registers, Burials 1677-1719
Wrigley & Schofield	EA Wrigley & RS Schofield, *The Population History of England 1541-1871* (London, 1981)

Wrigley et al.	EA Wrigley, RS Davies, JE Oeppen & RS Schofield, *English Population History from Family Reconstitution 1580-1837* (Cambridge, 1997)
Youings	J Youings, *Sixteenth-Century England* (Middlesex, 1984)

Additional sources used in confirming Portmoot litigants and their provenance:

Barratt — DM Barratt, *Diocese & Archdeaconry of Oxford Probate Records 1516-1732*, British Record Society 1981

Bladon Parish Registers 1545-1700

Howard-Drake — J Howard-Drake, *Calendars of Oxford Church Court Depositions 1542-1596* (Oxford 1991-98)

International Genealogical Index (IGI) – Oxfordshire, 1988

Oxfordshire Marriage Index 1538-1837 (in O.R.O.)

Wootton Parish Registers 1546-1700

INTRODUCTION CONTENTS

INTRODUCTION

Woodstock has never ranked amongst the larger towns of Oxfordshire, but as a former royal borough it was distinguished in being the seat of courts of record including its civil court, the Portmoot. In this respect the town belonged to a select group, along with Oxford and Banbury, in having probably the only such recognised courts among Oxfordshire boroughs in the late 16th century. Moreover the borough has the good fortune of possessing some record of its court proceedings stretching from the 13th century to recent times. More particularly over the period 1581 to 1847 there are extensive court books of various dates for the portmoot and frankpledge courts and the borough sessions court.[1]

Court Documents

For the present calendar three manuscript volumes of minutes have been drawn upon. The first, WBM B78/1, is a contemporaneous minute book of the borough Portmoot court covering the period 7 October 1588 to 22 December 1595. It has been edited to produce almost all of this calendar, and is referred to as B78/1. The second volume, WBM B77/1, contains a 'Fair Copy' of these Portmoot proceedings over the first two-thirds of the above period; it is referred to as B77/1. The third volume, Bodleian MS. Top. Oxon. d.47 (referred to hereafter as 'd.47'), also contains a 'Fair Copy' covering most of the remaining third of the period. The latter two volumes have been used to supplement the material from the first one where required. Manuscripts B78/1 and B77/1 are in the care of Oxfordshire Record Office archives through whom they may be consulted. Manuscript d.47 is available to readers of the Bodleian Library.

WBM B78/1

In book B78/1, from the general cast of the drafting and writing, with occasional entries curtailed or abandoned, and the change of handwriting with the change of town-clerk, it is clear these are minutes made at the time of the courts. The Portmoot proceedings are recorded, in the main, in abbreviated law-Latin with memoranda in English in some cases of witness examination before juries, conveyances and arbitration decisions. Apprenticeships and corporation business such as assize of bread and ale and victualler licensing are largely in English with occasional titling in Latin.

1 Rodwell, 200; Hallisey and Shipp, 240.

Nevertheless fair copies B77/1 & d.47 do carry some significant material not now present in B78/1.

(i) The Portmoot meetings for 14th & 28th June 1591 are absent from B78/1 apparently on a sheet now removed, and the accounts are taken from B77/1.

(ii) Most of a sheet originally between B78/1, f.6v and f.7r is missing, as are parts of ff.7r & 8r. The entries for the Portmoots 21 April and 5 May 1589 are taken from B77/1.

(iii) Two proclamations of the Rayer/Norwood conveyance B78/1, f.118r & f.123r are given in far more detail in d.47.

(iv) Though no officers are listed for Portmoot 2 December 1594 in B78/1, they are in d.47.

This suggests that when fair copies B77/1 and d.47 were made some complementary papers on actions were available in addition to those preserved in B78/1.[2]

In addition to the Portmoot proceedings B78/1 contains records of six assizes of bread and ale, and single entries on each for: flesh in Lent, a breach of the assize by a baker, an order for grain dearth survey, a licensing of victuallers, recognisances for victualler and for butcher licences, a mayoral election, shop rental, child maintenance, and an apprenticeship.

The first part of the text is in the hand of Thomas Duffild the town-clerk, who about this time had been ordered to bring in the mayor's book 'fair written' each year at Michaelmas; and to keep the records in the town hall in a chest under two keys, one held by the mayor.[3] From March 1594 the handwriting changes to that of the new town-clerk, Edulphe Dingley.

This manuscript volume is written on paper of uniform size 20cm. by 14cm. in parchment wraps. The folios now numbered to 165 are mainly in good condition (see exceptions above) and bound to a thickness of about 3cm. The rear cover is sewn on to double thickness, and the spine bears a leather tab at the top to secure the binding but appears to have lost a corresponding tab at the bottom. There is no titling on the cover. This is a quarto book made up of pairs of sheets each cut in half before folding to make gatherings of 8 leaves, 16 pages. Watermarking on the pages has horizontal chain lines about 20mm. apart and the tranchefiles at the tops of pages 12mm. apart. There are no countermarks and parts of the watermark emblem show on half of the pages – see Fig.1A. The tracings of Fig.1 give a typical example from each book of its mark which moves and changes to some degree with the wear, tear and repair of usage.[4]

2 Dance, xxxii

3 WBM 82, clause 56

4 Gaskell, 106

Figure 1: Watermarks in 16/17th C. Portmoot Court Books

Fig.1A

Chain-lines 22 mm apart
B78/1 ff.26/7
Pages 20 x 14 cm
marks across
mid-spine
1588/95 records

Fig.1B

B77/1 f.84
Pages 30 x 20cm
marks centre page
1594/5 records
Fair copy B78/1

Fig.1C

Bodl.MS.Top.Oxon. D.47
f.37
Pages 30 x 20 cm
marks centre page
Fair copy B78/1

3 cm

Fig. 1 D

B78/2 ff.55/56
Pages 20 x 14cm
marks across mid-spine
1607-14 records

Fig. 1E

B78/3 ff.18/19
Pages 20 x 15 cm
marks across mid-spine
1614-22 records

The watermark has been identified by Briquet and by Stevenson as marking one of a series of French "Pot" papers made in Normandy in the 16th & 17th centuries for the English market. The mark bears a crown on top of the 'pot' surmounted by fleurons on the jewels. There is a horizontal band across the belly of the pot bearing the initials 'R A', above which is another 'bande composee' divided by four vertical lines: the bearings of the city of Evreux. This latter feature conforms to paper produced in the second half of the 16th century.[5]

The B78/1 mark is one of a family of similar types also found on the papers of B78/2, B78/3, B77/1 and d.47; which are respectively the Portmoot records for 1607-14, for 1614-21, and the books described here B77/1 and d.47. See Figure l. Such Norman paper was that commonly used in English books in the 16th and 17th centuries, with the paper export trade largely carried out by the Dutch.[6]

In contrast to B78/1 which is filled with a sequence of Portmoot proceedings, both of the books B77/1 and Bodl. MS. Top. Oxon. d.47 contain several distinct items spaced out on their pages, bearing various dates and written at various times.

WBM B77/1

The main item in B77/1 is a 'Fair Copy' of the Portmoot proceedings covered by the first two-thirds of the contents of B78/1, probably made by Anthony Noble, local scribe and curate, who died in 1617. This is set out on ff.1r to 61r. The pages of this volume are 30cm. by 20cm. now numbered to 90 folios. They are bound in a parchment cover bearing the written title "Portmoot Court from the 7th October ani 30th of Queen Eliz. to the 17th of September inclusively in the 35th of the said Queene." This is a folio volume made up of gatherings of 8 leaves, two leaves to the sheet, bearing vertical chain-lines about 22mm. apart and tranchefiles about 13mm. apart. There are no countermarks and half of the leaves bear in their centres the typical Normandy-pot watermark shown in Fig.1B.[7]

Overall the contents of this book are as follows:

(i) First two folios unnumbered. On verso of second folio is signature 'G.George Ryves Jun., January 17th 1675/6', together with separated names 'Margaret Susanna Mary R Ryves' all associated with the Ryves family. It is not altogether clear that this was the George Ryves, town clerk, buried 1677 as 'senior'.[8]

5 Briquet IV 'POT' Figs 12740-12801; Stevenson, 34.
6 Stevenson, 34.
7 Gaskell, 83
8 Woodstock Parish Registers; *VCH Oxon,* xii. 382.

(ii) Numbered folios 1r-61r. 'Fair Copy' sequence of Portmoot Court 7 Oct. 1588 to 17 Sept. 1593. In general this text follows that of B78/1 rather closely; the commonest changes tend to be in details of names. The handwriting is the same as that of the Portmoot 'Fair Copy' in d.47; it appears to match that of scribe Anthony Noble in the wills of Phillip Barnesdalle 1584, Roger Norwood 1592, Robert Banting 1598, and of himself in 1613. Although differences in the hands do exist, that of the 'Fair Copy' seems to lie within the range of Noble's hands over these years. If he was the scribe this copy will date somewhere between 1595 and 1617.[9]

Folios 61v to 77v are blank.

The entries in the rest of the book work with the pages turned from top to bottom, and progressing from the back of the book towards the front. Proceeding from the back of the book, the items are:

Folios 90v & 90r are blank.

(iii) Folios 89v-87r. Full folios of notes pertaining to some 100 potential and actual Portmoot actions, from 6 December 1594 to 16 December (1595, deduced). The dates given are not Court days, some anticipate Portmoot dates others follow them; no progress on actions is given. Thus these notes are contemporaneous with the courts and the handwriting does match that of town clerk Edulphe Dingley in B78/1. Since these records are directly relevant to that in B78/1 details of the contents are given in Appendix 2.

Folios 87v-81r are blank.

(iv) Folios 80v-78v. A precisely scribed 'Fair Copy' account of a debt/detinue action for £85, from Portmoot 26 Oct.1584, referring to an action of 20 Aug.1582, by Thomas Prestman against William Skelton, lately mayor. This extended account clearly derives from papers other than Portmoot minutes. The litigation does not appear to be directly connected with the political court quarrels between Skelton and George Whitton at this time. From its placing within the book the entry is provisionally dated as several years after the court business, probably after 1595.[10]

Folios 78r-61v blank.

The placings of the items within the book suggest the sequence of use was as follows:

Firstly the contemporary 1594/5 Portmoot notes by Dingley on ff.89-87r, at what was then the front of the book. Secondly the Portmoot 'Fair Copy' Oct.1588-Sept.1593 was entered at the opposite end of the book turned top to bottom, and the titling was put on the cover that end. Anticipating that the rest of this 'Fair Copy' (in the event 67 folio sides) might not fit within the

[9] MS.Wills Oxon, 3/4/40, 47/2/2 & 31/1/66; MS.WillsOxon. c.22, f.254.

[10] *VCH Oxon.* xii. 374.

remaining space the scribe continued the text in d.47. Subsequently a scribe entered his 'Fair Copy' of the 1584 Portmoot action Prestman vs. Skelton in the middle of this gap between f.6lv and f.86v.

Bodleian MS. Top. Oxon. d.47

Bodleian MS. Top. Oxon. d.47 consists of 48 numbered folios of paper 30cm. by 20cm. bound in a parchment cover with the written title "Portmouth Court from the first of October in the 35th year of Queene Elizabeth to the eighth of December in the 38th year of the S--- Queene". As the title indicates the main item of contents is a 'Fair Copy' of most of the last third of the proceedings in B78/1, following on directly from that in B77/1, and in the same hand.

This also is a folio book made up of gatherings of leaves, two to the manufactured sheet, bearing vertical chain lines about 21mm. apart and tranchefiles about 12mm. apart. As now constituted the book has varied gatherings of between 6 and 10 leaves, and there are signs that a number of sheets, leaves and parts of them have been removed. Such removals are not manifest from the written contents of the book. In the centre of half its leaves is the Normandy-pot watermark exemplified in Fig. 1C; there are no countermarks.[11] The initials "PO" have been used as the mark of Pierre Ollivier, a paper-maker of Pont-Authou, Normandy. The greater height of this pot (68mm.) suggests this paper may be of a later date than that in B77/1.[12]

Overall the contents of this book are as follows:

(i) ff.1-2v. End jottings, including the signature of George Ryves.

(ii) ff.3r-36v. Portmoot Court 1 October 1593 - 8 December 1595. As noted for B77/1, the text in the main follows that of B78/1 rather closely, but here with the following major omissions:

(a) from 16 December 1594 onwards there are numerous omissions of the last four to twelve case entries in a court. There are 150 actions/entries in B78/1 (30% of the total) that are omitted between B77/1 and d.47.

(b) bread and ale assize Jan. 1595.

(c) witness examinations: **357**, **397**, **447**.

(d) conveyance **384**.

(e) many examples of suitors' provenances.

(iii) f.37r. Five-line memo.of 1673 - crossed out.

(iv) f.37v-f.42r blank.

(v) f.42v-f.47v. Written from back of book to front, and inverted on the page: "List of all the Country Bushels 1671, in time of Thomas Sparrow, mayor, by George Ryves, town clerk".

[11] Gaskell, 83.

[12] Stevenson, 34.

Court Officers

Court officers over this period are listed in Appendix 1. As mentioned above the court minutes were recorded by the town clerk who at the start of this period was Thomas Duffild and from March 1594 was succeeded by Edulphe Dingley. Duffild died soon after retirement; a number of local wills were drafted by him including those of Roger Norwood and his own. Dingley subsequently, in 1598, complained of wrongful dismissal and forcible ejection from the town clerk's house by the mayor and was disfranchised. During the 1580's the clerk was put in seniority among the common councillors whereas in the earlier l6th century and the l7th he was listed with the aldermen.

In the manner of similar office-holders elsewhere, these men and their successors such as Edmund Hiorne, may have trained in law at an Inn of Chancery, though direct evidence is lacking. The only information we have on these clerks' pay concerns fees for entering apprenticeships (12d), foreigners' freedom (4d) and marriage of freemen's widows (12d); whereas for Hiorne it is also known he had a salary of 45s a year.[13]

On matters of dispute, or of an exceptional nature, expert advice came from the recorder of the borough. The earliest known holder was James Bury in 1551, and at this time he was Sir Lawrence Tanfield of Burford who was M.P. for Woodstock from 1584 and known to be recorder by 1598. There is no mention of the recorder in these minutes, though he or his deputy were supposed to form a quorum with the mayor for the court of record, in addition to attending the borough court of sessions and the leet.[14] As in minute book B78/2 covering 1607-14 there is no record here of the high steward in court proceedings.

The borough commonalty was based on a common council, fixed in 1580 at twenty members, together with four or five aldermen and some sixty other freemen. Over the seven years of Portmoot the numbers of such litigants were slightly more; so the proportion of these inhabitants using the court at least once in the period is very high. A smaller population is quoted for 1581 when a list of only 58 freeman names including councillors is given.[15] This council, governing the borough, largely came at this time from leading businessmen and other notables of the town. The mayor and aldermen were justices of the peace within the borough by virtue of their office, and their courts of record and other legal functions were usually held before the mayor.[16] Under the 1580 borough constitution (WBM B82) the mayor must have served as chamberlain, and he was elected annually from the aldermen but was usually re-elected for a

[13] MS.Wills Oxon 189:57 (1594) ; MS.Wills Oxon. c.22, 254; P. Brand, personal communication 1998; Brooks, 151-65; *WCA*, xv; WBM B82, f.l4v; WBM B82, ff.13&15; *WCA*, xviii.

[14] WBM B83/4; *Rep.Com.Mun.Corpns,* H.C.116, App.I, p.141 (1835),xxiii.

[15] WBM B82, f.4; *VCH Oxon.* xii. 377.

[16] Dalton, 6.

second year. These elections were on the Monday before St. Matthew's Day (21 Sept.) and office was assumed at Michaelmas (29 Sept.); examples are given in **151** & **459** with election by majority of commonalty of freemen. Finish of the mayoral year is noted on f.15v of B77/1 & f.4lv of B78/1.

The sergeant-at-the-mace kept his office for life (**151**) although he was elected annually in September. In the Portmoot he dealt with the execution of writs, and was sometimes noted as intermediary in conveyances "according to the custom of the borough". His duties included charge of the town prison used for detention in both civil and criminal cases. Henry Redgate, the holder at this time also acted as attorney on occasion though he is recorded as making his mark rather than his signature in 1600.

Of the other officers of the Portmoot, the aldermen, five in number, were elected for life; the chamberlains were elected at their annual audit, and the rest, constables, tithingmen and ale-tasters, at view of frankpledge.

Provision of a leather fire-bucket each at their election to freemen, as required by the Borough Orders of 1580, is noted for Michael Nurse and Thomas Colgrave (**184**).[17]

Portmoot Court

New Woodstock was founded in the 12th century and by the 13th the borough court or portmoot, meeting on Mondays, was frequently recorded. The town was taxed as a borough in the early 14th century and from 1338 onwards the office of mayor was regularly noted. Criminal jurisdiction seems to have been exercised by 1402. In 1453 the borough's charter, based closely on that of New Windsor, granted wide jurisdiction to the mayor and commonalty thereby confirming much that had been long enjoyed. About this time the term Portmoot was applied more specifically to the regular sessions of the borough court, held fortnightly on Mondays. Most recorded business before the 1580's dealt with land transfers and the document by that date was usually called a final concord.

Actions initiated by writ of right were explicitly recorded from the early 16th century though they had long been in use, and by charter the court had return of writs. In 1580 it was agreed that actions between freemen for less than 5s. should be settled out of court by the mayor or any alderman (WBM B82). Also freemen were given two court session days longer than any foreigner to answer an action in the Portmoot. Whereas here in B78/1 there are few examples of these privilege days being invoked (**116**, **290** & **173** by a widow), twenty years later in B78/2 twenty-nine freemen used them over 48 actions. These regulations also formalized the money to be paid to the mayor's private profit: he would no longer handle profits from all the courts in the borough; instead he would receive an annual fee of £10 and retain fees from the Portmoot and from

[17] WBM B82, clause 17.

licences, recognisances, and warrants granted by him, but would still pay the fee farm together with charges for sessions and lawday dinners.[18]

Overall the Portmoot was called fairly regularly on Mondays at fortnightly intervals over these seven years: but there were six occasions when the interval was 1 week, twenty times an interval of 3 weeks, ten times a 4-week interval, five times a 5-week break, once a 6-week break, and twice a 7-week interval. The timing of meetings is sometimes influenced by the number of suits in the following court. And thus some of these longer intervals occur in proximity to one another over periods of less business: Dec.1589-Mar.1590; Aug.-Sept. 1590: Dec.1590-Mar. 1591; Jan.-May 1592; April-May 1593; Feb.-May 1594; Jan.-Feb. 1595; May-June 1595.

Although court meetings were fewer per year than in 1607-14 the average number of cases dealt with per year were similar in both periods. However there was a marked change in the recording of usage during this earlier period when the new town clerk took over. (see below).

There were six occasions when the date recorded for the court did not correspond to a Monday; these were:

24 Sept. 1589 - a Wednesday; 2 Oct.1589 - a Thursday
20 Dec. 1590 - a Sunday; 26 April 1593 - a Thursday
18 Sept. 1593 - a Tuesday, extension to Monday's business
12 Jan. 1594 - a Saturday, extension to Monday 7 Jan.

These non-Monday meeting dates are given in both B78/1 and the fair-copy versions. According to a note the court on 2 October 1589 was intended to be on the previous day, a Wednesday. The Sunday court paralleled four such sittings in 1612-17 (B78/2 and /3). The first two dates are for successive courts with an 8-day gap, the last held by mayor John Pyman and he may have been clearing his back-log; contents of the proceedings offer no clue for not being on a Monday. The 20 December 1590 session fell on the fourth Sunday of Advent, was followed by a 36-day gap, and the proceedings again provide no help. The meeting of 26 April 1593 came after a 31-day gap and was followed by a 32-day one, with only four entries plus five 'continuations' dealt with; the complement of supporting officers was very variable at this time. The last two dates were both drafted as simple continuations of their Monday Portmoots, but with no hint in their extent, content, or context as to their need.

Sittings of both the Portmoot and other borough courts seem to have been held regularly in the Guildhall at this time and this location was quite often identified in the proceedings.

As a borough court of record the Portmoot employed common law process: actions generally started with a plaint entered in a court book (see p.xxii & Appendix 2), rather than by writ; followed by the usual methods for obtaining

[18] WBM B82, clauses 4-6,16,40.

attendance in court and then the formal stages of pleading in joining the issue.[19]

Usage of Actions

In the seven years covered by this court-book a total of 489 Portmoot actions were recorded, comprising:

- 40% for debt, and account (2%);
- 31% for trespass and trespass on the case (20%);
- 6% for *Assumpsit;*
- 6% for conveyance, rental, Dower, and Ejectment;
- 6% for *Qui Tam*;
- 2% for detinue and trover;
- 1% "other" actions; including one trust obligation and one general controversy;
- 8% unspecified.

Over the period 1589-95 there was a sharp increase in the recorded number of actions per year for the last two years from the time Edulphe Dingley took over as clerk of court. From 1589-93 the average rate was 47 suits, which jumped to 115 suits/yr. for the last two years; this change arose from the large increase in single-entry plaints from around 13 to around 70 a year.

This may be compared to the period 1608-13 under clerk Edmund Hiorne where recorded usage was relatively steady at about 70 suits a year of which 20 were single-entry plaints.

Muldrew has noted the widely differing forms of record-keeping in various borough courts and the variations in the quoted proportions of plaints to actions processed. Dingley's records of Appendix 2 are equivalent to part of a plaint book (a rare surviving example of such), and in B78/1 he has apparently included a notably higher proportion of plaints not proceeding to declaration and beyond than did Duffild and Hiorne. Nevertheless numbers of his single-entry plaints are noted as 'Discharged'.

In fair copies B77/1 and more particularly Bodl.d.47 (which covers Dingley's period) far more single-entry plaints have been omitted; and attention has been drawn to the habit of clerks recording earlier courts of omitting suits which had been resolved before declaration, in order to save space and time.[20]

Progress and outcome of Actions

The average number of entries on the progress of each case is between three and four; with over two-fifths of cases having just a single entry, and only an eighth having more than six entries. Just over a tenth of all cases record an immediate discharge at the first entry, and in those examples where the

[19] WBM B78/2 Calendar, vii; Gilmore, *passim*; Muldrew, 205.

[20] WBM B78/2 Calendar; Muldrew, 335, 337.

recorded finish is the plaintiff's declaration some at least may have been settled out of court directly after being registered there. In contrast to such brevity a few actions proceeded for twenty or so entries followed by referral to the Westminster courts (**12**, **116**, **149** & **299**), satisfaction of debt (**290**), execution of action granted (**242**), or merely a continuance (**251**).

About 40% of all suits were eventually discharged or satisfied. For all the other cases not so finished their final entries fall into the following categories of progress:

Progress: final entry	Proportion of all actions
Plaintiff declaration	30% (3% suitors on bail)
Plaintiff/defendant defaults	4%
Arbitration/Imparlance/Compounding	3%
Referred toWestminster/Return	3%
'Continues'	10%
Jury called	2%
Judgment passed, execution issued, *scire facias* & renewals issued	8%
	60%

Thus 30% of actions did not proceed beyond the plaintiff's declaration and 10% "continued" unresolved; 10% ended on a default or arbitration/imparlance or referral to the Westminster courts; while the remaining 10% finished at a stage beyond calling a jury, up to and including renewals of *scire facias* on the execution of judgment.

Pledges

In the earlier part of this court-book names of sureties are often quoted as a pair of pledges to prosecute and a pair of pledges that the defendant would respond. The first pair were supposed to prevent vexatious actions by undertaking that the plaintiff would pursue his claim, but there was little necessity for them. The latter pair ensured the defendant did all that was required of him.[21] In contrast to this book that for the 1607-14 Portmoot bears little direct reference to such pledges, though in the execution of judgments the names of defendants' sureties sometimes suddenly appear in order to bear the costs.

About 3% of actions ended going to arbitration, imparlance or compounding a settlement. There were over four times as many arbitrations here as in 1607-14, and although some went before borough aldermen many were directed to outside arbitrators and umpires. Imparlance was requested in thirty-four suits (twice as often as in 1607-14) and its usage had surges of popularity; for example in March & May 1591, May 1592, November 1593,

[21] Gilmore, 9.

July 1594, and May 1595. Compounding was used in the settlement of *Qui Tam* actions for determining the amount of the monetary penalty to be paid via the borough chamberlains to the Queen.

Wager of law

Whereas there was just a single case of wager of law in this period 1588-95 (**114**), there were eleven cases in 1607-14 and ten cases in 1614-21. This seems an anachronistic change of procedure since its usage was in marked decline in the central courts over this time, and Slade's Case in 1602 is said to have resulted in its complete replacement by jury trial. In the Witney Borough Court (not one of record) over the period 1538-1610 wager was used in 1565, 1568, 1578 & 1598 but not after that. Nevertheless in the Bedford Borough Court two cases came as late as 1636, with the latest attempt to use the procedure in 1667. Perhaps the Portmoot procedure in the time of Edmund Hiorne and his advising Recorders was swayed by consideration of the private nature of local contracts such as debt and detinue between two parties, typically characterised by lack of witness and evidence.[22]

The mayor and commonalty took action against individuals on two occasions; in January 1593 for trespass on the case against George Clay (**217**); and at the end of December 1595 for trespass, against the goods of John Browne (**495**). In neither case are there any details, or any development of the action.

Provenance of Portmoot Litigants

The provenance of litigants in Portmoot actions was broadly as follows: in a fifth of actions both suitors were borough inhabitants, in a slightly higher proportion the plaintiff was a borough man versus an outsider; just under a sixth of cases had outsider plaintiff versus borough defendant, and in the remaining two-fifths of suits both parties were outsiders.

Provenance of litigants	Proportion of actions
Borough inhabitants pl. & def.	21%
Borough pl. v Outsider def.	22%
Outsider pl. v Borough def.	15%
Outsider pl. & def.	42%
	100%

Overall 38% of litigants were from the borough, and by 1607-14 this had fallen to 30%.[23]

The proportion of women in suits was low: in total less than 5% of all litigants; and those without male partners in suits made up only 3½%. Their

22 WBM B78/3; Baker, 394/5; *Witney Courts*, 38, 47, 85, 155; Gilmore, 34, 36; Maitland, 63.

23 WBM B78/2 Calendar, Introduction.

proportion of all plaintiffs was 4%, compared to 9% in King's Lynn borough court in the 1680's. Twenty years later the proportions of women in Portmoot actions had risen appreciably to nearly 7% of all litigants and to over 6% of plaintiffs.[24] (see also under 'Dower').

(i) Borough Inhabitants

Named aldermen averaged just over one Portmoot suit per year each, whilst named freemen averaged just over one suit each every two years. The average for all borough households was 0.43 suits a year. This compares on the one hand with over one suit/yr. initiated per household for large towns at this time; and on the other hand with the countrywide average of 0.25 suits per household at the present day.[25]

The total number of borough freemen, including councillors and aldermen, using the court in this period was seventy-five, with an average of some four actions each, and appearing as plaintiff three times for every two as defendant. They constituted 14% of the individuals using the court and provided 32% of the suitors; combined with the Woodstock non-freemen (less readily identified and enumerated) they made up 22% of individual users.

As a body the freemen were obliged to use the court against one another, and no doubt found it convenient and more speedy for local business compared with more central courts. Just over half these freeman suitors (42) engaged in 52 actions against fellow freemen in this way.[26]

All eight borough aldermen listed in these minutes engaged in Portmoot litigation, for an average of eight actions each, acting as plaintiff some three times for every time as defendant. Individual participation ranged from:

William Medcalf 18 actions;
William Ryley 14 actions, including pl.for £25, & def.for £20;
William Skelton 12 actions, including *assumpsit* def. for £200;
Thomas Browne 12 actions, of which 9 were against Woodstock men; one for £11, another for £5;
down to 3 actions by John Pyman and 1 action against John Williams.

Twenty-eight borough councillors are mentioned in B78/1 of whom twenty-five engaged in actions here at an average of four actions each. They were plaintiffs more often than defendants in the ratio 3:2. Those most using the court were, in descending order:

Henry Fletcher in 11 suits, seven against borough inhabitants, plaintiff in eight, one for £22;
John Phillips pl. in 10 suits;
Nicholas Tailor pl. in 2 out of 10 suits;

24 Muldrew, 246.
25 Muldrew, 227, 236.
26 WBM B83, 111.

William Ball pl. in 9 suits, all against Woodstock non-freemen;
Ralph Bradshaw pl. in 8 of 9 suits;
John Taylor pl. in 5 of 9 suits;
Francis Collingwood pl. in 2 of 7 suits;
Roger Norwood pl. in 5 of 7 suits, leaving £160 in trust on death;
Henry Redgate pl. in 7 suits, 3 of them leases;
Thomas Blythe pl. in 4 of 6 suits, all versus Woodstock aldermen or councillors;
Richard Meade pl. in 3 of 5 suits, including one for £5;
Thomas Bradshawe pl. in 2 of 4 suits;
Humphrey James pl. in 1 of 4 suits, a defendant for £25;
Robert Banting pl. in 1 of 3 suits;
and John Raunson defendant in 3 suits.

Henry Redgate and Humphrey James in the above list were regular attorneys in the court but others so acting had few personal suits, for example: Thomas Cave one; Nathaniel Sharpe nil; Richard Wright one; Edulphe Dingley two, plaintiff for £4.

All but four of the forty-six non-councillor freemen identified in these minutes partook in Portmoot actions, and these litigants averaged 3-4 suits each, divided equally between plaintiffs and defendants overall. Their usage varied widely, downwards from:

butcher John Coles in 30 suits, pl. in 12; debtor for sums of £14, £5:7s, £5;
James Dissell bringing 14 *Qui Tam* actions plus 2 others; with two informations worth £18 each and one on hides worth £10;
George Fones pl. in 7 of 9 suits;
Thomas Paynter def. in 5 of 6 suits;
Hugh Hamond in 5 suits;
John Heath pl. in 2 of 5 suits, one for £5:7s.;
John Bruce def. in 3 of 4 suits;
John Button pl. in 2 of 4 suits;
Robert Winter defendant in 4 suits.
John Batt, Richard Brown, Henry Johnson, John Pulchroe, John Wells, Willm Rathbone, Richard Smyth, & John Willis each partook in 3 actions.
Michael Glover's only suit was as debtor to alderman Thomas Browne for £10 plus £1 charges.

Forty-three non-freeman borough inhabitants are identified as parties in the Portmoot actions here. Since the 1607-14 minutes, which include census lists, show only a third of non-freeman house-heads using the court a similar fraction may apply here.[27] These litigants averaged about 1½ actions each in a ratio of two defendants for every claimant in their number.

[27] WBM B78/2 Calendar, Introduction.

In terms of usage:

butcher Richard Coles heads the list, as defendant in 27 actions;

followed by John Brown, pl. in 4 of 7 suits, but defendant on £27 claimed by Robert Symons of Hensington;

Richard Pyman pl. in 4 actions vs. Rob. Symons, in total of 5 suits;

widow Magdalen Bruce, clerk Anthony Noble and Benedict Norwood each in 4 suits;

each in 3 suits: Ann Bailies as landlord and John Tomlyns as tenant in conveyances; and also John Price.

In their sole actions widow Mary Riley def. was charged on £28 versus Richard Ayres of Hensington; and Edward Robinson as debtor for £16 to Evan Hollway of Water Eaton.

As a whole, inhabitants of the borough were claimants 1.2 times as often as they were defendants.

(ii) Borough - Neighbours

Certain people living in Old Woodstock and in Hensington were intimate neighbours of the borough and took part in much of its activities so, although this relationship did not apply to all their co-habitants, people of Wootton and Bladon parishes have been separately noted here.

Thirty-nine people of these parishes have been identified in Portmoot actions (largely using Bladon & Wootton parish registers), averaging just under two actions each and slightly more often defendant than plaintiff. The main litigants in the court were:

Robert Symons of Hensington in 11 suits, all versus borough people, one for £27, defendant in 8;

John Gregory of Hordley pl. in 3 suits (one for £100) of 5 versus borough inhabitants;

Richard and Elizabeth Kent of Wootton; 5 suits; defendants in 4, one was for detinue of rents worth £200, and another for a debt of £22;

Hercules Nashe of Wootton def. in 5 suits, all brought by borough men;

John and Elizabeth Phillips of Wootton defendants in 5 suits;

John Scott of Wootton pl. in 4 of 5 suits, three for trespass by slander by Alice Pickiver;

Thomas Symons of Bladon 4 suits;

Each with 3 suits: Thomas Osborne of Hensington and William Heynes of Bladon (one for £10);

William Jauncey of Bladon in a single action was plaintiff for £300; as was Richard Ayres of Hensington for £28.

(iii) Outsiders

Of the 390 litigants accounted as coming from outside New Woodstock borough and Bladon and Wootton parishes the provenance of a quarter is quoted in the minutes. For nearly another half of them it is reasonably well identified from other sources such as: B.78/2; *Woodstock Chamberlains' Accounts 1604-50*; *Victoria County History*; *Calendar of Witney Court Books* ; Oxford Diocese Church Court records; Oxfordshire Probate records; Oxfordshire Marriage Index and International Genealogical Index (Oxon). Provenances so identified are distinguished in this section by an asterisk. Within the remaining quarter (107 suitors) provisionally adjudged to be outsiders there may be some who, if further information such as the contemporary Woodstock parish registers or tithing lists were available, would prove to be Woodstock non-freemen, or common-sort, or casual residents.

Some 42% of the Portmoot actions had no apparent Woodstock borough interest, and outsiders formed 62% of suitors and 78% of individuals using the court. These proportions are much greater than those of 6% for outsider/outsider actions and of 21% for outsider users, quoted for the manorial or town court of Witney Borough Court over the period 1538-1610.[28] The large difference may be mostly attributable to the wider attraction of the Portmoot as a court of record. However considering the relative sizes of the two towns and their hinterlands, Woodstock with 600 inhabitants would have much less local commercial attraction than Witney with a population around 2,000.[29]

These outsiders averaged about one and a third actions each, so that most engaged in just a single suit, slightly more often as defendant than as claimant. Within this category the most frequent users were, in descending order:

William Harris pl. in 18 *Qui Tam* and 1 debt actions, def. in another;
Thomas Bodie of Hanborough pl. in 6 of 8 actions;
Edward Hanckes alias Warr, of Tackley, def. in 5 of 6 suits;
Richard Stutter of Hanborough def. in 4 of 6 suits, 3 versus Richard Richardson of same place who was in 4 suits;
Edmund White of Hampton Poyle in 6 suits versus near neighbours;
Thomas Freeman of Kiddington was involved in 6 suits and quoted as a borough tenant;
Thomas Bowles in 5 suits, defendant in 3 versus councillor Richard Meades, one for £5;
Thomas Bromryck gent. in 5 suits, pl. in 3 against Edw.& Mary Huffer of Kirtlington, and debt def. to Edulphe Dingley in £4;
William Teasler, Waterperry* in 5 suits;

[28] *Witney Courts*, xxxviii.
[29] Taylor, (1991), 248; Rodwell, 200; *Witney Courts*, lvi.

Arthur Machin and Giles Collier were tangled in a web of 4 simultaneous actions concerning arrearage of accounts;

Others engaged in 4 suits were: William Borman, Tackley*; Robert May, Kidlington*; Richard Merry, Hanborough*; John Norwood, Deddington*; Richard Pokins of Wolvercote & Robert Street, Islip.

Those partaking in 3 suits include: Richard Merrywether of Burford; William Parsons, Witney*; and William Wise, Eynsham*.

Some of the larger sums of money in dispute included:

Thomas Wilkinson, Hook Norton* def. in trespass for £100;

Thomas Yate, Witney* suing for debt of £20; Evan Hollway, Water Eaton* for £16; widow Margaret Yate of Deddington for £14;

Sums around £10 were in dispute by Roger Flie, by John Coles, Chipping Norton*; between Richard Clempson, Witney* and John Lane, Warwick*; and by Thomas & Mary Barton, Oxford*.

Sums around £7 were obtained by Richard Bennet, Adderbury*; and by Richard Wakefield of Cleveley;

and sums of around £4 by Thomas Norwood of Reading, and from Ethelbert Doa of Thrupp, and by John Golding of Dean (Spelsbury) from Henry Allis, Charlbury*.

Numbers of these actions were the sole occasions that the litigants appear in these court records. The sums of money involved in the suits of this period were of the same order as those in the Portmoot minutes for 1607-14, and in particular they do not appear notably smaller.[30]

In addition to cases given above, numbers of litigant neighbours came some distance to refer their local disputes to the jurisdiction of the Portmoot court of record. The transactions themselves must have been based on Woodstock, within the borough's 'liberties', but such pairings would arise from the closer interactions of neighbours and their greater knowledge and confidence of their respective credit standings. Examples of such neighbour-pairs are identified here in terms of their locality and suit numbers (numbers with asterisk represent suitors whose provenance is taken from sources other than the court minutes - see Abbreviations; see distribution map Fig.2):

North Aston/Kirtlington **252***; N.Aston/Shipton-on-Cherwell **254**;
Banbury/Steeple Aston **400***; Bicester **343**, **344**, **354**;
Bletchingdon/Hampton Poyle **351**; Brackley/Aynho **284**;
Burford/The Grange (Bruern?) **90**; Burford/Witney **345**;
'Chelkes'/Somerton **303**; Chipping Norton both **220***;
Chipping Norton/Kiddington **360**; Cleveley both **192**, **236**;
Cleveley/Lew **448***; Coventry/Banbury **362**;

[30] WBM B78/2, Calendar, Introduction.

Figure 2. Distribution of Portmoot Outsider Litigants

- ● Places identified in Woodstock Court Books.
- x Places identified from other sources.

Places within 2 miles of Woodstock omitted.

The circles are of 10 and 15 miles radius from Woodstock.

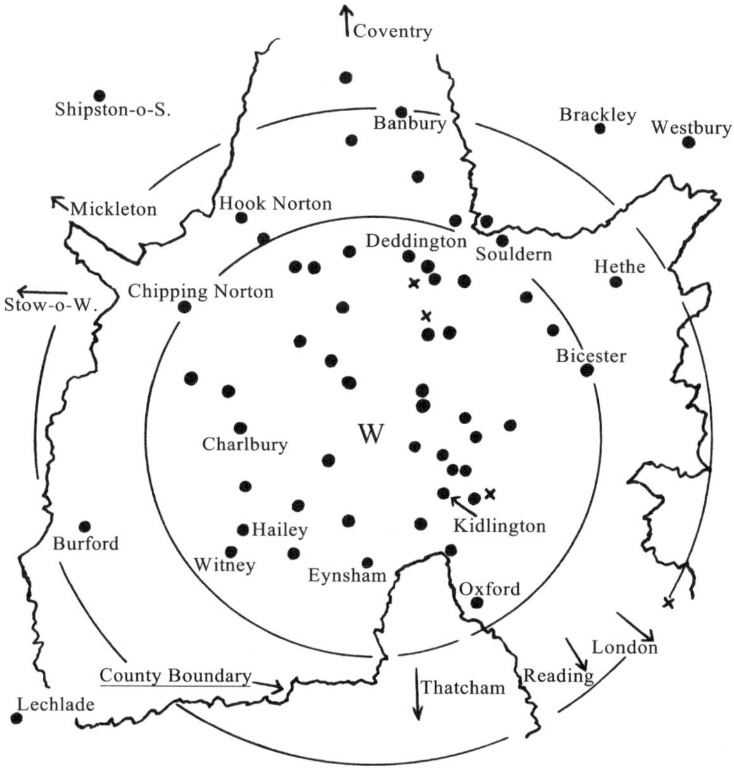

Whereas some places had lone litigants, Bicester, Deddington, Burford each had 4, and Witney, Kidlington & Hanborough each had 3. Of Portmoot individuals 7% came from beyond 10 miles and brought that amount of business; and just 3% of individuals and business from beyond 15 miles. By 1607-14 (WBM B78/2, Cal., Fig.1) the proportion coming beyond 10 miles had nearly tripled, but that beyond 15 miles had fallen.

Some 'distant' actions had special features: litigants from Lechlade, Burford and Stow-on-the-Wold were defendants probably sought out by the penal-statute informers (see below); customers from Shipston-on-Stour and from Thatcham (Berks.) were involved in land conveyances.

Deddington both **353***, **428**; Eynsham/Stanton Harcourt **450***, **451***;
Glympton/Combe **226***; Hailey/Ramsden **346**;
Hampton Poyle/Hampton Gay **447***;
Hanborough both **114***, **126***, **127***, **225***, **392**, **420***, **494***;
Hanborough/Witney **398**; Heyford both **107**; Islip both **49**, **50**, **51**;
Islip/Fewcott **264**; Islip/Tackley **342**; Islip/Yarnton **419***;
Kirtlington/Hampton Poyle **71**; North Leigh/Combe **130***;
North Leigh/Swerford **418***; South Leigh both **225**, **402***;
Rousham/Deddington **279***; Stanton Harcourt/Hanborough **502***;
Swerford/Nether Worton **174**; Tew/Spelsbury **412**; Duns Tew both, **485***;
Great Tew/Chadlington **449***; Witney both **31***, **58***;
Witney/Charlbury **117***; Witney/Ramsden **372**; Yarnton/Kidlington **258**.

Other individual suitors came from such places as
Adderbury **189**; Middle Aston **319**; Steeple Aston **293**; Banbury **280**;
Bletchingdon **198**; Brackley **363**; Broughton **299**; 'Brucsyde' **306**;
Bucknell **89**, **101**; Burford **90**, **267**, **306**; Charlbury **199**;
Chipping Norton **347**; Cleveley **324**; Deddington **285**, **290**, **358**;
Eynsham **291**, **325**; Glympton **390**; Hampton Gay **266**; H. Poyle **320**;
Hethe **240**; Hordley **501**; Islip **138**; Kidlington **203**, **233**, **288**;
Lechlade **262**; Ledwell **287**; London **15**; Mickelton (Glos.) **293**;
Nethercott (in Tackley) **381**; Nether Worton **240**; North Leigh **386,517;**
South Leigh **200**, **375**; Oxford **517**; Radford (Kiddington) **91**; Rousham **273**;
Sandford **376**; Shipston-on-Stour **296**; Somerton **196**; Souldern **61**;
Stow-on-Wold **216**; Thatcham (Berks.) **259**; Thrupp **268**;
'Wawking' (Watlington?) **138**; Water Eaton **76**; Westbury ('Northants') **367**;
Weston-on-the-Green **260**; Witney **231**; Wroxton **240**.

Central Courts at Westminster

Over this span of seven years a total of 13 Portmoot suits were referred to the central courts at Westminster:

5 by *habeas corpus cum causa* to courts not specified, but most likely to Common Bench, (**26**, **133**, **176**, **213**, **353**);
5 by writ of error; one to Chancery (**5**), at least three to Queen's Bench (**11b**, **116**, **299**), the latter and **426** recorded as returned to the Portmoot;
2 by writ of *certiorari* to unspecified courts (**12**, **429**), the latter action going on to
1 writ of *procedendo*, and subsequent return to the Portmoot;
1 writ of privilege, issued out of Queen's Bench (**168**).

Twenty years later, over the six years 1607-14, the court had 22 such referrals; and apart from the increased numbers of *habeas corpus* cases the usage of the various writs was broadly similar (numbers of each writ, in the order as above 13:4:1:2:2).[31]

Some forms of Action

Actions of Debt & Trespass on the case

In the late 16th and early 17th centuries most of the litigation in the country was taking place in the borough courts and most cases (up to 80% in some places) concerned unpaid debts or broken contracts dealt with by the actions of debt, trespass on the case, and *assumpsit*. The proportion of such cases in the Portmoot 1588-95 was 66%, and in 1607-14 had risen to 80%. Most of the underlying bargains were generated by oral agreements on unpaid sales credits and reckonings on consumer goods. In contrast in the Central Courts most debt cases concerned bonds. (see p.xxii).[32] In the present book bills obligatory are recorded on only four occasions: **5**(3/6); **111**:12/17 a future provision; **84** (15/15), two bills; and **240**:1/2, two trusts at £80 each. Bonds are specified in only four suits: **10**:11/12; **35**:2/5, and the final two entries above.

Most credit was extended orally in front of witnesses since these, rather than badly-kept or non-existent account books, were regarded as the most important form of security for debts and other agreements, throughout all levels of society.[33] A number of such witness statements are included in the present entries, giving details of oral bargains on money credits, land tenure, and on food, cattle, ironmongery and service barters etc.: **11a**:5/7; **12**:17/22; **149**:10/19; **173**:6/10; **180**:10/16; **192**:7/12; **220**:6/12; **245**:6/9; **251**:10/22; **271**:1/1; **288**:8/11; **299**:1/24; **320**:11/14.

Credit was commonly exchanged through chains of borrowers and lenders, as shown by the third parties and other participants occasionally mentioned in the brief entries provided here: **35**:2/5; **95**:7/7; **136**:2/3; **213**:13/15; **221**; **252**:1/1; **267**:11/11.

An example of a reciprocal cancellation of at least a proportion of outstanding debts and credits seems to have taken place in the 'even reckoning' of **290**:8/16. It has been estimated that money as coinage formed less than 10% of exchanges at this period and perhaps less than 7%.[34]

31 WBM B78/2, Calendar, Introduction.

32 Muldrew, 204; WBM B78/2, Calendar, Introduction.

33 Muldrew, 63, 96.

34 Muldrew, 98 - 100.

Actions of Account

This type of action continued in use at this time against bailiffs, common receivers, or other agents where debt was precluded because of the uncertainty as to the balance between the parties.[35]

Eight such suits took place:

2 of them (**11**, **11b**) started a tangle of litigation on arrearage of accounts between Giles Collier & Arthur Machin;

5 of them (**110**, **169**, **327**, **328**, **373**) involved borough councillors as one or both parties;

2 of them (**429** for £9, as well as **11b**) were referred to Westminster.

Arrears

Two of the actions of account (**11**, **328**) and one of debt (**251**) concern arrears of payment and Holderness has pointed out their importance as forms of credit, particularly when occurring as deferred rents, in smoothing over the worst consequences of money shortages in the fluctuating cycles of economic life.[36]

Actions of Assumpsit, Detinue, Trover & Replevin

In this period there were 32 actions of *Assumpsit* which made up 6% of the total: two of them (**21**,**109**) refer to debt and three others (**90**, **299**, **392**) refer to trespass.

In some contrast to this, in the 1607-14 Portmoot no such suits appear. Towards the end of the l6th century a major difference had opened up between the central courts in their treatment of this form of action: the Queen's Bench encouraged its use in lieu of debt, whereas the Common Pleas made its use extremely difficult. Matters came to a head in the 1590's and were resolved by Slade's Case in 1602 which established the right to recover debts by action of *assumpsit*. This hardly explains a reduction in use of the actions; nevertheless in the Witney Borough Court over this period it is notable that there are 9 actions of *assumpsit* between 1574 and 1592, but not one from then to 1610: which parallels the Portmoot record.[37]

Assumpsit as a mutual promise to accept an arbitration award with an associated penalty for any lapse, was employed at the end of 13 suits (**95**, **107**, **111**, **161**, **174**, **175**, **177**, **186**, **191**, **236**, **256**, **264** and **436**)

In a total of four detinue actions over this period:

one was for a deed (**30**), and another for an inventory (**408**);[38]

one commenced as detinue but converted to 'trover & debt'.

As well as the last case above there were two others for trover:

34, and **252** against the arrest of a mare.

[35] Baker, 411-13.

[36] Holderness, 102.

[37] Baker, 392/3; *Witney Courts*, xxxvii; Maitland, 70.

[38] Jacob, 'Detinue of Deeds & Charters, concerning land'.

There was a replevin action for a cow (**23**); and perhaps one for goods (**386**) but since no surety is mentioned detinue seems more likely in this case.

Thus in 1588-95 the Portmoot had 5 detinue and 3 trover actions (one converted from detinue) compared with 6 detinue and no trover actions in 1607-14. This change is counter to that taking place in the central courts and elsewhere at this time. Thus Maitland describes Trover gradually supplanting Detinue from the middle of the l6th century and becoming the normal mode of trying the title to moveable goods; also Gilmore notes in the Bedford Court of Pleas that Trover was very nearly fully developed and actions in Detinue correspondingly rare by the end of the 16th century.[39]

Conveyance, Dower, Tenancy, & Ejectment

Conveyance by proclamation was customary in the borough with the claim made in open court asking that the grant be recorded and proclaimed on three, usually successive, court days.

In the 12 conveyances by proclamation in this period:

borough councillors were engaged in 6 of them, in 2 as plaintiffs (**82**, **371**), and as deforciants in **124**, **260**, **296** & **384** (very detailed);

there were other freeman plaintiffs in 2 (**235**, **259**); and non-freeman as plaintiffs in 2 (**120**, **124**), and as deforciants in 4 (**82**, **235**, **269**, **371**).

Some of the outsiders, having gained residence, became more involved in the borough's affairs. Such as:

William Rayer (**260**) who later became mayor;

Richard and Elizabeth Kent of Wootton (**93**);

Richard Pokins (**93**) who rented tenements;

and Robert Bicknell/Bignell (**296**) who took over The Black Hall.

Several of the conveyances took place by writ of dower by which a widow claimed her third share of her husband's land to enjoy for her life. Those so engaged were:

widow Magdalen Bruce (**111**) who was claiming she had received none of her share of her husband's land, (dower *unde nihil habet*);

Elizabeth Kent, widow of John Phillips (**75**, **93**, **213**, **218**);

widow Ursula Weller, later married to Edmund Oven, together with Ann Bulliphant (ex Weller) (**258**, **427**);

Elizabeth James, relict of Humphrey James (**481**).

In some cases property-owning widows had remarried and were privately examined by the justice(s) to ensure they were not acting under duress, since the fine would bar the wife of a marriage and her heirs. Such examinations took place in actions **93**, **213**, **218** & **259**; and in the case of **260** the wife's specific declaration on this situation is included.[40]

[39] Maitland, 71; Gilmore, 87.

[40] Baker, 552.

Certain suits relating to conveyances, particularly after dower transactions, involved tenancies and rentals. Richard and Elizabeth Kent were sued for detaining rents of £200 in **55**, and their tenants named in **75**. Those of Richard Pokins and their rents were detailed in **75**; and those resulting from the Justinian Weller inheritance in **258**. Tenants were listed as pledges in **251**; and tenants of the chief lords of the fee named in **82** and **384**. Details of a land rental or transfer in Hensington were given in **149**:10/19; a 60-year lease of extensive land is detailed in **243**, and of conveyance tenancy in **260**. Entry **93** also shows the court being used to witness a series of leases as does **75**.[41]

Four cases of ejectment were undertaken, seemingly as the lessee's remedy against being dispossessed of land he had leased: one (**19**) succeeded in recovering a lease and another (**89**) went to imparlance. Overall in this field of action business increased marginally by the period 1607-14: the number of proclamation conveyances rose from 12 to 21; actions of Dower fell from 7 to 1; actions of Ejectment fell from 4 to 3; and in the later period there were 3 suits for Common Recovery.

Qui Tam Actions

By the latter part of the 16th century *Qui Tam* actions had developed whereby informers could sue before JPs for offences against statutes forbidding something under penalty to be paid, half to the crown (via the chamberlains in the Portmoot) and half to themselves as plaintiffs. They were used as a frugal method of economic and labour regulation, and informers arose who tended to specialise in this type of action – sometimes on behalf of others.[42]

A total of 32 such actions were brought to the court over the period, thus making over 6% of its business:

19 by William Harris (**166**, **167**, **170**, **224**, **231**, **232**, **262**, **301**, **307**, **309**, **311**, **312**, **326**, **333**, **349**, **352**, **368**, **376** & **411**); and 13 by James Dissell (**198**, **199**, **200**, **202**, **203**, **204**, **205**, **206**, **216**, **222**, **223**, **233** & **237**).

This contrasts with only 5 cases brought in 1607-13, all by Harris.

James Dissell was a borough freeman who dwelt in Woolmarket St. and Cooperyware St., and acted as juryman and pledge on occasion. He was provided with a shroud by the town on his death in 1613 - a mark of relative poverty.[43]

The identity of William Harris is not established, evidence does not suggest he was a borough freeman. He may have been the husbandman[44] of Hailey who died in 1627 with an estate of £151; but others of that name were flourishing in the area at that time. Some of Harris's *Qui Tam* defendants came from places

41 *VCH Oxon.* xii. 392 (i).

42 Langbein, 44; Bellamy, 100-11.

43 WBM B78/1 *passim*; WBM B78/2 Cal. *passim*; *WCA*., xxv, 45.

44 *Witney Courts*, 1xxxvi/vii; MS.Wills Oxon. I. Acct.106, 154; 297/5/11.

such as Witney, Burford and Lechlade which perhaps supports his location being at Hailey; moreover his successor as informer around 1614 was John Taylor of Leafield, close by Hailey.[45]

Informations in the Westminster Courts tended to come in clusters, and they did so in the Portmoot: thus 3 arose in December 1591, 8 in October 1592, 3 in January 1593, 4 in March-May 1593, 6 in June-July 1594, and 3 in August-September 1594. Whether this arose mostly from the timing of the offences, was influenced by the Portmoot/chamberlain calendar, or largely by some purpose or convenience of the informers is not apparent. The last two clusters may have arisen from the reprinting of the Book Dearth Orders in 1594 as well as from the dearth itself.[46]

In certain entries some indication is given of the particular statute being contravened:

Thomas Rook was accused of purchasing unlawfully ("emptor"), **116**, presumably referring to commodities or livestock for re-selling at excessive profit, contrary to the statutes of 1551, 5, 6 Edward VI. c.14, re-issued a few years previously in the 1586 Book of Dearth Orders.[47]

Similarly four men of South Leigh stood indicted together of badging and selling sheep (**200**); and in December 1594 after a bad harvest Richard Buller of Sandford (**376**) was fined for purchasing and re-selling barley.[48]

Edward Roberts was fined 4s on information laid concerning 20 hides of leather worth £10 (**206**); as with Thomas Smythe's offence of selling certain leather goods with a fine paid to the chamberlains and Queen (**307**), the statute invoked may have concerned the area of sale or the sale of honest goods.[49]

Other cases suggest offences associated with leather trades:

Defendant Thomas Ryman of Charlbury was a glover (**199**), but this action ended in a charge of maintenance - presumably against plaintiff Dissell, as a case of an unjust or feigned suit relating to informations upon the penal laws.[50] Edward Klerk of Kidlington (**203**) was a tanner, whilst John Carter was accused of unlawfully practising the craft of shoemaking (**368**); similarly John London tallow-chandler of Long Combe (**204**), on "information worth £18", was fined 3s 4d for practising the craft of either rope-making or possibly cordwaining; both presumably contravening the Statute of Artificers 1563.[51]

[45] WBM B78/3 *passim*.

[46] Beresford, 223/4, 230; Slack, 3.

[47] Holdsworth, IV, 375; Beresford, 238; Slack, 3.

[48] Hoskins, 38; Dalton, 39; Everitt, 575; Youings, 275-7; Beresford, 238.

[49] Beresford, 238; Holdsworth, IV, 321, 342.

[50] Dalton, 32, statute 11.Henry VII, c.3.; Bellamy, 105.

[51] Sharpe, 209; Beresford, 238.

Henry Rowsham senior was fined 12d for offending by working in brass (**309**), probably relating to the licence for trading or to the sale of defective brass. Thomas Daniell of Burford was a collar-maker who compounded for a fine (**349**) and may have broken the trade laws. William Hunt of Witney was a cardmaker in the wool-trade (**231**), and may have offended in the importing of wool cards.[52]

Although in the country as a whole apprenticeships and usury were seen as fruitful areas for informer profit, there is no evidence of such actions in the accounts provided here.[53]

Sums of money awarded in the Portmoot were small, typically a few shillings, even though two of the informations were recorded as worth £10 and £18. Dissell appears to have died a pauper, and even a large-scale operator covering much of southern England is accounted to have done meagrely, so that overall the profits gained from these activities seem to have been modest.[54]

Other and Unspecified Actions

There were just two specific actions outside the categories dealt with above. The first was the execution of a set of trust obligations (**240**), on a sum of £160 distributed on the death of Roger Norwood. The second was an arbitration of "all controversies" dependant between Anthony Noble clerk and William Ball freeman (**300**); these matters may have resulted from their unfinished suit **88**. A total of 45 actions were not specified, equivalent to 9% of all suits: probably most of these were either debt or trespass cases.

Usage of Attorneys

Parties in Portmoot actions were represented by attorney 218 times, many with them on both sides. Several of the attorneys also acted as essoiners, on 52 occasions, providing acceptable excuses for the non-appearance of their clients. Most of the attorneys were borough councillors; and Thomas Hardwyck who seems to have been either a non-freeman or outsider, having gained some business over a brief period, then appears to have been forced out. Councillor Thomas Cave was attorney 14 times, essoiner 10 times, and operated up to May 1590, in which year he died; councillor Richard Wright covered this whole period, being attorney 79 times, essoiner 17 times; councillor Nathaniel Sharp was in 56 suits from the start of the book up to August 1592. The sergeant-at-mace Henry Redgate from May 1594 was attorney on 44 occasions and was still operating in 1607-14; essoiner 20 times. Councillor Humphrey James acted as attorney 6 times between December 1593 and the following July; essoiner once. This complement of attorneys seems generous compared

[52] Jacob Brass defective, statute 19 Henry VII, c.6; Jones, 93.

[53] Youings, 297; Jones, 93.

[54] Elton, 152; *WCA*. 45.

to the one or two found in most prosperous smaller towns of southern England at this time, and may indicate the relative significance of the Portmoot court of record. Generally numbers were limited by election by members of a town's common council, or by its recorder or its town clerk, and such control may lie behind the Portmoot dismissal of Hardwyck.[55]

At his first appearance in September 1592 Thomas Hardwyck seems to have been admitted as attorney only until the end of the suit (**180**:5/16), but he acted in the role 21 times up to January 1594; then the court ruled there should be only two attorneys, named as Humphrey James and Richard Wright, acting in the current suit: Hardwyck completed the case but never appeared again (**273**:3/6).

On a few occasions individuals were chosen as personal attorneys by clients for specific items of legal business. Thus Robt. Clarke of Bladon proffers a writ of *habeas corpus* to a Westminster court (**213**); alderman Thos. Browne and councillor Fras. Collingwood are given powers of attorney by letter to act in a conveyance (**260**), as is councillor Edulphe Dingley (**386**); and Gilbert Penley of Ascott acting for Edward Savage (**285**) in a case of debt.

Apprenticeships

Indentures of apprenticeship were enrolled in the Portmoot Court Books as decreed in the Borough Orders of 1580, with the payment of 12d to the town clerk. One indenture is recorded here: for Robt. Sear of Adstock (Bucks) apprenticed for seven years to Jn. Dubber shoemaker (**239**).[56]

Corporation Business

Rental; child maintenance

One rental of corporation property is included: this for a shop at 1d a year together with donation of a black staff for the town's use (**162**); sample tokens are kept in the borough's muniments.[57]

A single case of child maintenance is recorded, and there the mother offered surety to avoid charge on the borough (**221**). Just one is also noted for six years (1607-14) covered by B78/2; these calls on charity may be compared with an expected three illegitimate children over 6 years for Woodstock's population around 600, based on estimated rates for all-England.[58]

Licensing of victuallers and butchers

Near the end of the book are two victual licensing lists for the borough; neither is dated or given a heading but the lay-out and contents are similar to those in B78/2. The first list (**482**) comes within folios apparently recording the court

[55] Brooks, 41; Baker, 186.

[56] WBM B82, clause 10.

[57] *VCH Oxon.*xii. 391

[58] Wrigley et al. 224; Hodges.

22 Dec.1595; the second list (**515**) bears only 8 names, 6 from the earlier list of 13, with widow Mondye succeeding her husband. Licensing in the borough over the first decade or so of the 17th century has been reviewed.[59]

Included in **515** are the recognisances for three butchers in the borough, with licence fees for two.

Assize of bread & ale

In each of the years from 1590 to 1595 the mayor called a court of assize, with himself as clerk of the market under the sovereign's patent, to price commodities on sale in the town. Sometimes another JP and a councillor sat with him, whilst in 1592 (**193**) John Powell the royal clerk of the market joined him. That same year Powell had made a major assay of breadmaking costs used as the basis for assizes up to 1669, and in 1600 he issued the first of several editions of an influential handbook on the "Assize of Bread", which set down official guidance on these matters to local magistrates.[60]

At this and the following court (**193** & **246**) details of the findings are omitted, but market and assize prices at the other four sittings are shown in Table 1.

Table 1: Woodstock market & assize prices 1590-1595

COMMODITY	Oct '90 **102**	Aug '91 **146**	Jul '94 **317**	Jan '95 **385**
Market price per quarter				
Best Wheat	22s8d	17s4d	40s	40s
Second Wheat	20s	16s	25s	37s4d
Third Wheat	18s8d	14s		
Best Malt	21s4d	17s4d		24s
Second Malt	20s			
Bread Assize Weight, Troy oz				
Halfpenny White Loaf	8½	12	6½	6
Penny White Loaf	17	24	13	12
Halfpenny Wheaten Loaf		18	9¾	8
Penny Wheaten Loaf	27	36	19½	16
Penny Household Loaf			36	22½
Ale Assize:				
Under Hair Sieve/Gallon	3d	3d		
Good Stale Ale/Quart	1d	1d	1d	1d
Small Drinks/Gallon	1d	1d	1d	1d
Candles/Pound	3½d			

59 Taylor (1991), 251.

60 Sheppard & Newton, 51; Connor, 206.

These years, in the country as a whole, were notable for three good harvests in a row (1591, 1592 and 1593) but which were immediately followed by a series of four very bad years, with 1594 to 1597 perhaps being the worst sequence of the century. The prices shown above directly reflect this succession of supply fluctuation, with the modest prices of 1590 being even lower in 1591, but then nearly doubling by 1594 and 1595. Oxford market best-wheat prices were some 10% or so higher than Woodstock's at the 1590 and 1595 dates, but climbed to over 20% higher in 1591 and 1594; in 1596/7 the Oxford price was 50% above its early 1595 level. Worksop malt was up to 12½% dearer than Woodstock best in '90/'91 but rose to 30% dearer in 1595.

London bread prices were quite similar to the Woodstock ones in 1590 and 1591, but in the bad years of 1594 and 1595 had climbed to 25% higher.[61]

Only in the years of shortage is a price given for the lowest grade household loaf, yet no price is put on third wheat when it might be expected to be most used in low-grade food. Perhaps its sale was restricted, along with that of the barley normally destined for second malt.

Malt price changes palely reflect those in wheat. Bread and ale assize in the borough in the early 17th century has been reviewed.[62]

Dearth grain survey; Breach of the assize by a baker.

At the assize in January 1595 a jury was formed to make a grain dearth survey (**389**), though any results are not recorded. This followed the first reprinting in 1594 of the book of dearth orders of 1586. Hoskins sees the dearth of this and the following year as an immediate cause of the Oxfordshire Rising in 1596, in which Bartholomew Steere of Hampton Gay took the leading role (**447**). Other Portmoot litigants connected with the uprising included: Edward Huffer of Kirtlington (**248/9** & **252**) named as a rebel; and as intended victims land-owners Sir Henry Lee (**268**), John Rathbone (**339,407**), and George Whitton (**101**, **407**).[63]

A rare record of an assize offence is of John Bowell of Eynsham (**150**) giving short measure in his loaves; foreign bakers had to provide extra weight in their products.[64]

Flesh in Lent and Local Ethics

An old observance to abstain from flesh eating during Lent was reimposed after the Reformation, from economic motives rather than those of religion. The purpose was to encourage the home fishing fleet to provide a large reserve of seamen for national defence. Statutes forbade the killing and selling of flesh as well as its consumption. One sitting is minuted of a Flesh in Lent jury, in

61 Hoskins, 32-46; Thorold Rogers, 7-10; Hoskins, 4l.

62 Taylor (1992), 345-361.

63 Walter, 90-143; *VCH Oxon.*vi. 157; Slack, 3; Hoskins, 38.

64 WBM B78/2, f.48.

1591(**125**) at which they presented "a good declaration", presumably indicating judgment of no transgressions. This single instance, in the year that the original penal statute on political Lent (5 Eliz. c.5) had been augmented by 33 Eliz. c.7 (1591), seems wise obedience to statute rather than local 'Puritan' enthusiasm.[65]

The low call on base-child charity (see above) suggests a relatively sober community, particularly in resisting such temptations as those associated with visits of the royal court.[66]

Victualler numbers licensed in the borough, at 13 and 8, (see above) were well below those around twenty found in the period 1607-14, but the presence of three women out of eight total (**515**) indicates a fairly relaxed attitude in these matters. At least so compared with the town in the early years of the reign of James I, when the four women licensed in 1604 were totally removed by 1607, with a slow recovery only beginning around 1612. This loss may have reflected the influence of Jacobean anti-feminist literature and the obsession of the day. Lack of the borough church records curtails study, but the overall impression is of a town reasonably well conducted without fervour for moral crusades, and the Oxford church courts depositions of the time record no Woodstock cases on matters of morality.[67]

Perhaps feelings were more actively engaged and mounting over this period concerning the exercise of local power (e.g. between George Whitton and William Skelton) and land rights at a time of historically low levels of real-wages, successively poorer harvests, and aggressive enclosures of local land. Woodstock was the market centre of a troubled rural area at this time, directly involved in these grievances.[68]

Criminal Examinations.

Just two examples of criminal examination are minuted, either by accident, or perhaps arising from civil plaints as occurs occasionally in B.78/2. One case is referred to the Borough Sessions of the Peace (**208**) in which alderman William Metcalf and councillor Jerome White are bound over to keep the peace. Thomas Sheldon, gent. is similarly bound over, on unspecified cause for appearance at the next county assize or gaol delivery (**297**).

65 Beresford, 238.

66 *VCH Oxon.* xii. 371; Walter, 96; and see **220**:6/12.

67 Taylor, (1991), 256; Underwood, 38/9; Howard-Drake.

68 *VCH Oxon.* xii. 329, 394; WBM B82 clause 50; Walters, 90-125; Emery, 106; Wrigley & Schofield, 642.

EDITORIAL NOTE

The individual civil actions and items of corporation business are each given an entry number in bold type; successive appearances of each action etc. are then numbered consecutively out of the total number of appearances, e.g. **251**:14/22.

Abbreviated entries such as "A.B. vs. C.D." are read as A.B. bringing the plaint against C.D., unless specifically indicated to be otherwise.

For those actions under way prior to the start of B78/1 the appearance number is in brackets, e.g. **10**:(1/12) though the number of previous stages is not known; for those going beyond the end of the book the last appearance here includes a + indicating continuation.

Editorial additions are put in brackets. Years and dates have been put into historical years, beginning on 1 January.

Minutes of the Portmoot proceedings are mainly in abbreviated law-Latin and these have been calendared in modern English. Headings have been abbreviated, but an example of a full heading for a Portmoot court is given on p.1. Court business has sometimes been re-arranged for ease of calendaring, but only within a particular recto or verso.

The court officers are listed in Appendix 1.

The original spelling of surnames has been retained, specifically as found in B78/1; christian names have been put into a standard modern form except in cases of doubt: they are given in full for the first entry of each action, but any subsequent abbreviations are transcribed from the text. Place-names are given their modern spelling, together with the original spelling in brackets. Only entries from B78/1, B77/1 and d.47 are included in the Place-name Index; others in the Introduction are taken from supplementary sources (given at the end of List of Abbreviations) and are marked by an asterisk. The counties are those before the local government reorganization of 1974.

The relevant contents of the fair copies in B77/1 and d.47 are broadly described in the early pages of the Introduction and the location of the individual court meetings within them is set out in Appendix 3, correlated with the Calendar page and B78/1 folio numbers.

GLOSSARY

The definitions are taken from : *O.E.D.*; JH Baker; P Brand; RD Connor; Michael Dalton; F Emery; GD Gilmore; MH Havinden; CB Herrup; ERH Ivamy; G Jacob; W Lambarde; FW Maitland; R Milward. (see List of Abbreviations)

accord and satisfaction	an agreement to receive something other than the amount owed in lieu of full payment of the amount owed
account, action of (*computo*):	to compel a bailiff, receiver or guardian to render his accounts.
ale, good stale:	in context of assizes, here and in *Witney Courts,* x, this appears regularly with connotation of ale which has stood long enough to clear, i.e. is old and strong.
ale under the sieve:	ale strained to remove the impurities.
alias scire facias:	renewed *scire facias*. (q.v.)
amercement:	a punishment in the nature of a fine, imposed by the court with the fine assessed by the jury.
arbitrament, arbitration:	where two or more parties submit all matters in dispute to the judgment of *arbitrators*, who are to decide the controversy; if they do not agree it is usual to add that another person be called in as *umpire* to whose sole judgment it is then referred.
arrears:	indebtedness; an outstanding balance. Rent arrears, deferred payments, were a particularly important type of credit.
assumpsit:	a voluntary promise, for a consideration, to perform for another.
assumpsit, plaint of:	an action on the case for damages for breach of simple contract, not under seal.
assumpsit for debt:	assumpsit for breach of contract when, as often, for payment of money could be brought for an executory contract (a promise for a promise), but not for an

	executed contract - for this an action of debt was the only proper remedy, until action of *indebitatus assumpsit* was introduced in 1602.
attachment:	primarily, finding of sureties for the appearance of an individual.
attorney, personal:	one duly appointed to act for another in business and legal matters.
badging (forestalling):	buying goods privately with a view to enhance the price (a penal offence).
bail on his body:	a surety for defendant, rendering it unnecessary to take his body into actual custody.
bar:	a plea in answer to a claim that prevents the plaintiff recovering.
bond ('band'):	an instrument under seal, whereby a person binds himself to do or not do certain things.
butt:	a small piece of land separated from the adjacent lands.
capias, writ of:	writ to arrest defendant to compel him to appear before court.
capias ad satisfaciendum, writ of:	writ to arrest defendant & detain until judgment satisfied.
case, plaint on:	action for damages for wrongs or injuries not accompanied with immediate violence.
cepi corpus:	sheriff's & serjeant's return, indicating he has complied with a writ requiring him to seize the body of a party.
certiorari, writ of:	writ commanding proceedings to be removed into a superior court of review.
chief lords of that fee:	the lords of whom the grantor had held (rather than the grantor himself).
close (land):	an enclosure about or beside a building; or narrow pasture fields near the village (Emery, 133).
compounding:	arranging, coming to terms.
compromitted ('comprymitted'):	bound mutually to refer to arbitration.
compurgators:	those called, in waging law, to swear belief in the truth of the defendant's denial.

concordat:	a compromise.
coper:	horse-dealer.
corpus cum causa:	an order to produce someone under arrest or detention with a justification for their arrest.
country, put oneself on the:	submission to trial by jury after issue had been joined on the pleadings.
covenant, bill of:	an action to enforce a contract made under seal to do or not to do any act, most often used in disputes between landlords and tenants about repairs and the like.
covenant, deed of:	Also an agreement contained in a deed whereby a party stipulates for the truth of certain facts, or to do or not do any act.
curtesy:	the life estate which a husband had in the lands of his deceased wife.
debt on obligation:	debt on bond/deed.
deed of feoffment	a mode of transferring estates of freehold in possession.
deforciant:	a person transferring land by conveyance device known as a fine.
demurrer (*morat in lege*):	objection, in an action, to a pleading on ground that it is insufficient in point of law.
detinue:	an action to recover a movable item of personal property, unlawfully detained.
dicker ('dica'):	10 hides of leather (Jacob).
distringas, writ of:	writ issuing against the goods & chattels, & the land and its profits of a defendant who did not appear.
dower, action of:	action of a widow for (part of) her dower portion of the lands of her husband; one third of the lands held by her husband in his own right at any stage during their marriage, to be held by her for life.
dower *unde nichil habet*:	action brought by widow where none of the lands in a particular town or village had as yet been assigned to her in dower.
dower conveyance:	disposal of a married woman's freeholds.
ejectment (*ejectio firme*):	an action to recover damages for ejection from land as lessee, or to try the title of land.

engrossing:	to buy up wholesale a commodity.
entail:	settlement of land granting it to a particular individual or to a man and his wife and his, her or their descendants; in theory from the 15th century inalienable in perpetuity, but in fact alienable by means of collusive common recoveries.
error, writ of:	writ obtained from Chancery to obtain an annulment of proceedings on grounds of an error. For local courts of record, as here, error went to Queen's Bench.
escheat:	where land reverted to the lord of whom it was held when its tenant had been convicted of a felony or to have confessed it and abjured the realm, or died without heirs.
essoin (er):	excuse for non-appearance in court; (one who essoins another): function absorbed into that of attorney.
even reckoning:	having no balance or debt on either side: 'square'.
execution, writ of:	writ to put in force the sentence of a judicial proceeding; the final process (e.g. *fieri facias*).
false claim:	reason given for imposition of an amercement of an unsuccessful claimant, on grounds that he had failed to make a proper and justified claim.
felony:	a capital offence.
fiat executio:	an order for execution of an order or judgment whose execution has not yet been carried out.
fieri facias (fi.fa.):	writ of execution to levy debt or damages from a party against whom judgment has been awarded or given.
gaol delivery:	a session (normally part of the county Assizes) at which the prisoners currently in a particular gaol were tried for the offences with which they were charged.
goods & chattels:	in practice most frequently limited to things movable in possession.
habeas corpora juratorum:	a writ to summon a jury.

habere facias seisinam:	writ of execution to recover possession of seisin.
hands:	compurgators (q.v.).
imparlance (*licentia loquendi*):	an extension of time to put in a response in pleading a case.
in forma pauperis:	poor persons with total possessions less than £5 were admitted to sue or defend without fees or costs.
information:	of various kinds, including here: an information on a penal statute, giving the informer a right to a share in the penalty; see below '*Qui Tam*'.
inquiry, writ of:	writ for inquiry, by oaths of a 12-man jury, into amount of damages to be awarded.
land (s):	(**61**) a strip of arable land in open fields, usually about ½ acre in area.
launche:	lance (medical).
lift:	to take up out of the ground.
maintenance:	interference with other people's law suits; unlawful upholding of a person or cause (Jacob).
make away:	destroy, kill.
mandamus:	a Queen's Bench order to compel an inferior court to determine a case.
(the) mother:	(f.83r "..as well for the *mother* as to other.."); the one (person).
mound (s):	hedges or fences to delineate property.
nihil dicit (nil dicit):	a failure on part of the defendant to put his defence (or plaintiff his plaint in **142**).
nil debet per patriam:	plea to traverse a declaration in debt by verdict of a jury.
non-assumpsit:	the plea to the general issue in an action of *assumpsit*, to the effect that the defendant did not promise as alleged in the plaintiff's declaration.
obligation (written):	a bond containing a penalty, with a condition annexed, for the payment of money, performance of covenants, or the like.
overplus:	surplus.
pennyworth, a good:	well valued.

peppercorn rent:	a nominal rent.
peremptory summons:	a final and determinate summons.
pluries distringas:	third issue of a writ against goods & chattels of person for non-appearance.
private examination:	in a conveyance, of a wife to ensure that she was not acting under duress, since the fine would then bar the wife and her heirs.
privilege day:	the two extra court days allowed a Woodstock freeman to answer a Portmoot action (WBM B82, clause 46. (1580)).
privilege, writ of:	plea intended to oust jurisdiction of the court on grounds that the defendant is privileged (a form of *habeas corpus*).
procedendo, writ of:	a Chancery writ commanding the judge of an inferior court to proceed without delay to a judgment.
Qui Tam action:	a species of action of debt, where a statute forbade something under penalty to be paid, half to the Crown and half to anyone who sued for it.
recovery:	a true recovery is an actual or real recovery of a thing, or its value, by judgment.
rejoinder:	defendant's answer to plaintiff's reply; therefore the fourth stage in pleading.
release (*relaxacio*):	release from a deed.
replevin	a redelivery to the owner of his cattle or goods distrained on any cause upon surety that he will prosecute the action of replevin against the person who distrained.
replication:	plaintiff's reply to defendant's plea; third stage in pleading.
rescue ('*rescussus*'):	illegal recovery of goods or persons from custody when taken in distraint or arrested.
restitution, writ of:	most frequently used in Common Law for the setting a person in possession of lands & tenements where he has been unlawfully disseised of them.

rod:	here a measure of area; a square rod (5½yds.x 5½yds.).
satisfaction:	payment of the amount owed.
scire facias (sci. fa.):	a judicial writ equivalent to a summons to show cause why execution of action/ judgment should not take place.
alias scire facias:	renewed writ.
sicut alias scire facias:	writ renewed again.
seisin ('season'), livery of:	is a delivery of feudal possession. part of the process of feoffment (see above).
small drink:	weak beer.
special case:	apart from general cases of Trespass, all other writs had to set out the plaintiff's cause of action with some particularity in what was called his 'special case'.
specialty, or specialty debt:	an obligation contracted by matter of record, or by bond or other instrument under seal.
surcingle:	a large girth passing over a pack and keeping it in place on the animal's back.
tenant saw:	tenon-saw.
term:	an estate or interest in land to be enjoyed for a fixed period.
tod:	a wool weight, about 28lbs.; or that load of wool.
trover:	an action on the case to claim damages against the defendant for converting the plaintiff's goods to his own use; it became the normal mode of trying the title to movable goods.
truck, to:	to potter about.
umpire:	a third person called in to decide when two arbitrators cannot agree. (see 'arbitrament' above).
venire facias (juratores):	a writ commanding, when issue was joined in an action, the summonsing of a jury.
wager of law *('vadiatio legis'):*	procedure whereby defendant discharges himself from a claim on his own oath, bringing a declared number of his neighbours to swear their belief of his denial.

wanty: a girth by which burdens are tied to the back of a pack horse.

warrant: a precept authorising an officer to arrest an offender to be dealt with according to the law.

written bond: *(scriptum obligatorium)* as for bond (*q.v.*)

yardland: an area of land, usually of 30 acres; commonly taken as a fourth of a hide; for sizes of local yardlands see *V. C. H. Oxon*. xii. 527.

CALENDAR OF WOODSTOCK BOROUGH MUNIMENT WBM 78/1

Minute book of New Woodstock Borough courts October 1588 to December 1595.

[f 1r]

(Odd jottings concerning court cases **117, 296, 501, 502 & 503**).

[f 1v (Blank)]

[f 2]

The Portmoot court of our lady Queen held in the aforesaid borough of New Woodstock on the 7th day of October of the - year of the reign of our lady Elizabeth by the grace of god queen of England, France and Ireland etc. Before John Pyman mayor. According to the custom of this same borough since time immemorial as practiced and approved here etc.[1]

[No other officers listed.]

Actions unspecified:

1:(1/4) The jury between John Gregori plaintiff and Nicholas Tailor defendant assesses damages at £21:6:8d and amercement 2d. Therefore judgment that he should recover for his aforesaid damages & amercement 36s, but adjourn execution until *scire facias* is issued against sureties.

2:(1/3) Aforesaid Robert Chaundler through his attorney comes and requests imparlance with a copy to Thomas Flaxon in next court, therefore day given.

3:(1/1) Execution against Ursula Tucker adjourned to next court and day given.

4:(1/5) Court will consider between John Willis and Nicholas Lance.

7:(1/1) John Gregorie appoints attorney Nathaniel Sharp against Richard Meade, and William Medcalf and Humphrey James to deliver on bail and essoin by Henry Redgat in next court after feast of All Saints.

8:(1/1) John Williams and Roger Norwode gents arbitrators between William Ryley alderman and John Bruce, arbitrate that the aforesaid John should pay 10s at this court and 5s at the feast of All Saints for all causes and actions whatsoever.

9:(1/3) Execution is renewed on behalf of W Skelton ald against Henry Standard.

Actions of debt:

5:(1/6) *Pluries distringas* issued against jurors for Henry Johnson, Henry Fletcher & John Raunson in next court.

6:(1/4) Execution is renewed for Thomas Yate against Will Ryley.

[1] Following this example of a full heading to a Portmoot court, taken from B77/1, the rest are abbreviated to the date and the mayor presiding. Details of the supporting officers are given in Appendix 1.

10:1/12 William Skelton ald against W Riley ald plaint of debt.

[f 2v]

Portmoot court held 21 October 1588 before John Pyman mayor. (No other officers listed)

Actions of debt:

5:(2/6) Jury between Henry Johnson, Henry Fletcher and John Raunson assesses damages at 2d and expenses ld. Judgment adjourned to next court.

10:2/12 William Riley to be bailed on his body to John Riley & Humphrey James, and requests essoin for sickness on way to court, day given.

Actions unspecified:

1:(2/4) *Alias scire facias* given against Richard Wright & John Raunson sureties for Nicholas Tailor in the suit of John Gregori on the same day.

2:(2/3) Peremptory response ordered for Robert Chandler & Emma his wife in the action against Thomas Flaxne in next court, and day given.

9:(2/3) *Fiat executio* against Henry Standard in suit of Will Skelton & Alice his wife, in next court.

[f 3]

Portmoot court held 9 December 1588 before John Pyman mayor.

Actions of debt:

6:(2/4) Execution renewed for Thomas Yate against Will Riley until next court after the start of Hilary Term.

10:3/12 The action continues between Will Skelton and Will Riley who is essoined and carries bail until next court.

13:1/1 Will Stanley gent vs Thos Bradshew in plaint of debt.

Action of account:

11:1/15 Giles Collier vs Arthur Machin in plaint of arrearage of account, pledges as sureties for prosecution Thos Browne & Nathaniel Sharp, and to respond for Machin, Humphrey James & Jerome White.[2]

Action of trespass on case:

12:1/22 Arthur Machin vs Giles Collier in plaint of trespass on the case, pledges for prosecution Humph James, Jerome White, and to respond for Collier, Francis Collingwood & Nath Sharp.

Actions unspecified:

1:(3/4) Nich Tailor appears in person and discharges his sureties Jn Raunson & Ric Wryt because the aforesaid Nicholas is committed to the sergeant to give satisfaction to Jn Gregory.

2:(3/3) Response delivered in court on behalf of Chaundler through Thos Cave attorney. Writ of *venire facias* granted for Thos Flaxne against Robert & Emma Chaundler and day given in next court.

[2] Actions **11** and **12**, and their succeeding actions **11a** and **11b** are intertwined in their developments and confusing in their recording.

4:(2/5) The two actions between Jn Willis and Nich Lance are continued until the next court.
9:(3/3) Execution granted for Will Skelton vs Hen Standard until next court.

[f 3v]

Portmoot court held 23 December 1588 before John Pyman mayor.

Actions of debt:
10:4/12 Action continues between Will Skelton and Will Riley who is essoined the second time in bail until next court.
14:1/9 Roger Norwod vs Edward War alias Hanckes for £6:13:4d, bail by warrant by Thos Cave & Will Spittell.
15:1/2 Henry Parckhurst of London for £6:3:6d debt vs George Bridges; pledges for prosecution Thos Bradshewe & Humph James; bailors for Bridges, Thos Prestman & Robert Walker.
Action of account:
11:2/15 Giles Collier appoints Nath Sharp his attorney vs Machin.
Action of trespass on case:
12:2/22 Arth Machin appoints Thos Cave his attorney vs Collier.
Actions unspecified:
1:(4/4) Nich Tailor is held in custody of Henry Redgate sergeant and the borough gaol until satisfaction is done for Jn Gregori. According to the ordinance of the court and its warrant dated 23 December. Under seal of the court.
4:(3/5) The two actions continue between Jn Willis and Nich Launce, and day given until next court for imparlance.

[f 4]

Portmoot court held 13 January 1589 before John Pyman mayor.

Actions of debt:
5:(3/6) Memo that it is adjudged by the Court that Hen Johnson is awarded against Hen Fletcher & Jn Raunson and either of them for the debt of £40 upon an obligation due to the said Hen Johnson. Sued for and recovered in this court, the sum of £21 and 37s for his costs of suit, and execution adjourned until etc.
14:2/9 Edw Warr essoined by Thos Cave until next court.
15:2/2 Peremptory summons for Geo Bridges to respond to Henry Parkhurst at start of next court.
Action of trespass:
16:1/1 William Metecalf against Thomas Cave.
Action of trespass on case:
12:3/22 Arth Machin has day to amend his declaration against Collier.
Action of account:
11:3/15 Machin will present his response to Giles Collier's declaration in next court.

Actions unspecified:
4:(4/5) Peremptory day given Jn Willis to declare against Nich Launce in next court in the two actions.
6:(2a/4) John Yeades in essoin in next court, pledged by Humph James & Michael Mondye.

[f 4v]

Portmoot court held 27 January 1589 before John Pyman mayor.
Actions of debt:
5:(4/6) Execution against Hen Fletcher & Jn Raunson in suit of Johnson adjourned until court shall advise.
14:3/9 Rog Norwood appoints as attorney Nath Sharp against Edw War alias Hanckes until next court.
18:1/3 William Metecaulf vs George Newell - next court.
Action of trespass:.
17:1/1 Thomas Browne vs John Raunson; Raunson excused through Thomas Cave to next court.
Action unspecified:
4:(5/5) Since Jn Willis does not prosecute his actions vs Nich. Launce on the peremptory day therefore in pledge for the two actions, but judgment adjourned until etc. .
Actions continuing: **11**:4/15; **12**:4/22.

[f 5]

Portmoot court held 3 March 1589 before John Pyman mayor.
Actions of debt:
5:(5/6) Thos Cave delivers to the mayor in full court a royal writ of error vs the action of Johnson, therefore execution cannot be made.
6:(3/4) Execution renewed against Will Riley ald in action of Thomas Yate.
Actions continuing: **10**:5/12; **11**:5/15; **12**:5/22; **18**:2/3.

[f 5v]

Portmoot court held 17 March 1589 before John Pyman mayor.
Actions of debt:
18:3/3 Court discharges action between Will Metecalf vs Geo Newell.
20:1/8 Lady Margery Babington vs Edmund Cuper, with Nath Sharp & S Hurst holding bail.
Action of ejectment:
19:1/5 Richard Archard prosecutes William Skelton in a plaint of trespass & ejectment. Archard appoints Nath Sharp his attorney vs Skelton and declares. Skelton through his attorney Thos Cave acknowledges the action of ejectment. And it is adjudged by the court that Archard should recover his term and execution be adjourned.
Actions continuing: **10**:6/12; **11**:6/15; **14**:5/9.
It is ordered by the mayor that the next court be held on 24 March following.

[f 6]

Portmoot court held 24 March 1589 before John Pyman mayor.

Actions of debt:

14:6/9 Since Edw Hanckes alias Warr does not appear following his peremptory day to defend himself against the declaration of Rog. Norwood. gent, the court adjudges that Roger should recover the said £6:13:4d debt given in the declaration and 8s8d for amercement & costs from bringing the suit.

20:2/8 Lady Margery Babington appoints Thos Cave her attorney against Edm Cupper who is essoined by Nath Sharp to next court.

Action of ejectment:

19:2/5 *Fiat executio* granted against Will Skelton & his wife Alice in ejectment and that Ric Archard should recover his term in a special case by royal writ according to the custom of the borough.

Action of debt on assumpsit:

21:1/9 Samuel Hurst against Robert Winter, with pledges Nath Sharp & Michael Vaux.

Actions continuing: **10**:7/12; **11**:7/15; **12**:6/22.

[f6v]

Portmoot court held 7 April 1589 before John Pyman mayor.

Action of debt:

14:7/9 Action remains as before.

Action of ejectment:

19:3/5 *Fiat executio* issued against Will Skelton to make restitution and return to Archard his boundary.

Debt on assumpsit:

21:2/9 Robt Winter appears and delivered bail by Will Flye & Mich Fauxe. Sam Hurst appoints Nath Sharp as attorney.

Actions continuing: **10**:8/12; **11**:8/15; **12**:7/22; **20**:3/8.

[f6a][3]

Portmoot court held 21 April 1589 before John Pyman mayor.

Actions continuing: **10**:9/12; **11**:9/15; **12**:8/22; **20**:4/8; **21**:3/9.

Court adjourned to 5 May.

[f6av][4]

Portmoot court held 5 May 1589 at the Guildhall before John Pyman mayor.

Action of debt:

22:1/6 Margery Nursse widow vs Francis Collingwood; Nursse pledged by Ralph Bradshewe, and appoints Nath Sharp her attorney. Collingwood essoined by Thos Cave and draws bail from John Heath & William Hix.

[3] B78/1 folio largely missing (unnumbered); text from B77/1.

[4] B78/1 folio largely missing (unnumbered); text from B77/1.

Actions of account and trespass o. c.:
11:10/15 & **12**:9/22 Item: that a copy of the declaration of Arth Machin vs Giles Collier, and Machin's response to Collier are to be delivered before next court according to the law.
Action of debt on assumpsit:
21:4/9 Peremptory day for Robt Winter to respond to Sam Hurst in next court.
Action of replevin:
23:1/2 John Webbe vs Ambrose Saunders in plaint for one cow, pledged to prosecute by Michael Faux & Robert Monk. Saunders essoined by Thos Cave until next court; same day given to Webbe to find sureties for the return of the cow if its return is adjudged to the defendant.
Actions continuing: **10**:10/12; **20**:5/8.
Adjourned to Monday after Trinity.

[f7][5]

Portmoot court held 26 May 1589 before John Pyman mayor.
Actions of debt:
10:11/12 Skelton vs Riley continues to next court for defendant to have a copy of the bond.
14:8/9 Norwood vs Warr, fiat *scire facias* vs surety of Edw Warr to be returned in next court.
22:2/6 Second privilege day for Collingwood to respond to Margery Nursse.
Actions of account and trespass o. c.:
11:11/15 Collier replicates; and puts himself on the country and Machin similarly, therefore *venire facias* for return in next court.
12:10/22 Continues to next court and same day.
Action of debt on assumpsit:
21:5/9 And since Robt Winter (*nichill dic*) puts no defence in bar of the action of Sam Hurst therefore it is adjudged for plaintiff to have a writ of inquiry into damages executed in next court.
Action of replevin:
23:2/2 And since Ambrose Saunders does not appear to respond to Jn Webb for replevin of one cow and *nihil dicit*, court adjudges Webb should recover against Saunders the damages with expenses of the action.
Action continuing: **20**:6/8.

[f7v]

Actions of debt:
26:1/8 Richard Wansell vs Robert May, pledges to prosecute; Maye bailed to Thos Brown & Robt Banting.
27:1/2 Will Skelton vs Nicholas Tailor who essoins through Henry Redgat, bailed to John Tailor.

5 Bottom R H corner of B78/1 folio missing; text from B77/1.

29:1/10 Action continues(?) between John Slatter, his pledge Henry Fletcher, vs Richard Rynge. Rynge pledged by Will Tanner and essoined by Henry Redgat until next court.
Action of trespass on case:
24:1/10 John Dewe vs Robert Maye, day given in next court to declare and prosecute.
Action of assumpsit of debt:
25:1/8 John Tailor vs Robert Maye, Tailor appoints Nath Sharp his attorney.
Action unspecified:
28:1/5 Action continues(?) between Richard Saunders vs John Williams until next court.[6]
Court adjourns until 9 June.

[f8] [7]

Portmoot court held 9 June 1589 in Guildhall before John Pyman mayor.
Actions of debt:
10:12/12 Skelton vs Riley, continues, copy requested and same day given to each.
22:3/6 Marg Nurse vs Collingwood, third day of privilege for Collingwood to respond.
Actions of account and trepass o. c.:
11:12/15 Collier vs Machin; *habeas corpora juratores* given for return in next court.
12:11/22 Machin vs Collier; day given Collier to respond in next court.
Action of debt on assumpsit:
21:6/9 Jury to inquire into damages between Hurst and Winter assess damages at £10, costs at 2d & amercement imposed regarding the suit at 17s 4d. And court adjudges Hurst should recover the aforesaid sums. *Scire facias* returned against Edw Warr alias Hanckes.
Action of trespass o. c.
24:2/10 Dewe appoints N Sharp vs Maye.
Action continuing: **20**:7/8.

[f8v] (Sliver of folio missing)

Actions of debt:
27:2/2 Skelton vs Tailor; court discharges action.
29:2/10 Slatter appoints Nath Sharp his attorney vs Ringe.
Action of assumpsit of debt:
25:2/8 Maye appoints Thos Cave attorney to respond to Tailor's declaration; *venire facias* to be returned in next court with copy of Maye's response.
Action of ejectment:
19:4/5 Writ of Restitution renewed for Archard vs Will & Alice Skelton.

6 Bottom L H corner of folio missing; text from B77/1.
7 Central vertical sliver of folio missing; text from B77/1.

Action continuing: **28**:2/5.

[f9]

Portmoot court held at Guildhall 23 June 1589 before John Pyman mayor.

Actions of debt:

5:(6/6) Writ of execution made for Jonson delivered in court vs Hen Fletcher & Jn Raunson etc. The court wishes to consider because the record and process in the suit between Johnson and the said parties was sent to the court of Chancery on a writ of error and has not been returned.

20:8/8 Court discharges action between Babington and Cupper since Cupper has given satisfaction to her lady on the debt in the declaration, and acknowledged in court that the said debt was to be satisfied through Thomas Duffild clerk of the court.

22:4/6 Peremptory day for Collingwood to respond to Margery Nurce in next court.

Account:

11:13/15 *Habeas corpora* for pl. Collier returned this day, and appearance.

Trespass o. c.:

12:12/22 Peremptory day in next court given to Collier to respond to Machin.

24:3/10 Peremptory day given next court for Maye to respond to Dewe.

Assumpsit of debt:

25:3/8 *Venire facias* returned between Tailor vs Maye, and writ of *habeas corpora juratores* issued for return next court.

[f9v]

Actions of debt:

6:(4/4) Thomas Cave acknowledges in court that Thos Yate has satisfaction in the debt of £20 against William Riley which he recovers in this court; action discharged.

11a:1/7 Collier vs Machin:attorney Nath Sharpe appointed for Machin, and bailors Sam Hurst & James Dissell.

29:3/10 Peremptory day for Ringe to respond to Slatter in next court.

Action of Account:

11:14/15 Jury between Collier vs Machin present their verdict that 'we find for the defendant according to the Issue'.

Action of debt on assumpsit:

21:7/9 *Scire facias* against surety of Robt Winter.

Action of ejectment:

19:5/5 Writ of restitution returned in court, and that said Ric Archard is in possession by virtue of it.

Actions of trespass on case:

31:1/10 Nicholas Gun vs Richard Shaw: pledges for prosecution Hen Fletcher & Nath Sharp; for Shaw: Jn Williams & Humph James.

32:1/1 Robert Symons vs Nicholas Tailor: pledges for prosecution Jn William & Hen Fletcher.
Action of detinue:
30:1/2 Nicholas Tailor vs Robert Symons, for detinue of a deed; pledge for prosecution Jn Tailor; for Symons:Jn Williams & Humph James.
Action continuing: **28**:3/5.

[f10]

Portmoot court held at Guildhall 14 July 1589 before John Pyman mayor.
Actions of debt:
11a:2/7 Machin requests imparlance to respond to Collier in next court, same day.
29:4/10 Since Ric Ringe has peremptory day but *nihil dicit* in response to the declaration of Jn Sklatter the court adjudges that Slatter should recover his action against said Ringe.
Action of account:
11b:1/7 Arthur Machin given day in next court to respond to George Collier.
Action of detinue:
30:2/2 Nich Tailor given day in next court to declare: discharged.
Action of trover:
34:1/2 William Skelton vs Nicholas Howe; a pledge for Howe.
Actions continuing: **22**:5/6; **24**:4/10; **28**:4/5.

[f10v]

Portmoot court held 28 July 1589 before John Pyman mayor.
Actions of debt:
22:6/6 Nath Sharp for Margery Nurce wid vs Fras Collingwood acknowledges her to be satisfied and paid in full. Discharged.
29:5/10 Court adjudges that Jn Slatter should recover from his action vs R Ringe and his debt 19s 4d and for amercement & costs of bringing the suit 10s 9d.
35:1/5 Thomas Browne vs Arthur Machin: pledges to respond Humph James & Ric Lowe.
Actions of account:
11:15/15 Court adjudges that Machin should recover from his action vs Collier, and for amercement & costs of bringing the suit 18s 4d. *Scire facias* vs surety Robt Winter.
11b:2/7 Machin peremptory day to respond to Collier in next court.
Actions of trespass on case:
12:13/22 Peremptory day for Machin to replicate to Collier's plea in next court.
24:5/10 R May requests imparlance on declaration of Jn Dewe and makes demurrer; court will advise.

Action of trover:
34:2/2 Nich How essoined by Thos Cave; his pledges Fras Collingwood & Nich Tailor.
Action unspecified:
28:5/5 Saunders vs Williams. Discharged.

[f11]

Portmoot court held 11 August 1589 before John Pyman mayor.
Action of debt:
35:2/5 Machin given day in next court to respond to Browne.
Action of account:
11b:3/7 Machin imparls to Collier's declaration, and Thos Cave will replicate.
Action of assumpsit of debt:
25:4/8 Jury between Jn Tailor gent vs Robt Maie:

Humph James,	Hen Fletcher,	Will Medcalf,
Thos Prestman,	Ralph Bradshewe,	Thos Blythe,
Jerome White,	Sam Hurst,	Will Flye,
Jn Dissell,	Jn Wells	& Will Hix,

sworn: who say upon oath that they find for the plaintiff, in damages 32s 9d and for costs 12d.
Actions of trespass on case:
12:14/22 Machin replicates and puts himself on the country, with *ven. fac.* for return in next court.
24:6/10 Maye has day until next court to make a direct response to Dewe's declaration.
Action of trespass:
36:1/6 Richard Ollyver appoints Nath Sharp his attorney vs Robert May.

[f11v]

14:9/9 Norwood vs Warr:the sureties of Warr are discharged, because he comes here to court and surrenders himself to the custody of the sergeant. Discharged.
26:2/8 Ric Wansell appoints Nath Sharp his attorney vs Robt May.
29:6/10 *Scire facias* granted vs sureties of Ric Ring, namely Hen Fletcher & Will Tanner.
41:1/7 Humphrey James essoins through Hen Reddgat in next court to respond to William Skelton, with his pledges Hen Fletcher & Will Rabon.
Action of trespass:
37:1/8 William How vs John Tailor, has day to declare in next court.
Actions of trespass on case:
31:2/10 Shawe has day in next court to respond to Gun.
39:1/6 John Tailor has day in next court to declare vs Nic How.
Action of assumpsit:
38:1/2 John Brown appoints Thos Cave as attorney vs John Tailor.

Action unspecified:
40:1/3 Hercules Nashe essoins to next court through Hen Reddgat with pledges Hen Fletcher & Jerome White.

[f12]

Portmoot court held at Guildhall 25 August 1589 before John Pyman mayor.

Action of debt:
35:3/5 Since Machin does not come to respond and *nihil dicit*, court adjudges Thomas should recover his debt.
Action of account:
11b:4/7 Collier replicates to the response of Machin and has day for rejoinder in next court; copy of replication.
Actions of trespass on case:
12:15/22 *Habeas corpora* for Machin for return in next court.
24:7/10 Dewe has day to amend his declaration vs Maye next court.
Actions of trespass:
36:2/6 May has day to respond to Ollyver next court, and requests copy of declaration.
37:2/8 How appoints Thos Cave his attorney vs Tailor, who has day next court to respond & requests copy of declaration.

[f12v]

Actions of debt:
26:3/8 Peremptory day for May to respond to Wansell, next court.
29:7/10 *Alias scire facias* granted vs sureties of Ric Ringe.
41:2/17 First day for James to respond to Skelton next court.
Action of assumpsit:
38:2/2 Browne vs Tailor continues until the end of Michaelmas term next.
Actions of trespass on case:
31:3/10 Shawe responds to declaration of Gun, with copy for Gun to replicate to.
39:2/6 Peremptory day for Tailor to declare vs How, next court.
43:1/1 Ald William Riley vs George Banting; pledges to respond Robt Walker & Robt Banting.
Action of trespass:
42:1/6 William How vs John Tailor has day in next court to declare. Bailors: Will Skelton & Jn Williams.
Action continuing: **40**:2/3.

[f13]

Action of debt:
44:1/1 Samuel Hurst vs Roger Norwood gent, for payment.

Action of debt on assumpsit:
21:8/9 *Alias scire facias* granted against sureties of Robt White for return in next court.
Action of assumpsit of debt:
25:5/8 Court adjudges that Tailor should recover against Maye for his damages 32s 9d, for costs 12d, & for amercement of bringing suit to court 26s 9d.

[f13v]

Action of trespass on case:
12:16/22 Witnesses on behalf of Arth Machin vs Giles Collier to the issue in court, namely:
Will Rosse & Robt Webbe - sworn for plaintiff; Geo Collier, Thos Harris the elder, Cicely Mollington, Edmund Pryddy, Mary Addams & Ric Fletcher - sworn for defendant.

[f14]

Portmoot court held 8 September 1589 before John Pyman mayor.
Actions of trespass:
36:3/8 Peremptory day for May to respond to Ollyver, next court.
37:3/8 Peremptory day for Tailor to respond to How, next court.
Action of debt on assumpsit:
21:9/9 Sureties Will Fly & Mich Faux proffer Winter who commits his own body to the sergeant. Discharged.
Action of trespass on case:
24:8/10 Peremptory day for May to respond to Dewe in next court.

[f14v]

Actions of debt:
26:4/8 May requests imparlance to declaration of Wansell, and appoints Thos Cave his attorney to respond.
41:3/17 Second privilege day for James to respond to Skelton.
45:1/2 Richard Good vs John Ryley, first day to respond to Goodd who appoints Nath Sharp his attorney.
46:1/16 Thomas Browne vs Michael Glover; bailors Mich Mondy & Humph James.
Action of trespass:
42:2/6 Peremptory day for How to declare vs Taylor, next court.
Action of trespass on case:
31:4/10 Peremptory day for Gun to replicate vs Shawe.
Unspecified Action:
40:3/3 Discharged between Jn Tailor vs Hercules Nashe.

[f15]

Actions of debt:

29:8/10 Execution granted against Ric Ringe, Hen Fletcher & Will Tanner and any of them to the suit of Jn Slatter.

35:4/5 Court adjudges that Thos Browne, should recover against Art Machin his debt of 18s and for expenses and 8s 8d his costs in court on the suit required for his matter.

Actions of trespass on case:

12:17/22 Jury empanelled between Machin and Collier say: We find for the plaintiff in damages 8s 4d & in cost of suit 6d.

39:3/6 Tailor appoints Nath Sharp his attorney vs How.

Action of assumpsit of debt:

25:6/8 *Scire facias* granted for Tailor vs May; sureties Thos Browne & Robt Banting.

[f15v]

Action of debt:

11a:3/7 Since Machin does not come to rejoinder vs Collier then according to custom of court - *nihil dicit*, therefore court makes judgment. Machin requests imparlance and pleads *non-debet per patriam*. Therefore *venire facias*.[8]

[f16]

Portmoot court held at Guildhall 24 September 1589 before John Pyman mayor.[9]

Actions of trespass:

36:4/6 May responds to declaration of Ollyver with copy; day for rejoinder in next court.

37:4/8 Tailor responds to declaration of How and puts himself on country, therefore *venire facias*.

Action of trespass on case:

24:9/10 May imparls and responds to declaration of Dewe and *demurrs* on its insufficiency. Dewe through Nath Sharp requests copy of *demurrer* and is granted day in next court.

[f16v]

Actions of debt:

26:5/8 Peremptory day for May to amend response to Wansell's declaration, day in next court.

41:4/17 Third day for James to respond to Skelton, day given.

42:3/6 Will How appoints Thos Cave his attorney vs Jn Tailor in plaint of trespass and copy granted.

45:2/2 Court discharges John Riley since he has died.

[8] A plea to traverse a declaration in debt by verdict of a jury. Gilmore, Glossary 5.

[9] Court day a Wednesday.

46:2/16 Brown appoints Nath Sharp his attorney vs Glover who has first privilege day to respond.
48:1/4 William Skelton vs William Est; bailors Mich Faux & Jerome White. Continues.
Actions of trespass on case:
31:5/10 Gun replicates to response of Shaw and puts *demurrer* and copy returned.
39:4/6 How responds to declaration of Tailor, copy requested.
47:1/4 John Norwood vs John Castell, has day in next court to declare; pledges to respond Robt Monk, Jerome White.

[f17]

Actions of debt:
29:9/10 *Fiat executio* vs Ring, Fletcher & Tanner and any of them in the suit.
35:5/5 Memo. that Thomas Cave has appeared in court and has undertaken that Thomas Browne ald shall keep in his hands 6 tods ('toddes') of coarse wool belonging to Robert Webb and Arthur Machin, now in his possession until Machin has satisfied a debt of 18s and 8s 8d for costs and 6d for a bond, recovered in this court, by the said Brown against Machin. And that within 15 days either the money to be paid or else the wool to be sold for discharge of the debt, and the overplus to be restored to Webb, or Cave, to his use: fine etc.[10]
52:1/5 John Hiorn appoints Nath Sharp his attorney vs Edward Dodeswell.
Actions of trespass:

49:1/5 Robert Stret vs Henry Bolt	bailors for Bolt;
50:1/5 Robt Stret vs Hen Bolt	Francis Collingwood
51:1/5 Robt Stret vs Hen Bolt	& Samuel Hurst.

Action of assumpsit of debt:
25:7/8 *Alias scire facias* vs sureties of May in suit of Tailor.

[f17v]

Action of debt:
11a:4/7 *Habeas corpora* for Collier vs Machin for return in next court, namely Wednesday.[11]

[f18]

Portmoot court held at Guildhall 2 October 1589 before John Pyman mayor.[12]
Action of trespass on case:
24:10/10 Memo. that both the said John Dewe and the said Robert May are agreed to a *demurrer* in law as to the insufficiency of the count of the said John and they have a day to plead on the *demurrer* at the next court.

[10] 1 tod = 28 lbs. of wool.
[11] Court day planned to be a Wednesday?
[12] Court day a Thursday.

Actions of trespass:
36:5/6 May in response to declaration of Ollyver puts himself on country & Ollyver does likewise, therefore *venire facias*.
37:5/8 *Fiat habeas corpora* for How vs Taylor, return next court.
42:4/6 Peremptory day for Tailor to respond to How, next court.
Unspecified Action:
53:1/4 Peremptory day for John Tailor to respond to Nicholas How in next court.

[f18v]

Actions of debt:
11a:5/7 Witnesses on behalf of Giles Collier:
Thomas Brown ald sworn, John Quinny of Moreton-in-Marsh ('Merton Henmarsh'), and Thomas Collier sworn, do all confess that upon an accompt there was 33s 4d which Machin was found in arrearage and that he subscribed his hand to his book. The jury find for plaintiff the above said sum to be debt and for damages 6d and for costs 2d.
41:5/17 Skelton appoints Nath Sharp his attorney vs James, copy of declaration requested and bill.
46:3/16 Second day next court for Glover to respond to Brown.
Action of trespass on case:
31:6/10 Shaw responds vs Gonne & requests copy & day in next court.

[f19]

Actions of debt:
26:6/8 Wansell has day next court to replicate to May.
52:2/5 Peremptory summons for Dodeswell to respond to Hiorn in next court.
Actions of trespass on case:
12:18/22 Court adjudges Machin should recover for his damages 13s 4d & 47s 10d costs in suit against Collier.
47:2/4 Norwood appoints Thos Cave his attorney vs Castell and provides copy.
Action of assumpsit of debt:
25:8/8 *Fiat executio* granted against Maye, Brown & Banting in suit of Tailor.
Actions of trespass:
49:2/5 Peremptory summons for Stret to declare vs Bolt.
50:2/5 Peremptory summons for Stret to declare vs Bolt.
51:2/5 Peremptory summons for Strete to declare vs Bolt.
Action continuing: **48**:2/4.
(End of the book for one full year of the time of John Pyman, as mayor of the Portmoot Court of the said Borough.)[13]

[f19v] (Blank)

[13] Omitted from B78/1.

[f20]

Portmoot court held at Guildhall 13 October 1589 before John Williams mayor.

Actions of debt:

41:6/17 To this court comes Thomas Cave and confesses that the action against Humphrey James is true; he refers himself to the court's discretion.

46:4/16 Third day for Glover to respond to Browne.

Actions of trespass:

36:6/6 Fiat *habeas corpora* between Ollyver vs May to be returned in next court.

37:6/8 Jury between How and Tailor does not appear therefore both are in mercy.

Action of trespass on case:

31:7/10 Peremptory summons for Gonn to replicate to Shaw in next court.

Action unspecified:

53:2/4 Tailor asks to confer on declaration of How who has day next court to replicate. Nathaniel Sharp.

[f20v]

Action of debt:

26:7/8 Wansell replicates to response of May.

Actions of trespass, on case, & unspecified:

37:7/8, **39**:5/6, **42**:5/6 & **53**:3/4 Memo. that at this court all actions therein depending between William How and John Tailor, and between Nicholas How and John Tailor whatsoever they be and how so many they be, are referred to the arbitration and end of Roger Norwood and Thomas Duffild gents. And if they cannot agree then to be ruled and umpired by John Williams mayor, or by any two of them, this to be done at or before 20 November which arbitration to be published in writing and delivered by the said day or else void. And also to end all other causes & controversies & demands from the beginning of the world betwixt the said parties. Nich How for himself & his brother Will confess to owe Tailor & his wife £20 if they refuse the award; and Tailor confesses to owe Nich How & his executors if he shall refuse the award of the arbitration in the manner aforesaid £20 of lawful money of England and have delivered each to other 12d upon the assumption.

[f21]

Actions of Debt:

26:8/8 May produces royal writ of *corpus cum causa* for Wansell. [14]

56:1/2 Henry Fletcher vs Richard Lowe who is essoined by Thos Cave and delivered on bail by Humph James & Mich Mondy.

[14] Removal to a Westminister court.

Action of debt & detinue:
55:1/4 William James vs Richard Kent & Elizabeth his wife administrators of all and every one of the goods & chattels of John Phillipp deceased, in plaint that his rents of £200 are owed and detained by them; bailors Jn Pyman & Thos Brown, aldermen, and pledges to prosecute Nich Tailor & Hen Fletcher.[15]
Actions of trespass on case:
12:19/22 *Scire facias* for surety of Collier for return next court.
47:3/4 Peremptory summons for Castell to respond to Norwood in next court and has day.
Actions continuing: **48**:3/4; **49**:3/5; **50**:3/5; **51**:3/5; **52**:3/5.

[f21v] (Blank)

[f22]

Portmoot court held at Guildhall 27 October 1589 before John Williams mayor.[16]
Actions of debt:
46:5/16 Peremptory summons for Glover to respond to Brown, next court.
48:4/4 Discharged between Skelton and Este.
Actions of trespass on case:
12:20/22 *Alias scire facias* against surety of Collier.
31:8/10 Gun replicates to response of Shawe and *morat in lege*, and peremptory summons for Shawe to rejoinder in next court.
47:4/4 Discharged between Norwood and Castell.
*Actions continuing:***49**:4/5; **50**:4/5; **51**:4/5; **52**:4/5; **55**:2/4; **56**:2/2.

[f22v]

Actions of debt:
11a:6/7 Court adjudges that Collier should recover against Machin in plaint of account 33s 4d & for amercement costs 34s 2d & for his damages 6d.
41:7/17 Court adjudges that Skelton should recover against James for his debt of 40s & for amercement & costs 10s 8d & for damages 5s.
57:1/5 Evan Hollway has attorney Nath Sharp vs Edward Robinson, and brings a copy and has day in next court.

[f23]

Portmoot court held at Guildhall 10 November 1589 before John Williams mayor.
Action of debt:
46:6/16 Since Glover puts no defence in bar to declaration of Browne therefore court adjudges Browne should recover his said debt with costs.
Actions of trespass:
49:5/5; **50**:5/5; **51**:5/5 Discharged between Stret and Boult.

[15] Elizabeth Kent was widow of John Phillips of Wootton.
[16] Court day possibly '28th' (smudged) in B78/1.

Action of trespass on case:
31:9/10 Whereas this court was to have proceeded by awarding a writ of damages for plaintiff Gun, for lack of sufficient answer for defendant Shawe and thereupon plaintiff hath been driven to his several *demurrals:* Now upon request of defendant the court is contented that if defendant before next court shall make agreement with plaintiff by compromise or otherwise then upon information to this court the plaint to cease, or else plaintiff to be awarded a writ to enquire of damages & costs at next court.

[f23v]

Actions of debt:
29:10/10 Sklatter through his attorney Nath Sharp comes to court and confesses himself satisfied vs Ring for sum of 30s 1d with amercement. Discharged.
57:2/5 Peremptory summons for Robinson to respond to Hollway.
Action of Account:
11b:5/7 *Scire facias* against surety of Machin to respond to Collier.
Action of trespass:
58:1/2 Robert Cakbred vs Thomas Barber alias Buttler has day to declare next court. Bailors for Barber: Will Abraham, Jn Heath.
Actions continuing: **52**:5/5; **55**:3/4.

[f24]

Portmoot court held 1 December 1589 before John Williams mayor.
Actions of debt:
11a:7/7 *Scire facias* against surety of Machin, return next court.
46:7/16 Court adjudges Browne should recover vs Glover his debt of £10 & for amercement & costs of suit 11s 0d.
Actions of trespass on case:
12:21/22 *Fiat alias scire facias* against surety of Machin for return next court.
31:10/10 Discharged by the court between Gun and Shawe from the testimony of Nath Sharp.
Action of trespass:
58:2/2 Discharged by court between Cakebred and Barber alias Butler.
Action of debt & detinue:
55:4/4 Discharged by court between James and Kent.

[f24v]

Actions of debt:
41:8/17 *Scire facias* on surety of James in suit of Skelton.
57:3/5 Since Robinson gives no defence in bar of Holway's action, court adjudges Holway should recover £16 for debt & 7s 11d for amercement & costs of suit.

Action of trespass on case:
60:1/2 Thomas Sall vs Robert Turner, pledges for Turner: Mich Mondey & Jas Tasker.
Action of assumpsit:
59:1/5 William Ball vs Thomas Paynter, bail delivered by Mich Mondey & Jn Heath.
Actions continuing: **37**:8/8; **39**:6/6; **42**:6/6; **53**:4/4.

[f25]

Portmoot court held 15 December 1589 before John Williams mayor.
Action of debt:
46:8/16 *Fiat scire facias* against surety of Glover for suit of Browne, for return in next court.
Actions of trespass on case:
60:2/2 Sall appoints Thos Cave his attorney vs Turner. Discharged.
61:1/2 And the said Thomas Sall puts himself under the arbitration of Roger Norwood, gent and John Pyman ald, and Robert Turner does likewise.[17]
Action of account:
11b:6/7 *Fiat alias scire facias* against surety of Machin vs Collier, for return in next court.

[f25v]

41:9/17 *Fiat alias scire facias* against surety of James for suit of Skelton, for return next court.
57:4/5 *Fiat scire facias* against surety of Robinson in suit of Hollowey.
Action of trespass on case:
61:2/2 Memo. that Roger Norwood gent & John Pyman ald arbitrators elected between Thomas Sall plaintiff and Robert Turner defendant by consent of both parties touching their controversies in this court are agreed and pleased that the action of the Case began by the plaintiff shall was and forever be void. And whereas Sall has sowed 7 lands[18] with wheat of Turner in the fields of Souldern ('Soldren') that Sall & his assignees shall quietly have & take, half the crop arising & coming upon the said wheat being indifferently divided at

[f26]

harvest time, without the let trouble reparation or hindrance of Turner or any other person or persons to his use. And also we do further award that in consideration of other charges that is the wheat best rod of the other part of the said land and of tillage, charges in court Turner shall yield and pay to Sall the sum of 12s of good & lawful money of England in present pay & so this quarrel to cease. Witness whereof we the said arbitrators have hereunto put our hands this present 15 December 1589. And further that Turner shall have and enjoy

[17] Referred to in *VCH Oxon*.xii. 392ii, n. 73.

[18] lands = selions; strips in the common fields. Also see Glossary. Only 7 lines on this entry in B77/1.

the barley tilth which has been ploughed & dressed by Sall, without the let or hindrance of Sall his assignees from hence forth, and also over other actions in the County Court began between Turner and Sall shall cease and all debts duties and demands since the beginning of the world to this present day.
Roger Norwood John Pyman Discharged.

[f26v] (Blank)

[f27]

Portmoot court held at Guildhall 12 January 1590 before John Williams mayor.

Actions of debt:

46:9/16 *Alias scire facias* vs surety of Glover. Discharged. (?)

57:5/5 *Scire facias* vs surety of Robinson. Discharged.

Action of trespass on case:

62:1/5 William Ball appoints Thos Cave his attorney vs Thomas Paynter, day given for return of copy in next court.

Action of assumpsit of debt:

63:1/6 John Pyman vs William Skelton for a debt of £200; pledges to prosecute by Jn Phillips & Fras Collingwood.

[f27v]

Portmoot court held 9 February 1590 before John Williams mayor.

Actions of debt:

64:1/6 John Cobbett vs John Coles, with Nath Sharp his attorney. Pledges to prosecute Jn Heath & Humph James.

65:1/1 John Tailor vs Alice Cook; pledged to respond by Thos Prestman & Will Ball. Jn Coles(sic?) essoined by Hen Redgat and Alice Cook by Hen Redgat. Discharged.

41:10/17 *Fiat executio* vs James & surety in suit of Skelton.

Action of trespass on case:

62:2/5 Peremptory summons for Paynter to respond to Ball in next court.

[f28]

Actions of debt:

46:10/16 *Fiat executio* vs Glover and his surety.

68:1/16 Henry Johnson vs Humphrey James & Henry Fletcher, pledges to prosecute Thos Blith & Jn Heath.

69:1/2 William Medcalf vs John Batt; pledges Robt Monck & Humph James.

70:1/3 William Aris vs Matthew Fraunces:pledges Will Abram[19] (Medcalfe) & Humph James.

Action unspecified:

67:1/1 John Kempster vs John Tailor; pledged to prosecute.

[f28v](Blank)

19 'Wm. Abram' = William Medcalfe alias Abraham; see *WCA*, 235.

[f29]

Portmoot court held at Guildhall 2 March 1590 before John Williams mayor.

Actions of debt:

41:11/17 *Fiat executio* renewed vs James and surety.

46:11/16 *Fiat executio* renewed vs Glover and surety.

64:2/6 Second privilege day for Coles to respond to Cobbett.

68:2/16 Johnson appoints Nath Sharp his attorney; James & Fletcher & John Batt essoined by Thos Cave.

70:2/3 Aris appoints Nath Sharp his attorney vs Fraunces and requests day to amend his declaration in next court.

Action of trespass on case:

62:3/5 Paynter responds to declaration of Ball through his attorney Nath Sharp and copy requested.

[f29v](Blank)

[f30]

Portmoot court held 16 March 1590 before John Williams mayor.

Actions of debt:

41:12/17 Renewed *fiat executio* vs James & surety.

46:12/16 Renewed *fiat executio* vs Glover & surety.

64:3/6 Third day for Coles to respond to Cobbett.

68:3/16 Second day for James & Fletcher to respond to Johnson.

70:3/3 Discharged between Aris and Francis.

72:1/1 Robert Symons vs Nicholas Tailor; remains in force.

Actions of assumpsit:

71:1/5 Adrian Whicker vs Edmund Whit; essoined, day to declare.

73:1/1 NicholasTailor vs Robert Symons; remains in force.

74:1/5 Richard Pyman vs Robert Symons who is essoined by T Cave.

Action continuing:

69:2/2 Will Abram als. Medcalf vs Batt.

[f30v]

Action of Dower:

75:1/5 To this court come Richard Kent & Elizabeth his wife and seek claim in right of Elizabeth his wife of one third of one tenement lately in the tenure of William Bailies rent assessed @ 20s/annum; and one tenement in the tenure of Hugh Hamon @ 20s/annum; and one tenement in the tenure of Thomas Freman @ 20s/annum; & a piece of land in tenure of Henry Reddgat @ 9s/annum; & a stable in tenure of Richard Dodman @ 5s/annum; & a tenement held by John Tomlyns @ 26s 8d/annum; & a tenement held by Abraham Daunter @ 16s/annum. And it is ordered by the court to summon the said tenants to answer to said Richard & Elizabeth next court.

Action continuing: **59**:2/5.

[f31]

Portmoot court held at Guildhall 30 March 1590 before John Williams mayor.

Actions of debt:
41:13/17 *Fiat executio* vs James renewed again.
46:13/16 *Fiat executio* vs Glover & surety renewed again.
64:4/6 Peremptory summons for Cole to respond to Cobbett next court.
68:4/16 Third privilege day for James & Fletcher to respond to Jonson.
Actions of assumpsit:
71:2/5 Whicker appoints Nath Sharp his attorney vs Wite, and copy returned.
74:2/5 Pyman appoints Nath Sharp vs Symons.
Action continuing: **59:3/5**.

[f31v]

Action of assumpsit:
76:1/7 Frances Rollright of Water Eaton ('Eton') vs Matthew Frances, pledged by Will Medcalf & Jer White and essoined by Thos Cave.
Tenancy Rentals:
75:2/5 John Meadowes, John Tomlyns, Abraham Danter & Henry Redgate and each of them, having been summoned, do all confess to be the tenants of Richard Pokins. Hugh Hamon & Thomas Freman, having been summoned, confess to be tenants of Mildred Phillips. Anne Bailies, the old stable, tenant for her own self.
Action continuing: **77**:1/1.

[f32]

Portmoot court held at Guildhall 13 April 1590 before John Williams mayor.

Actions of debt:
41:14/17 Execution renewed in suit of Skelton vs James.
46:14/16 *Fiat executio* renewed vs Glover & surety.
64:5/6 Because Coles says nothing in bar of Action on Cobbett's debt plaint for 40s, therefore according to custom of the borough court adjudges Cobbett should recover 40s debt & 10s 6d expenses & costs.
68:5/16 Third day for James & Fletcher to respond to Johnson.
Actions continuing: **71**:3/5; **74**:3/5.

[f32v]

Action of debt:
80:1/8 William Skelton appoints Nath Sharp his attorney vs John Gregory, who has bailors Jn Pyman & Thos Prestman and has copy and day to respond in next court.
Actions of assumpsit:
63:2/6 Skelton is essoined by Nath Sharp to respond to Pyman.
76:2/7 Day given Fraunces to respond to Rowlright.

Action of trespass on case:
62:4/5 Ball replicates and demurrs on the insufficient response of Paynter.
Action of ejectment:
81:1/1 Robert Lyne vs Alice Wilkinson widow & Alice her daughter, complains against them unjustly holding a tenement with adjacent croft, being his right, and seeks restitution. (see also **101**:1/1).
Action of conveyance:
82:1/4 Memorandum that Thomas Danvers gent did acknowledge before John Williams mayor and John Pyman alderman, William Ryley & Thomas Browne ald A concord and fine of two tenements with the appurtenances lying within this borough before this time sold to Roger Norwood of the said borough gent, to be the right and inheritance of the said Roger and his heirs forever. According to his deed thereof to the said Roger made and sealed.

[f33]

82:1/4(cont.) First proclamation made for the two tenements in the tenure of Roger Norwood gent recently purchased from Thomas Danvers gent, and no one comes to claim.
Action of trespass on case:
83:1/1 Henry Fletcher vs Roger Jackson, pledge to respond.

[f33v]

Portmoot court held 27 April 1590 before John Williams mayor.
Actions of debt:
68:6/16 Peremptory summons for James & Fletcher to respond to Johnson in next court.
84:1/15 John Coles requests imparlance to respond to Roger Norwood; bailors Nich Tailor, Humph James.[20]
Action of assumpsit:
74:4/5 Symons responds and has day to amend to Pyman.
Actions continuing: **64**:6/6; **71**:4/5.

[f34]

Actions of debt:
41:15/17 *Fiat executio* renewed vs James & surety in Skelton suit.
46:15/16 *Fiat executio* vs Glover in Browne suit, return next court.
80:2/8 Peremptory summons for Gregori to respond to Skelton, next court.
Actions of assumpsit:
63:3/16 First privilege day for Skelton to respond to Pyman, and copy requested.
76:3/7 Peremptory summons for Fraunces to respond to Rollright in next court.

[20] First entry here of this action.

Action of conveyance:
82:2/4 Second proclamation concerning the two tenements with appurtenances in the tenure of Roger Norwood purchased from Thomas Danvers and no one comes to claim.
Tenancy/Rentals:
75:3/5 And to the said court comes Anne Balies widow and in court gives acknowledgement of her new landlord by payment of one penny and acknowledges herself to be the tenant of Richard Pokins in one tenement at present in her tenure, witness of the court.
75:4/5 And similarly Hugh Hamon tenant of Mildred Phillips by agreement with the said Mildred gives acknowledgement of his new landlord the aforesaid Richard Pokins, witness of the court.
Action continuing: **59**:4/5.
Adjourned for 15 days.

[f34v] (Blank)

[f35]

Portmoot court held at Guildhall 11 May 1590 before John Williams mayor.
Actions of debt:
68:7/16 James & Fletcher imparl through Thos Cave attorney; with copies requested.
84:2/15 Norwood appoints Thos Duffild his attorney vs Coles.
Actions of assumpsit:
63:4/6 Second day of privilege for Skelton to respond to Pyman.
74:5/5 *Venire facias* between Pyman and Symons, return next court.
Actions continuing: **41**:16/17; **46**:16/16.

[f35v]

Actions of debt:
80:3/8 Gregori imparls through Thos Cave to respond to Skelton & puts himself on the country, therefore *venire facias.*
84:3/15 First privilege day for Coles to respond to Norwood.
Actions of assumpsit & trespass on case:
59:5/5 & **62**:5/5 Court discharges between Ball and Paynter, and concordat through arbitrament of Thos Duffild & Jn Bentley.
Actions of assumpsit:
71:5/5 Discharged by court between Whicker vs Whit, because it is agreed.
76:4/7 Frances imparls through Thos Cave & returns assumpsit and puts himself on the country, therefore *venire facias.*
Action of conveyance:
82:3/4 Third proclamation for two tenements recently purchased by Roger Norwood from Thos Danvers & no one comes to claim, therefore it is adjudged that the aforesaid tenements are the right of the said Roger. (see *f70*)

[f36]

Portmoot court held at Guildhall 1 June 1590 before John Williams mayor.

Action of debt:

68:8/16 Court will advise if response of James is sufficient in law, if not then to be amended in next court.

Actions of assumpsit:

63:5/6 Continues between Pyman vs Skelton until court next before the Feast of St. Michael the Archangel next. Bailors for Skelton to respond: Jn Dissell & Jn Heath.

74:6/7 *Fiat habeas corpora* for Pyman vs Symons.

Action continuing: **41**:17/17.

[f36v]

Actions of debt:

80:4/8 *Hab. corpora* for Skelton vs Gregory, return next court.

80:5/8 Witnesses for Skelton: Nath Sharp & Will Easte.

84:4/15 Second day for Coles to respond to Norwood.

86:1/2 Lenard Brown vs William Holway for debt of 15s; pledge John Brown.

Action on the case:

87:1/4 Salloman Coles vs Anthony Hawthorn; bailors for defendant Jn Dissell & Jn Heath.

Action continuing: **76**:5/7 Wroleryght vs Frances.

[f37] (Blank)

[f37v]

Portmoot court held 15 June 1590 before John Williams mayor.

Actions of debt:

68:9/16 James responds to declaration of Johnson, requests copy.

80:6/8 Witnesses for Skelton: Sharp & Easte swear; Witnesses for Gregory: Joan Wryght & Henry Horn swear.

84:5/15 Third day of privilege for Coles to respond to Norwood.

Action of assumpsit:

74:7/7 Court discharges between Pyman and Symons.

[f38]

Actions of debt:

80:7/8 Jury between Skelton and Gregory; 'We find for defendant':
Nathan for plaintiff concedes.

90:1/2 Richard Merywether of Burford vs Robert Parrat of The Grange ('de le grainge') in plaint for 16s. Pledge for prosecution Will Abram; Robt Banting & Nich Tailor for Parat. [21]

[21] Bruern Grange was near Burford; otherwise perhaps Churchill, Middle Aston or Chesterton:see Gelling, & Emery, 105.

Action of Account:
11b:7/7 Machin proffers in court a royal *writ of error* for return on the quindene of Trinity.[22]
Action of ejectment:
89:1/5 Robert Smyth of Bucknell ('Buckmell') in county Oxon vs Alice Wilkinson widow & Alice Wilkinson daughter of Hugh Wilkinson deceased.
Action of assumpsit:
88:1/11 William Ball vs Anthony Noble clerk.
Action of trespass on assumpsit:
91:1/1 Richard Banting vs John Bradley of Radford.
Action continuing: **76**:6/7.

[f38v]

Portmoot Court held 6 July 1590 before John Williams mayor.
(No other officers listed.)
Actions of debt:
68:10/16 Court will advise on response of James to plaint of Johnson in next court.
80:8/8 Court adjudges that Gregori should recover vs Skelton for amercement & his costs for the action 17s.
84:6/15 Peremptory summons for Coles to respond to Norwood next court.
Action of assumpsit:
76:7/7 Court discharges between Rolright vs Francis.
Action on case:
87:2/4 Saloman Cole appoints Thos Duffild his attorney vs . Hawthorn.

[f39]

Portmoot court held 27 July 1590 before John Williams mayor.
Actions of debt:
68:11/16 Johnson replicates to response of James; copy requested. R Wryt.
84:7/15 Coles through Nath Sharp attorney comes to court & confesses action to be true. Thos Duffild.
90:2/2 Rich Merriwether appoints Nath Sharp his attorney vs Robt Parrett, and copy. Ric Wryte. Discharged.
Action on case:
87:3/4 Peremptory summons for Hawthorn to respond next court. Salloman Coles; Thos Dufild.
Action of ejectment:
89:2/5 Robt Smyth appoints Nath Sharp his attorney vs Wilkinson widow & Wilkinson daughter. Widow essoins herself and requests copy of declaration.

[22] Removal to the Queen's Bench.

[f39v]

Action of assumpsit:
88:2/11 Day for declaration next court for Ball vs Noble.
Action of trespass on case:
12:22/22 Nath Sharp proffers a royal *writ of certiorari*[23] for Collier for return on the octave of Michaelmas next.
Action of conveyance:
75:5/5 At this same Portmoot court comes Elizabeth Kent recent relict of John Phillips and privately examined before the mayor[24] acknowledged namely: that the several tenements separately held by John Meddowes, John Tomlyns, Abraham Danter, Henry Redgat, Hugh Hamon, Thomas Freman, Anne Bailies, that Richard Pokins of Wolvercote ('Wolvecote') recently purchased from the said Phillipes, to be the right of his, Ric Pokins & his heirs in perpetuity and disclaim from her dower and joint tenancy aforesaid in perpetuity.
Memo: that at the said court Rich Pokins did confess and grant that Anne Bailies shall hold & enjoy one rectory house or stable of his for 7 years paying a pepper corn if it be demanded to commence at Michaelmas 1590.
Action of ejectment:
89:3/5 Alice Wilkinson makes 'rescue' in Henry Redgat, sergeant[25] on attachment and is sworn.

[f40]

Portmoot court held 10 August 1590 before John Williams mayor.
Actions of debt:
68:12/16 Peremptory summons for James to respond to replication of Johnson in next court.
84:8/15 Court adjudges Norwood should recover from his action £8 vs Coles, & for amercement & costs of suit 10s 2d.
Action on case:
87:4/4 Since Hawthorn *nihil dicit* to declaration of Cole therefore adjudged *fiat* for *writ of inquiry for damages.*

[f40v]

Actions of debt:
97:1/5 Richard Castell vs John Coles:Nat Sharp; Jn Heth, Jer White.
99:1/2 George Doddyn vs John Veysie:bailors Rob Banting, Ric Lowe.
Action of ejectment:
89:4/5 Peremptory summons for Wilkinson to respond to Smyth in next court, day given.

23 Removal to a Westminster Court.
24 Private examination of wife - see Glossary. With respect to the tenement of Abraham Danter see also *WCA*, 32 & WBM 78/2, Cal. f 222v.
25 Rescue: illegal recovery of goods or persons from custody.

Action of trespass on case:
95:1/7 Edward Tynson vs Thomas Croftes: for defendant Robt Walker & Thos Browne, for plaintiff Humph James & Jer White.
Actions of trespass:
96:1/6 John Coles vs Robert Castell; Mich Mondy, Humph James witnesses.
98:1/6 John Coles vs John Harris; Ralph Bradshewe, Fra Collinwood.
Action of assumpsit:
94:1/4 Robert Hanwell vs Richard Tredwell; Will Medcalf, Jn Heth.
Action continuing: **88**:3/11.

[f41]

Portmoot court held 28 September 1590 before John Williams mayor.
Actions of debt:
68:13/16 Court will advise on rejoinder of James, next court.
97:2/5 Castell appoints Nath Sharp his attorney vs Coles.
99:2/2 Dotton appoints Nath Sharp his attorney vs Vesie, this day Hen Redgat proffers 33s 4d to satisfy the debt over and above the costs conceded to the hands of the mayor.
Actions of trespass:
96:2/6 Coles appoints Ric Wryt his attorney vs Castell.
98:2/6 Coles appoints Ric Wryght his attorney vs Harris.
Action of ejectment:
89:5/5 Wilkinson imparls & responds to declaration of Smyth.
Action of trespass on case:
95:2/7 Tynson appoints Ric Wryght his attorney vs Croftes.
Actions of assumpsit:
88:4/11 Ball appoints Nath Sharp his attorney vs Noble.
94:2/4 Hanwell appoints Ric Wryght his attorney vs Tredwell.

[f41v]

Actions of assumpsit:
63:6/6 Discharged by court between Pyman vs Skelton; for £20.
88:5/11 Noble given day next court to respond to Ball.
94:3/4 Hanwell has day next court to declare vs Tredwell; essoined by Nath Sharp.
Action of trespass on case:
95:3/7 Tynson has day to declare next court vs Crostes; essoined by Nath Sharp.
Actions of trespass:
96:3/6 Coles has day to declare next court vs Castell; essoined by Nath Sharp.
98:3/6 Coles has day to declare next court vs Harris; essoined by Nath Sharp.

Finish of this year and book of the time of John Williams for the whole year.

[f42]

Portmoot court held 12 October 1590 before John Williams mayor.

Actions of debt:

68:14/16 Court will advise next court in Johnson vs James.

97:3/5 Cole responds to declaration of Castell, and copy granted.

Actions of trespass:

96:4/6 Coles declares vs Castell.

98:4/6 Coles declares vs Harris.

Actions of assumpsit:

88:6/11 Noble has day next court to respond to Ball's declaration.

94:4/4 Court discharges between Hanwell vs Tredwell.

Trespass on case:

95:4/7 Tinson declares vs Crostes, copy requested.

[f42v]

Portmoot court held 26 October 1590 before John Williams mayor.

Actions of debt:

68:15/16 Court will advise between Johnson vs James, next court.

97:4/5 *Venire facias* between Castell vs Cole.

Action of trespass on case:

95:5/7 Croftes imparls on declaration of Tinson, therefore *ve. fa.*

Actions of trespass:

96:5/6 *Ve. fa.* between Cole vs Castell.

98:5/6 *Ve. fa.* between Cole vs Harriss.

Action of assumpsit:

88:7/11 Noble imparls on declaration of Ball, therefore *ve. fa.* .

Action for right of dower:

111:1/17 To this court comes Magdalen Bruce widow, recently relict of John Bruce senior, and requests her dower in the tenement of Robert Symons now in the tenure of William Ball, and the court will give judgment in the next court.

Action continuing: **86**:2/2.

[f43]

Action of conveyance:

101:1/1 Michael Harb & Alice his wife, Margaret & Francis Wilkinson daughters and co-heirs of one Hugh Wilkinson deceased have come into court and there, before John Williams mayor, George Whitton esq, John Pyman ald and the whole court, confess themselves to have released all their several interests in the late tenement of their father's to be the right of Robert Lyne of Bucknell as that he had from the said Hugh Wilkinson and so forever whosoever and hold up their right. Voluntary confession from them & their heirs to him & his heirs for ever. (See also **81** & **89**)

[f43v] (Blank)

[f44]

102. Court of the Assize of Bread and Ale held at Guildhall before John Williams mayor, Clerk of the Market; Roger Norwood gent & William Ryley alderman, 29 October 1590.

To inquire concerning the prices of grain and victuals:

William Metecalf, John Phillips, Robert Banting, Ralph Bradshewe, John Tailor, John Bruce, William Flye, Robert Winter, William Hix, George Fones, John Heath, John Wells, Richard Lowe, Robert Giles.

Their presentation that:

The best wheat is in value the bushel	2s10d
The second sort of wheat at the bushel	2s6d
The third sort of wheat the bushel	2s4d
The best malt the bushel at	2s8d
The second sort malt the bushel at	2s6d

The Assize gives by the mayor and assistants namely Roger Norwood & Wm Ryley:

The halfpenny White loaf to weigh	8½oz
The penny White loaf to weigh	17oz. troy weight
The penny Wheaten to weigh of Troy weight at	27oz

The brewers to sell ale under the hair seive at 3d the gallon
and of good & stale ale a quart for 1d.
and to sell good wholesome small drink for 1d the gallon;
and that candles be sold within this borough for 3½d the pound.

[f44v]

Action of assumpsit of debt:

103:1/6 Michael Chamber vs Richard Meades; pledges Robt Banting for prosecution, Humph James & Ralph Bradshewe for defendant.

Action of detinue:

104:1/4 John Tailor vs John Laurence; Nath Sharp, pledges Jn Pyman & Fra Collingwood.

Action of debt:

105:1/3 Edulphe Dingley vs Thomas Brombrick, for £4; Humph James, pledges to respond Thos Bradshew, Nich Tailor.

[f45]

Portmoot court held 9 November 1590 before John Williams mayor.

Action of debt:

105:2/3 Dingle requests day to declare through attorney R Wryte, vs Brombrick essoined by Nath Sharp.

Action of detinue:

104:2/4 Tailor through attorney Nath Sharp requests day to declare next court.

Action of assumpsit of debt:
103:2/6 Nath Sharp requests day for Chambers to declare next court, Meades himself appears & essoins himself to respond.
Actions continuing: **68**:16/16; **88**:8/11.

[f45v]

Actions of trespass:
96:6/6 *Hab. corpora* for Coles vs Castell in next court.
98:6/6 *Hab. corpora* for Coles vs Harris in next court.
Action of debt:
106:1/4 John Davye vs Thomas Freman; bailors for defence Thos Bradshew, Jn Coles; for prosecution Ric Wryt & Robt Winter.
Action of trespass on case:
95:6/7 *Fiat hab. corpora* for Tinson in next court.
Action continuing: **97**:5/5.
Adjourn court for 15 days.

[f46]

Portmoot court held 7 December 1590 before John Williams mayor.
Action of trespass on case:
95:7/7 Witnesses for Tinson vs Croftes:
Joan Wyckins, Edward Atkins, John Benett, Margaret Atkins, Mary Colborn all sworn and examined.
Memo. that all touching the controversy between Edward Tynson plaintiff and Thomas Croftes defendant and Thomas Rainford gent it is agreed by consent of all the parties to abide the award of Messrs Pyman, Ryley and Brown arbitrators for Mr mayor to be umpire and have delivered each to the other money upon the *assumpsit* of £5 a piece. Touching the killing of Tinson's hogge and of all actions that may be brought by Mr Rainford for these causes to be ended this present day.

[f46v]

Actions of debt:
105:3/3 Court discharges between Dingley vs Brombryck in accordance with a writ of privilege.
106:2/4 Davy appoints Ric Wryt his attorney vs Freman, and has day to declare in next court.
108:1/2 James Dissell vs William Warner.
Actions of assumpsit:
103:3/6 Chambers appoints Nath Sharp his attorney vs Meades.
107:1/1 William Harbord vs George Norton.
Action of trover & debt:
104:3/4 Tailor appoints Nath Sharp his attorney vs Laurence.[26]

[26] Starting in Detinue but changing to Trover & Debt this action paralleled procedural trend of the time:see p. xxxiv.

Action continuing: **88**:9/11.

[f47]

Portmoot court held 20 December 1590 before John Williams mayor.[27]

Actions of assumpsit:

103:4/6 Second day for Meades to respond to Chambers.

107:2/2 Harbard requests arbitrament of Nath Sharp & Hen Redgat and with assumpsit of £5 by payment of 6d before next court and by arbitration 31s is paid by Harbard & agreement is made 'Concordat'.

Action of trover & debt:

104:4/4 Lawrens responds to declaration of Tailor & puts himself on country & asks for copy, and costs given. Discharged.

Actions of debt:

84:9/15 *Fiat scire facias* vs sureties of Coles in suit of Norwood, return next court.

106:3/4 Since Davy does not prosecute his suit vs Freman or his pledges, then court adjudges he is in mercy & Thomas should recover for expenses & costs unjustly imposed at 6s 5d.

[f47v]

Action of debt on assumpsit:

109:1/6 George Bridges vs Richard Meriwether in plaint for 38s which is attached for pledges.

Action continuing: **88**:10/11.

[f48]

Portmoot court held 25 January 1591 before John Williams mayor.

Action of assumpsit:

103:5/6 Meades confesses action of Chambers vs himself to be true and that he would pay said debt, together with expenses to feast of Annunciation of Blessed Mary next, & continue action.

Actions of debt:

84:10/15 *Fiat alias scire facias* vs sureties of Coles in suit of Norwood.

108:2/2 Dissell essoined by Ric Wright vs Warner, day to declare.

Action of debt on assumpsit:

109:2&3/6 Merriwether appoints Ric Wright vs Bridges; pledge 38s.

[f48v]

Action of assumpsit:

88:11/11 *Fiat ve. fa.* for return next court in Ball vs Noble.

Action of account:

110:1/6 William Riley granted day to declare vs Nicholas Tailor who is essoined by Hen Redgat; pledges Mich Mondy, Ric Lowe.

[27] Court day a Sunday.

Action of Dower:
111:2/17 Magdalen Bruce vs Robt Symons & Will Ball.[28]

[f49]

Portmoot court held 1 March 1591 before John Williams mayor and others.
Actions of debt:
84:11/15 Suit of Norwood, *fiat als scire facias* vs Coles' surety.
114:1/3 Richard Merry vs Thomas Bodie, copy; Jn Dissell, Wm Hix.
Actions of trespass on case:
112:1/1 John Whitton gent vs William Wells, copy; pledges Hugh Hamon, John Wells. Discharged.
113:1/6 John Coles vs Edward Camby; pledges H Jemes, Mich Monday.
115:1/10 William Jahncy vs William Powys, for £300, and imparls. Powys appears in own person.
Actions continuing: **109**:4/6; **110**:2/6.

[f49v]

Actions of debt:
106:4/4 Court will advise between Davie vs Freman - Discharged.
116:1/25 William Ryley ald vs Humphrey Jeames; prosecution pledges: Jn Heth, Will Hix.
117:1/3 Thomas Yate senior vs Thomas Buckner; bailors Fra Collingwood & Wm Spittel.
118:1/2 Thomas Symons vs Richard Lowe.
119:1/2 Thomas Symons vs John Bruce.
Action of trespass on case:
113:2/6 Camby essoined by Ric Wright in next court.
Action of Right of Dower:
111:3/17 Magdalen Bruce widow vs Robt Symons & Will Ball in *writ of dower unde nihil habet*, and declaration in court this same day. Copy.
Adjourned till 15th.

[f50]

Portmoot court held 15 March 1591 before John Williams mayor.
(No other officers listed.)
Actions of debt:
114:2/3 Merry vs Body who requests to wage his law in next court, conceded for himself and four hands.
116:2/25 Riley appoints Nath Sharp his attorney vs Jeames who requests privilege of said borough & conceded to through Ric Wright attorney.[29]

[28] 'Plaint of Dower' taken from B77/1; omitted from B78/1.

[29] Presumably a freeman's privilege referred to in WBM 82, cl. 40 of the two extra privilege court days in answering Portmoot actions; or, less likely, exercising any trade.

117:2/3 Yate vs Buckner, day to declare next court. Buckner essoined by Hen Redgat.
Action of debt on assumpsit:
109:5/6 Peremptory day for Bridges to declare vs Merriwether in next court.
Actions of trespass on case:
113:3/6 Coles vs Camby, imparls and copy.
115:2/10 Peremptory day for Powys to respond to Jancey in next court and the days between.
Action of Dower:
111:4/17 Peremptory day for Symons to respond to Bruce next court.
Action continuing: **110**:3/6.

[f50v]

Actions of debt:
84:12/15 *Fiat alias scire facias* vs surety of Cole; suit of Norwood.
121:1/15 William Metcalf vs Thomas Paynter; Mich Mondy, Jn Heath.
123:1/2 Smyth vs Francklen, this is discharged.
Action of trespass:
122:1/3 Richard Merrywether vs George Bridges.
Action of conveyance:
120:1/3 First proclamation concerning a burgage messuage or tenement within the borough of New Woodstock in the tenure of William Phillips, William Toe and Henry Johnson who by a deed of feoffment made by John London and Ellinor his wife makes over to Richard Foster and his heirs in perpetuity, and no one comes to the claim made in open court.[30]

[f51]

Portmoot court held 29 March 1591 before John Williams mayor.
Actions of debt:
114:3/3 Memo. that this present day being given for Bodye to come in with his four hands to wage his law, and Merry having the same day to be here the said wager is to stand to his action, who being solemnly called did not appear. Therefore being adjudged to pay costs.
116:3/25 Second day for James to respond to Riley.
Action of trespass on case:
113:4/6 Peremptory day for Cambie to respond to Coles next court.
Action of conveyance:
124:1/1 Memo. that a fine and concord between Thomas Bradshewe & Elizabeth his wife knowledged before John Pyman mayor of this borough in the 27th year of the reign of our lady Queen Elizabeth to Thomas Silvester and his heirs and not finished until this day, was by consent of John Williams mayor and divers others, namely:William Riley ald., John Pyman ald., Roger Norwood gent., Thomas Duffild clerk of the Court, the sergeant of the mace Henry

[30] Deed of feoffment: see Glossary.

Redgat, the chamberlains above said and the other officers present at this court allowed for true and a record there of being made by consent of all the persons have there unto put their common seal for Ric Wrytes house.[31]

[f51v]

Actions of debt:

84:13/15 Suit of Norwood: return *alias scire facias* vs surety of Cole & does not come. *Fiat executio* vs Coles & sureties, return next court.

117:3/3 Discharged between Yat vs Buckner.

Action of Dower:

111:5/17 Imparl by Symons through Ric Wright, and copy.

Action of conveyance:

120:2/3 Second proclamation for the tenement in the tenure of Phillips, Toe and Johnson and no one comes to claim etc.

Action of debt on assumpsit:

109:6/6 Memo. that Bridges in court does confess his action against Merrywether and has delivered the money arrested[32] to the use of Merewether 38s beside his costs and so the court is discharged.

Actions continuing: **110**:4/6; **115**:3/10; **116**:4/25; **118**:2/2; **119**:2/2.

[f52]

Flesh in Lent.

125. The jury for flesh in Lent, namely:

Robert Banting,	Richard Wryght,	John Bruse,
William Flie,	John Heath,	William Hix,
John Dissell,	George Fones,	John Wells,
Robert Wynter,	Abraham Danter,	Richard Lowe,
Robert Giles	& Thomas Fitter:	

present a good declaration.[33]

Actions of plaint on case[34]

126:1/11 Richard Merry vs Thomas Body.

127:1/11 Thomas Body vs Richard Merry.

[f52v] (Blank)

[f53]

Portmoot court held 12 April 1591 before John Williams mayor.

Actions of debt:

116:5/25 Third day for Jeames to respond to Riley.

121:2/15 Second day for Paynter to respond to Metcalf.

[31] Omitted from B78/1 but in B77/1 are phrases 'to Thomas Silvester & his heirs' & 'for Ric Wrytes howse'. See also *WCA*, 36.

[32] Arrested = attached.

[33] Omitted from B77/1.

[34] Case: Action for damages for wrongs or injuries free of immediate violence i. e. where covenant or trespass did not apply.

123:2/2 Court discharges between Smyth vs Franclen.
Action of trespass on case:
115:4/10 Powis responds to declaration of Jauncey, and copy.
Action of Dower:
111:6/17 Peremptory day for Bruce to replicate to response of Symons in next court, day given.
Actions continuing: **110**:5/6; **113**:5/6; **122**:2/3.

[f53v]

Actions of plaint on case:
126:2/11 Merry has day next court to declare; Body essoined by Nath Sharp.
127:2/11 Body appoints N Sharp his attorney, Ric Wryt for Merry requests copy.
Action of conveyance:
120:3/3 Third proclamation for the tenement with appurtenances in the tenure of Phillips, Toe & Johnson, and no one comes to claim, therefore court adjudges aforesaid tenement is the right of Richard Foster and his heirs in perpetuity according to the customs of the said borough.

[f54]

Portmoot court held 17 May 1591 before John Williams mayor.
Actions of debt:
116:6/25 Peremptory day for Jemes to respond to Riley next court.
121:3/15 Metcalf vs Paynter, peremptory day to respond.
Action of account:
110:6/6 Discharged between Riley vs Taylor.
Action of trespass:
122:3/3 Discharged Merywether vs Bridges.
Actions of trespass on case:
113:6/6 Discharged between Coles vs Cambye.
115:5/10 Jancey replicates vs Powes, and copy and *ve. fa.*
128:1/7 John Gregory vs Thomas Wilkins essoined by R Wryt next court.
129:1/3 Thomas Gardner vs Ashpole; Ralph Bradshew pledge & essoin for Ashpole.
Action of Dower:
111:7/17 Bruce to replicate in next court vs Symons.
Actions of plaint on case:
126:3/11 Peremptory day for Body to respond to Merry next court.
127:3/11 Peremptory day for Merry to respond to Body next court.

[f54v] (Blank)

[f55]

Portmoot court held 31 May 1591 before John Williams mayor.
Actions of debt:
116:7/25 Jeames imparls to declaration of Riley, and copy.

121:4/15 Paynter imparls to declaration of Metcalf, and copy.
Actions of trespass on case:
115:6/10 Powis to replication of Jancey puts himself on country, therefore *ve. fa.*
130:1/3 John Grevill gent, attorney R Wryt, pledge to prosecute H James, vs Nicholas Gye, bailors Robt Walker & Ric Meades.
Action of Dower:
111:8/17 Peremptory day for Bruce to replicate to Symons next court.
Actions of plaint on case:
126:4/11 Merri appoints Ric Wryght his attorney vs Bodie, copy.
127:4/11 Merrie imparls to declaration of Bodye, and copy.

[f55v]

Actions of trespass on case:
129:2/3 Gardner appoints Nath Sharp his attorney vs Ashpole who is essoined & bailed by Ralph Bradshew.
130:2/3 Gye essoined in next court and Greville to declare in next court.
131:1/2 William Clemson vs Nicholas Launce who is essoined by Hen Redgat & bailed by Jer White & Humph Jemes.
Action unspecified:
132:1/1 Vincent Cowper executor of the will of Richard Cowper citizen of York complainant against Matthew Crostacces: discharged.
Action continuing: **128**:2/7.

[ff56-59v] (Blank)[35]

[f32(B77/1)]

Portmoot court held 14 June 1591 before John Williams mayor.
Action of debt:
116:8/25 Riley vs Jeames *morat in lege.*
Actions of trespass on case:
115:7/10 *Hab. corpora* between Powys vs Jancey, return next court.
129:3/3 Court discharges between Gardner and Ashpole.
130:3/3 Court discharges between Gryvell and Guy.
Action of Dower:
111:9/17 Bruce vs Symons responds & day & copy for Symons.
Actions continuing: **126**:5/11; **127**:5 /11; **128**:3/7; **131**:2/2.
Adjourned for 15 days.

[f32v (B77/1)]

Portmoot court held 28 June 1591 before John Williams mayor.
Actions of debt:
84:14/15 The body of Coles committed to sergeant for debt to Norwood.
116:9/25 Peremptory day for Jeames to respond to Riley and *morat in lege.*

[35] In B78/1 binding cord is exposed here, where folios may have been removed. Minutes for Portmoot courts held 14 & 28 June 1591 are taken from B77/1.

121:5/15 Peremptory day for Paynter to respond to Metcalf in next court.
133:1/9 John Pryce clerk vs William Teasler.
Action of trespass on case:
115:8/10 Request whether the *writ of distringas* could not be returned to next court between Jancey and Powys then by the court entering judgment against Jauncey.
Action of Dower:
111:10/17 Magdalen Bruce and Robert Symons proffer themselves to arbitrament by William Metcalf, Humphrey Jemes, John Pyman & Thomas Duffild arbitrators between them with regard to their suits and pending actions in this court and all their mutual assumpsits on the £20 in hand, stand until the next court as the aforesaid parties prosecute.
Actions continuing: **126** & **127**:6/11; **128**:4/7.

[f60 (B78/1)]

Portmoot court held 12 July 1591 before John Williams mayor.
Actions of debt:
116:10/25 *Ve. fa.* between Riley vs Jeames, return next court.
121:6/15 *Ve. fa.* between Medcalf vs Paynter, return next court.
Action of trespass on case:
115:9/10 Since Jancey does not come to court and prosecute his action vs Powys it is adjudged by the court that Powys should recover the costs & expenses of bringing his suit, and pledges for plaintiff.
Actions continuing: **126** & **127**:7/11.

[f60v]

Action of debt:
133:2/9 Price declares vs Teasler and appoints Nath Sharp his attorney; similarly Ric Wryt for Teasler; copy requested & granted.
Action of Dower:
111:11/17 Symons responds to replication of Bruce, and puts himself on the country, therefore *ve. fa.*
Action of assault & battery:
134:1/4 John Phillips vs Hercules Nash; & appoints Nath Sharp his attorney; Nashe essoined by Ric Wryte; pledges Jer Whit & T Brown; copy requested & granted.
Action of assumpsit:
135:1/8 William Durant vs Michael Denett who is essoined by Ric Wryt; bailors T Brown, Fra Collingwood; prosecution pledge Mr Pyman.
Action continuing: **128**:5/7.

[f61]

Action of Dower:
111:12/17 Citation: The award and arbitrament of Jn Pyman ald, Thos Duffild town clerk, Will Metcalf & Humph Jeames arbitrators indifferently chosen and

agreed by each by Magdalen Bruce as Robert Symons did. And Roger Norwood gent umpire as follows: first whereas there is an action brought in the court of this borough upon a writ of Dower by the said Magdalen against Robert Symons and others for a dower third to be had furth of the tenement or burgage now in the use of William Ball in this borough: it is now agreed that the said Magdalen shall secure her action and claim for the said dower and shall release by a sufficient release to the said Robert Symons & his heirs for ever the said dower whatsoever; upon the sealing of such bonds ('bands') as the said Robt shall seal to the said Magdalen. We the said arbitrators do award that the said Symons & his heirs executors and administrators or one of them shall pay unto the said Bruce her executors and assignees the sum of fifty ('fyvetie') pounds namely: £6 thereof upon Michaelmas Day next 1591; and £6 residue thereof on the day of St. Michael the next following 1592 - if the said Magdalen so long shall live, and he the said Robert shall before the next court deliver Magdalen a sufficient obligation for the payment of the said £5 and then she to release.[36]

[f61v]

Actions of debt:
136:1/3 John Garet vs Richard Hudson. Mr Piman, Fra Collingwood.
137:1/1 John Cuddington vs Robert Bruce.
138:1/1 William Lion(?) of Wawking(?) vs Hix of Islip.

[f62]

Portmoot court held 26 July 1591 before John Williams mayor.

Actions of debt:
116:11/25 *Ve. fa.* returned between Riley vs James.
121:7/15 *Ve. fa.* returned between Medcalf vs Paynter.
121:8/15 *Hab. corpora* for return in next court.
133:3/9 Teasler imparls on declaration of Pryce; court will advise on sufficiency of response.
Action of Dower:
111:13/17 *Ve. fa.* returned between widow Bruce vs Symons.
Actions continuing: **126** & **127**:8/11.

[f62v]

Actions of debt:
116:12/25 *Hab. corpora* between Ryley vs Jeames, return next court.
136:2/3 Hudson on arrest[37] of a horse in suit of Garrett, the jury find that it is not his own personal goods but the goods of Richard Hardyman & John Hardman his son. Judgment that the goods are Richard Hardman's and so it (the horse) should be surrendered.
139:1/4 Thomas Groves vs Richard Hudson, plaint for £4.

[36] Not in B77/1.
[37] arrest=attach.

Actions of trespass on case:
115:10/10 In suit of Powys (def.) for his amercement & costs vs sureties of Walker and *fiat executio* vs Walker for 12s[38] arising from suit.
140:1/1 Richard Hardman vs John Garet. (see also **136**)
Action of Dower:
111:14/17 *Hab. corpora* between Ryley vs Jeames, return next court.
Action of assault & battery:
134:2/4 Peremptory day for Nashe to respond to Phillips.
Actions continuing:**128**:6/7; **135**:2/8.

[f63]

Action of trespass on case:
128:7/7 Memo. that Nath Sharp attorney for Jn Gregorie vs Thos Wilkinson for £100 does confess Wilkinson has satisfied and fully contented Gregory and thereupon the court to be exonerated and his sureties fully discharged, 29 July 1591, 33rd year of Elizabeth, before John Williams mayor, Thomas Browne ald, John Pyman ald.

[f63v]

Action of debt:
141:1/3 Salloman Wesburn vs John Grey; pledges Wm Medcalf, Nath Sharp; and Robt Banting, Jn Dubber.[39]
Actions of trespass on case:
142:1/8 John Grey vs Robert Smyth alias Dyckinson; pledges Robt Banting, Ric Lowe; and Robt Walker, Thos Blith.
143:1/10 George Fones vs William Riley; pledges Ro Walker, Thos Blith.[40]

[f64]

Portmoot court held 9 August 1591 before John Williams mayor.

Action of debt:
116:13/25 The names of the jury between Will Ryley vs Humph Jeames:

William Ball,	Michael Faux,	Jn Phillips,
Thos. Blith,	Jerome White,	Michael Nursse,
Jn Bruce,	Jn Dubber,	Hugh Hamon,
Jn Wilkinson,	Rich Lowe	& Jn Wells:

sworn. We find that James has not paid Ryley according to the conditions of the obligation and assess damages @ 2d & costs 2d.

[f64v]

Action of debt:
133:4/9 Peremptory day for Teasler to make a better response at next court.

[38] Judgment vs plaintiff & Walker.
[39] Washbroke'in 3/3.
[40] Plaintiff Will Fones in **143**:4& 5/10; ends on a continuance. Action **143a** with plaintiff Geo Fones vs Riley is immediately discharged.

Action of trespass on case:
149:1/19 Robert Symons vs John Browne.
Action of Dower:
111:15/17 The names of the jury between Magd Bruce widow vs Robt Symons, namely:

Hen Fletcher,	Jn Phillips,	Robt Banting,
Thos Blithe,	Mich Vaux,	Jer White,
Ric Meed,	Will Flie,	Jn Dubber,
John Dissell,	Geo Fones	& Jn Heath;

Who are charged and on their oaths say they find for the tenants.

[f65]

Actions of debt:
121:9/15 The jury between Will Meatcalf vs Thos Paynter:

Humph Jeames,	Nic Taylor,	Will Ball,
Will Hix,	Mich Nursse,	Jas Dissell,
Jn Wilkinson,	Abraham Danter,	Robt Wynter,
Thos Fytter,	Hugh Hamon	& Jn Coles:

sworn. We find for the plaintiff damages at 2d with costs of court.
136:3/3 Ric Hudson essoined by Ric Wright in next court.
Action of assault & battery:
134:3/4 Herc Nashe through Ric Wright attorney confesses the action between himself and said Jn Phillips to be true and because it is not known what damages he sustained; *fiat* for a writ for damages.
Actions continuing: **126** & **127**:9/11; **135**:3/8.

[f65v]

Actions of debt:
84:15/15 Rog Norwood confesses himself to be satisfied before the mayor as far as 2 obligations for debt by Jn Coles, and in the borough court prosecutes and confesses himself delivered of the bonds aforesaid.
144:1/1 23 August (in margin) Roger Norwood gent vs Magdalen Bruce.
Action of trespass:
145:1/1 John Phillips vs Hercules Nashe; pledge to prosecute. (see also **134**).

[f66]

Portmoot court held 23 August 1591 before John Williams mayor.
Actions of debt:
116:14/25 Judgment adjourned in Will Metcalf vs Thos Paynter.
121:10/15 Judgment adjourned in Will Ryley vs Humph Jemes.
Action of assault & battery:
134:4/4 Names of jury to inquire into damages between John Phillips pl. vs Hercules Nashe def.:

Wm Metcalf,	Humph Jemes,	Ralph Bradshew,
Jn Heath,	Jn Bruce,	Thos Blith,

Ric Meede,	Jn Coles,	Will Hix,
Jn Wilkinson,	Mich Faux	& Hugh Hamon:

Which jury find for the plaintiff damages to the value 26s8d.

[f66v]

Action of debt:
133:5/9 Teasler imparls on declaration of Jn Price.
141:2/3 Westburn through Nath Sharp appears and Grey essoins through Ric Wright.
Actions of trespass on case:
142:2/8 Grey appoints Ric Wryght his attorney vs Smyth, copy granted.
143:2/10 Geo Fones appoints Ric Wright his attorney vs Will Riley who essoins through Nath Sharp; day & copy given.
Actions Continuing: **126**:10/11; **127**:10/11; **135**:4/8; **139**:2/4.

[f67]

146 Court of Assize of Bread and Ale held at Guildhall 25 August (1591) before John Williams mayor, and clerk of the market, Roger Norwood & William Ryley assistants. (Regnal year etc.)

Jury:

Jn Phillips,	Nath Sharp,	Will Flie,
Ralph Bradshewe,	Geo Fones,	Hugh Hamon,
Jn Coles,	Jn Bruce,	Will Hix,
Robt Wynter,	Jas Dissell,	Robt Gieles,
Ric Lowe,	Abraham Danter,	Jn Wilkinson
& Thos Fytter;		

we present:

The best wheat	2s2d the bushel
The second wheat	2s the bushel
The third wheat	21d the bushel
And the bushel of malt	2s2d.

The assize given by the clerk of the market and the said Roger Norwood and Will Riley assistants:

The penny white loaf to weigh	24 ounces only.
The penny wheaten loaf to weigh	36 ounces.
The halfpenny white loaf	12 ounces.
The halfpenny wheaten loaf	18 ounces.

[f67v]

A gallon of ale under the hair seive	3d.

And that every brewer have and do sell good and wholesome drink for one penny the gallon. ld. the gallon.

And that every victualler or alekeeper shall sell a quart of stale ale of the best both within and without doors for a penny and this assize to hold until the next court.

Action of debt:

147:1/1 Edward Hanckes pl. vs Richard Borman, for 11s 8d, pledges for prosecution Mich Faux, Will Hix.

Action of trespass on case:

148:1/1 Richard Borman pl. vs Edward Hanckes.

[f68]

Portmoot court held 6 September 1591 before John Williams mayor.

Actions of debt:

116:15/25 Court adjudges that Will Riley should recover vs Humph Jeames his debt for £23 and for amercement & costs of suit 32s 10d, execution adjourned.

121:11/15 Court adjudges that Will Medcalf should recover vs Thos Paynter his debt with amercement & costs of suit, execution adjourned.

133:6/9 *Ve. fa.* for Jn Pryce vs Teasler.

141:3/3 Washbroke confesses satisfaction through Nath Sharp attorney, for the debt of Jn Grey.

Actions of trespass on case:

142:3/8 Jn Grey vs Robt Smyth, day to respond.

143:3/10 Second day for Will Ryley to respond to George Fones.

[f68v]

Actions on the case:

126:11/11 Discharged between Mery vs Body.

127:11/11 Discharged between Body vs Mery.

Action of debt:

139:3/4 Groves vs Hudson continues.

Action of assumpsit:

135:5/8 Durant vs Denett continues.

Action of trespass on case:

149:2/19 Robt Symons has day to next court to declare vs John Brown.

150 *Baker's assize*: 13 October 1591.

John Bowell baker of Eynsham ('Ensham') wanted in his penny white loaf – 6 ounces, and his penny wheaten loaf – 12 ounces.

He is in mercy.[41]

[f69]

Portmoot court held 20 September 1591 before John Williams mayor.

Actions of debt:

116:16/25 *Fiat scire facias* vs sureties of Humph Jeames.

[41] A rare recording of an assize offence in B78/1 or B78/2; and this case involves a foreign baker who typically had special conditions of sale (see B78/2, f48).

133:7/9 *Fiat bre de hab. corpora* for Jn Pryce vs W Teasler, return in next court.
139:4/4 Court discharges between Groves vs Hudson.
Action of trespass on case:
142:4/8 Peremptory day for Robt Smyth to respond to Jn Grey, and copy.
Action of assumpsit:
135:6/8 Peremptory day for Durant to declare in next court.
Actions continuing: **121**:12/15; **143**:4/10.

[f69v]

Action of trespass on case:
149:3/19 Robt Symons appoints Ric Wryt his attorney vs Jn Brown, and gives copy.
151 *Election of Mayor*: Thomas Brown clerk is made to the office of mayor of this said borough through the choice of the majority of the free burgesses. And Henry Redgat to office of sergeant-at-mace according to the liberties of the said borough.
Conveyance fines:
152 Memo. that at this court certain fines were sealed which were acknowledged before the said mayor and therefore not recordat before this court unto which several fines proclamations having been made accordingly as appeareth in their several courts of proclamation are annexed to the said fines under the common seal of this said borough in full court and before such of Credit are subscribed witnesses as followeth in the next leaf. (**82**:4/4)

[f70]

Final Concord:
82:4/4 This is the final concord made in the court of the said lady Queen of the said borough on 13 April in the thirty-second year of the reign of our lady Elizabeth, queen of England, France and Ireland and defender of the faith in accordance with the custom of the same borough used from time out of mind till now and approved in accordance with the liberties conceded to the mayor and community of the same borough by the charters of the said lady Queen and of her various progenitors late kings and queens of England before John Williams mayor, William Ryley, John Pyman & Thomas Browne aldermen and others the lieges (or subjects) of the said present queen then present. Between Roger Norwood gent plaintiff through Thomas Duffild his attorney to win or to lose. And Thomas Danvers gent deforciant for two messuages, burgages or tenements, two tan-houses, two gardens with appurtenances in New Woodstock and two pasture closes. Which Roger Norwood has as the gift of Danvers and which are handed over in this same court having and holding the same, Roger Norwood and his heirs to hold of the chief lords of that fee which belongs to these tenements. And moreover Danvers grants that he himself and his heirs will warrant to Roger & his heirs to hold the aforesaid

with appurtenances & closes against the said Danvers & his heirs in perpetuity. And for this fine etc. . For those witnesses of the document of the present deed the common seal is affixed.[42]

[f70v]

And further, because the said Roger comes to this court and claims to hold for himself & his heirs in perpetuity the said two tenements with other premises with their appurtenances described above and puts his Claim according to the custom of the said borough in open court solemnly proclaimed and recorded. And this records and proclaims for the first time. And the above at the Portmoot court held 27 April of the above year proclaimed and recorded the claim in the manner & form as above in open court proclaimed the second time. And by the above manner to this court held here 11 May in the coming year the said Roger, through Thos Duffild his attorney and seeks that the said claim be proclaimed a third time by oral proclamation according to the custom of the borough. And thus three oral proclamations are made for the Claim as above. And because no one comes to court to contradict or challenge the claim. Therefore in accordance with custom of the said borough since time out of mind it was approved and attested by John Williams then & there mayor of the said borough, and William Riley, John Pyman & Thomas Browne aldermen (Margin note:witnesses: aldermen aforesaid & Thos Duffild, Jn Phillips, Nath Sharp, Hen Redgat clerk, Ric Wryt clerk.). For which proclamation and enrolment . . . Roger Norwode gave four shillings by way of fine. And thus also by said Jn Williams mayor and other of his aldermen of the borough according to the custom of the borough . . . It is adjudged in accordance with the custom of the same borough that said Roger shall have, enjoy, occupy and hold, for himself & his heirs in perpetuity, the two tenements and closes with appurtenances. In the court with the common seal affixed dated 11 May 32 Elizabeth.

[ff71&71v] (Blank)

[f72]

Portmoot court held 4 October 1591 before John Williams mayor.

Actions of debt:

116:17/25 *Alias scire facias* for surety of Jeames, return next court.

133:8/9 W Teacher has day to replicate to declaration of J Pryce since court finds that insufficient.

Action of trespass on case:

142:5/8 Robt Smyth through Nath Sharp pleads not guilty to declaration; *ve. fa.*

Action unspecified:

154:1/6 Troylus Boucher appoints Ric Wryght attorney vs Robert Hanwell.

[42] The charter of 1453 granted the corporation the right to a common seal. *VCH Oxon.* xii. 390ii, n29.

Action continuing: **143**:5/10.

[f72v]

Action of debt:
121:13/15 *Fiat sci. fa.* for Will Medcalf vs surety of Thos Paynter, next court.
Actions of trespass on case:
149:4/19 Peremptory day for Jn Brown to respond to Robt Symons.
155:1/3 John Price appoints Nath Sharp his attorney vs William Teasler.
157:1/1 Edward Gosse of Bladon vs Thomas Hollway; court discharges.[43]
158:1/1 John Browne vs Richard Browne.
Actions of assumpsit:
135:7/8 Since Durant does not come to declare vs Denet after peremptory summons order for non-suit continues.
159:1/1 John Browne vs Richard Browne.
Action of debt on case:
156:1/1 Thos Smythe vs Samson Morley for £3 17s; Nathan Sharp.

[f73]

Portmoot court held 18 October 1591 before Thomas Browne mayor.
Actions of debt:
116:18/25 *Fiat sci. fa.* vs surety of H Jeames in suit of W Riley.
121:14/15 *Fiat sci. fa.* vs surety of T Paynter on behalf of Metcalf.
133:9/9 Will Teasler has peremptory day to respond vs Jn Pryce who court adjudges has material sufficient for a royal writ[44] of *habeas corpus cum causa*.
Actions of trespass on case:
142:6/8 Jn Gray vs Robt Smyth; *ve. fa.*
143:6/10 George Fones vs Will Riley continue in next court.
149:5/19 Robt Symons vs Jn Brown, continues by assent.
155:2/3 Jn Pryce vs Will Teasler, copy of declaration requested.
Action of assumpsit:
135:8/8 Durant vs Denet, court discharges.
Action unspecified:
154:2/6 Troilus Butcher vs Robt Hanwell continues.

[f73v]

Portmoot court held 8 November 1591 before Thomas Browne mayor.
Actions of trespass on case:
142:7/8 Jn Grey vs Robt Smythe, since *nihil dicit* in bar,[45] court adjudges 9s 5d costs for defendant.
149:6/19 Jn Brown has day to improve his response.

[43] Actions **157-159** omitted from B77/1.
[44] Removal to Westminster.
[45] Interpreted as plaintiff not appearing, to make his case, so action is in *bar* and judgment given to defendant by default.

Actions of assumpsit:
160:1/2 Peremptory day for Will Teasler to respond to Jn Pryce.
161:1/2 Richard Mead made assumption to Mr Norwood in £10, Roger Norwood gent made assumption to Ric Mead in £10 to stand to the end, and arbitrament of Thomas Browne mayor, Will Riley, Jn Pyman, Jn Williams and Will Metcalf aldermen, for a mound in variance between them, so that the end be made by the feast of Purification next.
Action unspecified:
154:3/6 Robt Hanwell to imparl next court & requests copy of declaration of Troilus Butcher.

[f74]

Portmoot court held 22 November 1591 before Thomas Browne mayor.
Actions of trespass on case:
142:8/8 *Fiat executio* vs pl. Jn Grey and he is mainprised for the expenses and costs adjudged by the court because he is non-suited vs Robt Smythe etc.
149:7/19 Robt Symons vs Jn Brown copy to respond.
155:3/3 Between Jn Pryce vs Will Tesler, court discharges.
Action of assumpsit:
160:2/2 Between Jn Price vs Will Tesler, court discharges.
Action unspecified:
154:4/6 *Ve. fa.* between T Butcher vs R Hanwell, return next court.
162 Corporation rental:
Memo. it is agreed by Mr mayor, Will Riley, Jn Williams, Mich Faux, Humph Jemes, Nath Sharp, Ric Wryt, Hen Redgat, Jn Phillips, Jn Tailor, Nich Tailor & Ric Meade of the common council that John Button shall have and enjoy the shop of the late John Coles which was escheated ('excheted') to the town for 1d by the year if it be asked ('axat') by the chamberlains, and giveth the black staff ('stafe') to the town's use.[46]
Actions continuing: **116**:19/25; **121**:15/15.

[f74v]

Portmoot court held 6 December 1591 before Thomas Browne mayor.
Action of trespass on case:
149:8/19 *Ve. fa.* for R Symons vs J Brown, return next court.
Action unspecified:
154:5/6 *Fiat hab. corpus* for Tr Butcher vs R Hanwell, return next court.
Actions of debt:
163:1/2 Richard Pyman vs Robert Symons; pledge to prosecute Nath Sharp, for response Jn Heth & Jn Wells.
165:1/3 Henry Fletcher vs Jerome White, essoined by H Redgat.

[46] Black staff: staffs retained in borough muniments; see *VCH Oxon.* xii. 391i.

Action of assumpsit of debt:
164:1/7 Henry Fletcher vs Francis Collingwood, copy. Pledges Jn Pyman, Hen Redgat.
Actions of Qui Tam:
166:1/4 William Harris on behalf of the Queen & himself vs Thomas Rook for purchasing against the penal statutes.[47]
167:1/5 William Harris vs William Springall in plaint of tresp. o. case.
Action continuing: **116**:20/25.

[f75]

Portmoot court held 20 December 1591 before Thomas Browne mayor, William Riley and John Pyman.

Actions of debt;
116:21/25 *Fiat alias sci. fa.* vs surety of H Jemes in suit of W Riley.
163:2/2 Court discharges between Ric Pyman and Robt Symons.
165:2/3 H Fletcher vs J White continues next court.
Action of trespass on case:
149:9/19 *Fiat hab.corpus* for R Symons vs J Browne, return next court.
Actions unspecified:
154:6/6 Between Tr Butcher vs R Hanwell, *distringas* given until Monday following the feast of the Epiphany.
168:1/6 Stephen White appoints Nath Sharp his attorney vs Thomas Hart; copy requested.
Action of assumpsit of debt:
164:2/7 Fras Collingwood requests first privilege day, granted.
Actions of Qui Tam:
167:2/5 Will Harris proffers information for declaration vs W Springall, who essoins himself and requests copy of information.
166:2/4 Will Harris similarly proffers information vs T Rook, who requests copy.
Action of account:
169:1/2 Thomas Bradshewe vs William Tanner who acknowledges himself indebted to 24s. and is committed to the sergeant-at-mace.
Memo. If Will Tanner before next court does not satisfy Thos Bradshewe (B77/1-'T. Bucher') of the former action, then if he yields himself to the sergeant at the next court, Mr Williams is discharged; if not, to take order.

[f75v]

Portmoot court held 10 January 1592 before Thomas Browne mayor.

Action of assumption of debt:
164:3/7 Second day for F Collingwood to respond to H Fletcher.
Action of debt:
165:3/3 Discharged between Jerome White in suit of H Fletcher.

47 Purchasing contrary to the penal statutes - see p. xxxvi.

Action of trespass on case:
149:10/19 Witnesses examined on the part of Robt Symons p1. vs Jn Brown def.
On oath: John Manying deposed says that 20 marks to be paid in hand and 20 nobles at sealing of the writing, for the Land, being a Close and 3 Butts, as also for Legacies.
Sworn: John Sklatter was present at Mr Williams at A bargain making between Robt Simons and Jn Brown 20 marks was to be paid in hand and 20 nobles at the making up of the assurance as well for the Land as Legacies.
Sworn: Henry Elsby says that he was at payment of 20 marks at two times, and 20 nobles more should be paid at sealing of his writings.

[f76]

Sworn: John Bently deposed says that he was not at the bargain making between Robt Symons and Jn Browne, but yet both of them came to him and told him that R Simons was to have of J Browne a Close and 3 Butts ('butta') in Hensington and that Symons should pay him £20 and one cow as well as in consideration of the Land as of Legacies and other curtesies, and that £13. 6s. 8d was paid at two times, and a cow delivered and 20 nobles the rest at the sealing of the writing for the Land. Names of the jury impanelled between Robt Symons p1. vs Jn Brown def.:
12 sworn.

Hen Fletcher,	Humph Jeames,	Ralph Bradshewe,
Thos Blithe,	Robt Walker,	Jn Phillips,
Jn Tailor,	Ric Meed,	Mich Faux,
Fras Collingwood,	Jer Whit,	Jn Dissell,
Robt Banting,	Thos Paynter,	Will Flie,
Will Hix,	Geo Fones,	Jn Coles,
Jn Bruse,	Jn Wilkinson,	Hugh Hamon,
Jn Heath,	Jn Wells	& Robt Winter

who charged on their oaths say, we find for the plaintiff in damages £6. 14s; and for costs of the suit - 2d.

[f76v]

Action unspecified:
168:2/6 Peremptory day for Thos Hart to respond to S White in next court.[48]
Action of debt:
116:22/25 Will Hix & Jn Heth sureties for Humph Jemes for that they brought not in the said Humphrey at the second *scire facias*, by the order of the court and their own process with the consent of Mr Riley either to bring in Jemes or £23 and 32s 0d for the costs recovered or to yield their bodies, for the said debt at the next court.

48 This entry omitted from B78/1, taken from B77/1.

Action of assumpsit:
161:2/2 Memo. that the award made by the arbitrators between Mr Norwood of the one party and Ric Meades of the other party was sealed and published this present 10th January 1591/2 and does remain under their seals and hands, the said day amongst the records in the Chest.[49]
Actions of Qui Tam:
166:3/4 Peremptory day for T Roke to respond to W Harris's information in next court.
167:3/5 W Harris is contented if W Springall and he cannot agree before next court then to refer it to the court order.
Action of account:
169:2/2 Court discharges between T Bradshewe vs Tanner.

[f77]

Portmoot court held 24 January 1592 before Thomas Brown mayor.
Actions of assumpsit of debt:
103:6/6 Michael Chambers through Nath Sharp confesses himself to be paid and satisfied by payment by Richard Medes of the debt of 40s & 7s for costs of bringing the suit. (see *f48*)
164:4/7 Third privilege day for F Collingwood to respond to H Fletcher; copy.
Action of trespass on case:
143:7/10 Third day for W Riley to respond to G Fones.
Actions of Qui Tam:
166:3/4 Permission to compromise for W Harris vs T Rooke.
170:1/1 Permission to compromise for W Harris vs Ball and day agreed - 12d John Phillips.
Action unspecified:
168:3/6 T Hart imparls on declaration of S White next court, Ric Wright his attorney.
Actions continuing: **116**:23/25; **167**:4/5.

[f77v]

Portmoot court held 21 February 1592 before Thomas Browne mayor.
Action of Dower:
111:16/17 Court will advise on judgment handed down for the party R Symons vs Magd Bruse (see *f64v*).
Action of debt:
116:24/25 Humph Jemes proffers *royal writ of error* and delivered by the mayor in open court vs suit of Will Riley.
Action of trespass on case:
149:11/19 Court will advise on judgment handed down for the party Robt Symons vs Jn Brown.

[49] Borough chest: see *VCH Oxon.*xii. 391i and *WCA*, xv.

Action of assumpsit of debt:
164:5/7 Peremptory day for F Collingwood to respond to H Fletcher in next court.
Action unspecified:
168:4/6 Peremptory day for S White to replicate to T Hart next court.
Actions continuing: **143**:8/10; **166**:4/4; **167**:5/5.

[f78]

Portmoot court held 6 March 1592 before Thomas Browne mayor.
Action of Dower:
111:17/17 The above court to advise on the judgment handed down for Symons vs Magd Bruce in next court.
Actions of trespass on case:
149:12/19 The above court to advise on the judgment handed down for Symons vs Jn Brown in next court (see *f83v*).
143:9/10 Peremptory day for W Riley to respond to G Fones in next court; and copy.
Action of assumpsit of debt:
164:6/7 H Fletcher vs F Collingwood submit themselves to the arbitrament of Roger Norwood gent and Will Metcalf ald in certain plaints of *assumpsit* and each their *assumpsits* for himself and the other in sum of £10 for 4d to stand and remain for arbitrament on this side of next court.
Action unspecified:
168:5/6 Stephen Whit *morat in lege* on the reponse of Thos Hart.
168:6/6 Thos Hart to the same court through his attorney Ric Wryt proffers a *writ of privilege* out of Queen's Bench for return on Wednesday next following Easter three weeks, therefore court will advise.

[f78v]

Portmoot court held 3 April 1592 before Thomas Browne mayor.
Actions of trespass on case:
143:10/10 Continues between Geo Fones vs Will Riley.
172:1/2 Ralph Bradshewe appoints Nath Sharp vs Thomas Riley.
173:1/10 Richard Ayres appoints Ric Wryt vs Mary Riley and declares, and Mary through Nath Sharp requests day to respond, and copy in next court. Pledges:pl. Jn Williams; def. H James & Jer White.
174:1/8 John Baily vs Robert Payne; pledges:pl. Th Duffild; def. Mich Nursse & Jn Heath.
Action of assumpsit of debt:
164:7/7 Court discharges between Hen Fletcher vs Fr Collingwood.

[f79]

Portmoot court held 17 April 1592 before Thomas Browne mayor.
Action of asssumpsit:
143a:1/1 Court discharges for Geo Fones vs Will Riley.

Actions of trespass on case:
172:2/2 To this court comes Ralph Bradshewe and acknowledges satisfaction on the debt of Thos Riley for the sum of £3 9s; and discharged.
173:2/10 Mary Riley requests privilege day to respond to Ric Ayres in next court, day given.[50]
174:2/8 Jn Baily appoints Ric Wryt vs Robt Payne, and copy.
175:1/4 Thomas Osburne vs Henry Coles; pledges to respond H Fletcher & Je Whit.

[f79v]

Portmoot court held at Guildhall 8 May 1592 before Thomas Browne mayor.
Action of debt:
116:25/25 Will Riley vs Humph Jeames; plaint & record for return in Queen's Bench in Easter term.
Actions of trespass on case:
173:3/10 Ric Ayres vs Mary Riley, Riley imparls.
174:3/8 R Payne imparls on declaration of J Baily, copy & day to respond in next court.
175:2/4 H Coles imparls to response of T Osburn, copy & day given in next court.
176:1/2 Henry Flemyn vs Simon Collins.
177:1/5 Richard Getty vs Roger Wheler; H Jemes, Mic Mondy for Wheler.

[f80]

Portmoot court held at Guildhall 1592 before Thomas Browne mayor.[51]
Actions of trespass on case:
173:4/10 *Ve. fa.* between R Ayres vs M Riley for return next court by assent between parties with court's permission.
174:4/8 *Ve. fa.* between J Baily vs R Payne for return next court.
175:3/4 Peremptory day for H Coles to respond to T Osburn in next court.
176:2/2 Simon Collins proffers royal writ here in court for *hab. corpus cum causa* for return on Monday following the octave of Trinity and upheld.[52]
177:2/5 Peremptory day for R Whelare to respond to R Getty in next court, and day given.
Action of debt:
178:1/2 Henry Fletcher vs Leonard Yate ; pledges to respond Will Flie, Thos Colgrave.

[f80v]

Portmoot court held at Guildhall on 5 June 1592 before Thomas Browne mayor.

[50] Mary Riley is granted a freeman's privilege extra court-day to respond, with no comment.
[51] Day & month of Portmoot court omitted in B78/1 & B77/1; (likely to be 22 May 1592).
[52] Removal to a Westminster court.

Actions of trespass on case:
173:5/10 *Fiat hab. corpora* for jury between R Ayres vs M Riley, for return in next court.
174:5/8 *Fiat hab. corpora* between J Baly vs R Payne for jury, for return in next court.
175:4/4 T Osburn vs H Coles in £10 each, put themselves in arbitrament by Roger Norwood and William Medcalf as they settle in next court.
177:3/5 R Getty vs R Whelar by assumption in £10 each to other; stand to the award of John Pyman ald, Roger Norwood gent, William Metcalf & Thomas Duffild town clerk, to be made within the month.
Action of debt:
178:2/2 Peremptory day for Leo Yate to respond to Henry Fletcher in next court, therefore day given.

[f81]

Portmoot court held at Guildhall on 19 June 1592 before Thomas Browne mayor.

Actions of trespass on case:
173:6/10 John Winsmore of the age of 55 years or thereabouts sworn and examined in court touching the debt challenged by Richard Ayres of Mary Riley, says that Mary Riley widow promised after her late husband's death to satisfy the said Ayres for all such wares as he should deliver to her son Thomas at any time.
Names of the jury between Ric Ayres pl. vs Mary Riley wid. def. in this plaint of trespass-on-the-case:

Hen Fletcher,	Robt Walker*,	Jn Phillips*,
Humph Jemes,	Fra Collingwood,	Jn Dubber,
Robt Banting*,	Jer White,	Jn Taylor,
Nich Tailor,	Ric Medes*,	Geo Fones*,
Will Ball*,	Mich Faux,	Jn Heath*,
Jn Dissell*,	Will Hix*,	Jn Bruce*,
Jn Coles*,	Robt Wynter*,	Jn Dysell,
Ric Lowe,	Will Rabon	& Jn Pulco.

*= sworn

[f81v]

Which jury, having been tried and sworn on their oaths, say: we find for the plaintiff in damages - £27, and for costs of his suit 2d.
174:6/8 Jn Baily pl. and Robt Payne def. have put themselves and cause in various to the arbitrament and order and end of Will Riley, Jn Pyman, Jn Williams & Will Medcalf alds. to be decided by them, within one month and their award to be put in writing under their hands and seals, within that time, and have bound viz. the said Baily to the said Payne by 6d to him given in the sum of £10 and the said Payne by giving 6d to the said Baily hath bound

himself in £10 to stand to their award which if they finish not within this month then to leave them to their trial as before.

[f82]

Portmoot court held at Guildhall on 3 July 1592 before Thomas Browne mayor.

Actions of trespass on case:

173:7/10 Court will advise between R Ayres vs M Riley on handing over judgment, until next court.

177:4/5 R Gettie vs R Whelar by assumpsit in £10 either to the other and gave 6d to make arbitrament by Jn Pyman ald, Will Medcalf ald, Rog Norwood & Thos Duffild to end their cause and to put it in writing before next court, or else in peril for Whelar.

[f82v]

Portmoot court held at Guildhall on 17 July 1592 before Thomas Browne mayor.

Actions of trespass on case:

173:8/10 Court adjudges that R Ayres should recover vs M Riley widow for his damages in the recent action for £27 and for amercement & his costs of bringing the suit of 25s 8d.

174:7/8 Memo. that in same court a certain arbitrament between J Baily vs R Payne has been publicly read in court and is under the seals and hands of the arbitrators.

177:5/5 Memo. that such arbitrament to be published in court between R Getty vs R Whelar the same day, and court discharges.

180:1/16 William Fly vs Francis Collingwood; pledges Jn Pyman, Jn Hethe.

183:1/4 John Phillips vs Edmund Barnes.

Actions of debt:

179:1/2 Isabel Freeman vs John Heath; Freeman essoined by Redgat; pledges Thos Paynter, Jn Coles.

181:1/1 William Metcalf vs Elizabeth Pole widow.[53]

182:1/1 Ralph Bradshew vs Elizabeth Pole widow.

[f83]

Portmoot court held at Guildhall on 31 July 1592 before Thomas Browne mayor.

Actions of trespass on case:

173:9/10 *Fiat scire facias* vs sureties of M. Riley; return next court.

174:8/8 Memo. that R Payne has paid this present day in court to J Bayly for the award made in his suit the sum of £3 and Baily has released 10s. and each have sealed releases to the other from the beginning of the world to this day as well for the mother as other unto whom this appertains and all is discharged.[54]

[53] Entries on **179** to **183** omitted from B77/1.

[54] ". . . . . the mother. . ." : see Glossary.

180:2/16 Will Flie vs Fra Collingwood, day to declare next court.
183:2/4 Jn Phillips essoined by Nath Sharp vs Edm Barnes in next court and upheld.
Action of debt:
179:2/2 Court discharges between Isabel Freeman vs John Heath.

[f83v]

Action of trespass on case:
149:13/19 Court adjudges that R Symons should recover vs J Broun in this certain plaint for his damages the sum of £6. 14s and for his amercement 2d, and for further damages & costs of bringing his suit 25s 10d; in total sum £8.
184 Corporation business:[55]
Item: Michael Nursse and Thomas Colgrave brought into the Guildhall each 1 bucket. 2 buckets.

[f84]

Portmoot court held at Guildhall on 14 August 1592 before Thomas Browne mayor.
Actions of trespass on case:
180:3/16 W Flie declares vs F Collingwood who requests privilege day which is granted. Renewed first *sci. fa.* since it is delayed coming, return next court, *fiat* for renewal.
183:3/4 J Phillips appoints Nath Sharpe vs E Barns; pledge Jn Heath. Attachment for Barns, return next court, & to respond.
Action of assumpsit of debt:
185:1/3 Richard Mead appoints Nath Sharp his attorney vs Thomas Bowle, & pledges Will Metcalf, Jn Phillips. Bowle essoined through Hen Redgat.

[f84v]

Portmoot court held on 28 August 1592 before Thomas Browne mayor.
Actions of trespass on case:
149:14/19 For R Symons court will advise in next court for execution vs J Browne (see f131v).
173:10/10 *Alias sci. fa.* for Ayres vs M. Riley, return next court.
180:4/16 Second privilege day for Fra Collingwood.
183:4/4 Discharged between Jn Phillips vs E Barns.
Action of debt:
187:1/1 Edmund Clodhill vs Ball for debt on demand of 40s.; pledges for prosecution Th Duffild, He Redgat.
29 August: Discharged.
Action unspecified:
186:1/10 Thomas Paynter appoints Ric Wryt his attorney & requests day to amend; granted in next court.

55 By 1580 all new freemen provided a leather bucket for fire fighting; or an equivalent fee of 2s6d in the late 16th century. *VCH Oxon*. xii. 376ii; WBM 82: Borough Orders 1580, Clause 17.

Action continuing: **185**:2/3.

[f85]

Portmoot court held at Guildhall on 11 September 1592 before Thomas Browne mayor.

Action of trespass on case:

180:5/16 Third privilege day for F Collingwood. Thomas Hardwycke admitted attorney for W Flie until end of suit.

Actions of assumpsit of debt:

185:3/3 R Mead vs T Bowle in plaint for £5.

189:1/1 Richard Bennett of Adderbury vs John Ossendie alias Hostelds in plaint for £6. 13s 4d on demand; pledges for prosecution Th Coles, Jn Sket senior.

Action unspecified:

186:2/10 Nich Tailor requests privilege day; granted.

Action of debt:

188:1/1 Powell Thomas vs William Teasler.

[f85v]

Actions of debt:

190:1/1 Richard Pyman vs Robert Symons; pledges:pl. Jn Pyman, def. Hen Fletcher, Jer White.

191:1/6 Nicholas Taylor vs Thomas Paynter; Mich Mondy, Jn Heth for Paynter.

192:1/12 Richard Wakfield of Cleveley ('Clevley') vs Richard Fawdrey son of same place, for £6. Jn Coles, Jn Wells for prosecution.

[f86]

193 Assize of Bread & Ale.

Court of the Queen held at Guildhall 13 September 1592 before Thomas Browne mayor and clerk of the market and before Powell esquire clerk notary of the household of our lady Queen as follows.[56]

[f86v]

Portmoot court held at Guildhall on 9 October 1592 before Thomas Browne mayor.

Action unspecified:

186:3/10 Second privilege day for N Tailor to respond to T Paynter.

[56] Although royal clerks of the market were barred from the borough by the charter of 1453, the corporation welcomed clerks general and clerks of the verge during the frequent royal visits of the late 16th & early 17th centuries, and allowed them to declare the assize. (*VCH Oxon*. xii. 371i reference to this entry; and WBM 79, *passim*. Also see p. xxxix.).

Actions of trespass on case:[57]
180:6/16 F Collingwood responds and W Flie given day & copy.
196:1/1 John Symes vs Nicholas Symes of Somerton, to return.
Actions of debt:
194:1/1 Thomas Gibson gent vs William Skelton.
195:1/2 Edward Roberts vs George Fones, for 20s. ; pledges Ro Walker, T Duffild.
Action of trespass & ejectment:
197:1/1 William Hardwyck vs James & Thomas Coles & John Raunson.
Actions of Qui Tam:
198:1/1 James Dissell on behalf of Queen & himself vs Henry How of Bletchingdon ('-ton'), plaint of debt.
199:1/5 James Dissell vs Thomas Ryman of Charlbury glover, plaint of debt.
200:1/1 James Dissell vs John Sharp of Southleigh ('-ly') senior yeoman & John Sharp junior & William Austine of same & John Hart of same, for badging and selling of sheep, in plaint of debt.[58]
202:1/4 James Dissell vs James Watts, in plaint of debt.
203:1/1 James Dissell vs Edward Klerk of Kidlington ('kyd-') tanner, plaint of debt.
204:1/5 James Dizell vs John London in plaint of debt.

[f87]

Portmoot court held at Guildhall on 23 October 1592 before Thomas Browne mayor.

Action of trespass on case:
180:7/16 Peremptory day for W Flie to replicate to response of F Collingwood in next court.
Action unspecified:
186:4/10 Peremptory day for N Taylor to respond to T Paynter in next court.
Actions of debt:
191:2/6 Nic Tailor appoints Thomas Hardwyck his attorney vs Thos Paynter, day next court to declare.
195:2/2 Paid in court before Mr mayor the full demand of Edward Roberts' action by George Fones, 19s 10d in full discharge of all actions, and to and from the beginning of the world.
Actions of Qui Tam:
199:2/5 Jas Dissell puts information in court vs Thos Ryman glover on behalf of the Queen & himself as suitors, and Thomas requests day & copy to respond in next court.

57 Rest of this court omitted from B77/1.
58 'Badging and selling of sheep' in contravention of the statutes 5, 6 Edward VI, c. 14 re-issued in 1586 in Book of Orders (see also f141 and p. xxxvi). *Qui Tam* was a species of action of Debt. (Gilmore, 101).

205:1/4 James Dissell on behalf of the Queen & himself prosecute together vs Nicholas Brydges on information to the value of £18 and delivered said information in court. And Brydges through Ric Wryt his attorney says that in no manner is he guilty of this and so puts himself on the country. And plaintiff similarly.

[f87v]

Actions of Qui Tam:

204:2/5 Jas Dizell *qui tam* for Queen & himself proffers in court information according to the form of the statutes vs Jn London chandler in action on the statutes to value £18. And London through attorney Ric Wryt requests a copy and is granted day to respond in next court.

206:1/4 James Dissell proffers information in court vs Edward Roberts, with suitors the Queen & himself concerning 2 dickers ('dica') of leather to value of £10. And Roberts requests copy and given day to respond in next court.[59]

Action unspecified:

207:1/3 Richard Pyman appoints Ric Wryt his attorney vs Robert Symons who is essoined by Hen Redgat; day to declare next court.

208 Keeping the peace.

Wiliam Metcalf recognises his debt to the Queen of £10 and John Pyman proffers £5 on behalf of William that he will keep the peace towards all people of our lady Queen and particularly towards Jerome White in any manner.

Jerome White recognises his debt to the Queen of £10 and to keep the peace against all people and especially against Will Metcalf, to appear at the Sessions next.

[f88]

Portmoot court held at Guildhall on 6 November 1592 before Thomas Browne mayor.

Action of trespass on case:

180:8/16 W Flie replicates to F Collingwood, *ve. fa.* granted next court.

Action unspecified:

186:5/10 N Tailor responds to T Paynter, who requests day to replicate in next court.

Actions of Qui Tam:

199:3/5 T Ryman responds and Jas Dissell requests copy & day to respond next court.

204:3/5 J London responds by putting himself on the country and Jas Dissell through Ric Wryt is granted copy and day to imparl in next court.

205:2/4 Jas Dissell imparls with N Brydges until next court.

206:2/4 Edw Roberts responds & Jas Dissell requests copy & day next court. Dissell & Roberts, thro' Wryt, granted imparlance.

[59] Dicker ('dica') of leather is ten hides. An offence presumably in contravention of the leather-trade statutes 24 Henry VIII, c. 1 or 5 Eliz. c. 8 (see also f122v and p. xxxvi).

[f88v]

Action of debt:
192:2/12 Ric Wakefield appoints Ric Wryte his attorney and Ric Fawdry requests copy & day to respond next court. Will Hix, Nich Tailor.
Action of Qui Tam:
202:2/4 Jas Watts essoined by Ric Wryt at next court and responds to Jas Dissell, & granted copy & permission to imparl. Not guilty.
Action unspecified:
207:2/3 Action continues between R Symons & R Pyman for 1 month.

[f89]

Portmoot court held in Guildhall on 20 November 1592 before Thomas Browne mayor.

Action of trespass on case:
180:9/16 Let there be made a *habeas corpora* for W Flie vs F Collingwood for return next court.
Action unspecified:
186:6/10 Peremptory day for T Paynter to replicate to N. Tailor in next court.
Action of debt:
191:3/6 N Tailor given day to amend declaration vs Paynter.
Actions of Qui Tam:
199:4/5 *Ve. fa.* for Queen & Jas Dissell vs T Ryman, return next court.
204:4/5 Concord for London, & refer to chamberlains and others.
205:3/4 *Ve. fa.* for Queen & Jas Dissell vs N Brydges, return next court.
206:3/4 *Ve. fa.* for Queen & Jas Dissell vs E Roberts, return next court.

[f89v]

Actions of debt:
192:3/12 Peremptory day for Fawdry to respond to R Wakfild next court.
209:1/2 Roger Flie vs Frideswide Edges for £10, and appoints Thos Hardwyck his attorney. And to this court comes Frid Edges and confesses the action to be true.
209:2/2 Rog Fly in person confesses himself satisfied in the aforesaid plaint vs Fr Edges and of the 2s. thereof and the court discharges.
Actions of Qui Tam:
202:3/4 *Ve. fa.* for Queen & Jas Dissell vs J Watts, return next court.
204:5/5 To this court comes Jn London and made fines for trespass according to the form of the statutes for not entering the trade as rope-maker, and said London by assent of the court makes fine of 3s 4d.[60, 61]

[60] Entries on **204**, **210** & **211** omitted from B77/1.

[61] John London, chandler, is sued for entering trade as rope-maker without licence thereby contravening the statutes (21 Hen VIII. c. 21 - Holdsworth IV, 343). Reads as 'cordarius' (rope-maker) ; possibly 'cordonarius' (cordwainer)

Actions unspecified:
210:1/1 And to this court comes Katherine Abram alias Medcalf and appears in the suit of William Ball, and because he does not come and prosecute in respect thereof so he pays amercement for the defendant 2s 10d for court. Discharged.
211:1/1 Anthony Noble clerk appears in suit of William Ball and he does not come to plead, therefore no suit, and to pay court amercement - 2s 10d.

[f90]

Action of assumpsit of debt:
212:1/4 Thomas Brown vs Ethelbert Doe, for £4 8s.

[f90v]

Portmoot court held in Guildhall on 4 December 1592 before Thomas Browne mayor.

Action unspecified:
186:7/10 And T Paynter replicates to response of N Tailor & puts himself on the country; *ve. fa.*
Actions of debt:
191:4/6 N Tailor appoints Thos Hardwyk in plaint of trespass on case vs T Paynter; copy & day granted.
192:4/12 Fawdry through Thos Hardwyke his attorney responds to R Wakfild; & copy & day granted.
Action of trespass on case:
180:10/6 Jury betweenWill Fly p1. vs Fra Collingwood def.:

Robt Walker,	Ralph Bradshew,	Jn Phillips,
Will Ball,	Robt Banting,	Jerom White,
Mich Nursse,	Thos Blith,	Geo Fones,
Jn Bruce,	Jn Wylkinson	& Jn Heathe:

all sworn.

[f91]

Witnesses for plaintiff's party: Jn Wodsroff, Fras Gryffyn, Robert Wynter, William Hiche & Michael Harles: sworn.
John Woodsroffe says William Fly brought the gelding upon May over to Fra Collingwood and loaded the horse with 8 todd[62] and not above and Fly did help to load him and at the going over the bridge Fly said he doubted that his gelding would not hold out because he had lent him forth the week before, and so the gelding travelled with his burden to Cirencester ('Cysseter'), and was there well kept and travelled homewards within 5 miles of home, and because he had charge about him he left him at Hailey with the smith, the morrow after

62 1 tod=281bs. of wool; packhorses could carry 3cwt. =12 tods (Wood, 419).

being Monday, and was loaded with nothing but saddle and wanty and surcingle.[63, 64]

Francis Gryffyn says that he overtook, about twelve months past, Francis Collingwood betwixt the new gate and Gorrel ('gorell') gate and rode upon the horse being loaded from new gate almost to Gorrel gate, and that it was Will Flie's horse and that the horse came hence well to Flye's house for that time.

Robert Wynter says that Fly called this deponent to go with him, and found him (the horse) a furlong's length from Gorrel gate laid on the ground on one side and left him so and said that John Wodsroff gave him 6d to stay with him and gave him meat, and said that the horse's back was broken; as the flaying of him well proved.

[f91v]

Sworn: Michael Harles says that Will Fly willed him as he had also Winter to go see the gelding and found him as Wynter said and received 6d of Wodrofe to watch him and gave him meat.

Sworn: William Hiche says that at the flaying of the said horse he found the back of the horse broken.

Sworn: Francis Heath says that he met with John Wodrofe at the park wall who did drive the said gelding and went well until he came almost to Cirencester and then began to truck but performed the journey.[65]

Action of Qui Tam:

206:4/4 Edw Roberts in action of trespass against the statutes acknowledges the award and fine of the assessment for the Queen & for the court. Discharged.

Discharged by the court by assent of Jas Dissell & through the court for the defendant. Discharged.

4s. paid to the chamberlains, to the said Jn Phillips.

Action unspecified:

207:3/3 Continues between R Pyman vs R Symons until the feast of the Purification of the Blessed Mary next.

Action continuing: **212**:2/4.

[f92]

Actions of Qui Tam:

199:5/5 Jas Dissell vs T Ryman, concerning maintenance, committed to arbitrament of Jn Dubber & Jn Phillips until next court.[66]

63 This packhorse going on a likely wool-route from Woodstock to Cirencester travelled not by Bladon (c.f. *VCH Oxon*. xii. 98, 213, 362), but northwards by bridge (over the Holloway or at the Glyme causeway; *VCH Oxon*. xii. 337ii) to a new park-gate. This highway crossed the park to the Gorrel gate in the N. W quarter (map on *VCH Oxon*. xii. 442) and apparently onward to Hailey. The new gate may have been at the site of the Podge gate at the lower end of Old Woodstock *VCH Oxon*. xii. 423).

64 Wanty: a rope or girth by which burdens are tied to the back of a pack-horse (Havinden, 337).

65 to truck: to potter about.

66 Maintenance:(applying to plaintiff James Dissell), interference with other people's law; unlawful

202:4/4 Court discharges between Jas Dissell with Queen on breaking of form of statutes vs Jas Watts who confesses the action; court satisfied by payment of sum of 4s.
205:4/4 Court discharges between Jas Dissell vs Nic Brydges in which information on breaking the statutes is satisfied by a fine assessed at 3s6d.
Action of debt:
213:1/15 Henry Fletcher vs Richard Kent of Wootton his executor & Elizabeth his wife as administratrix of the goods and chattels which he brings from John Phillips lately called John Phillips of Wootton in a plaint of debt of his executor Henry.

[f92v]

Portmoot court held in Guildhall on 18 December 1592 before Thomas Brown mayor.

Actions of debt:
191:5/6 T Paynter requests day to respond to N Tailor next court.
192:5/12 R Wakfield replicates to response of R Fawdry & puts himself on country; def. similarly, therefore *ve. fa.* next court.
Actions unspecified:
186:8/10 Between T Paynter vs N Tailor *ve. fa.* returned; *hab. corpora* for return next court.
215:1/1 Court discharges between John Lawns vs William Page.
Action of Qui Tam:
216:1/4 James Dissell on behalf of Queen & himself vs William Page of Stow ('-e'), requests day to inform court in better manner.
Action continuing: **212**:3/4.

[f93]

Arbitrament:
186:9/10 & **191**:6/6 Memo: that in the two several actions brought between Thos Paynter pl. and Nicholas Taylor def. & also in other actions brought by Nic Tailor pl. and Thos Paynter def. and all other causes whatsoever are put to the arbitrament of John Pyman, John Williams aldermen, Ralph Bradshewe & John Phillips arbitrators indifferently chosen to end all causes and to deliver up in writing their award at or before the next court, and Mr mayor is chosen umpire and each party hath affirmed to stand to their order under pain of £10 upon assumption by giving each to other 4d.
Action of Qui Tam:
216:2/4 Will Page appoints Ric Wryte his attorney to respond to the plaint of the Queen & Jas Dissell.

---

upholding of a person or cause (statute of 11 Henry VIII, c. 3; Bellamy, 105). Dalton, 32, includes here unjust and feigned suits relating to informations upon the penal laws.

Adjourned 21 days.
Action of trespass on case:
217:1/1 Mayor and commonalty vs George Clay.

[f93v]

Portmoot court held 8 January 1593 before Thomas Browne mayor.
Actions of debt:
192:6/12 *Habeas corpora* for Wakfild, return next court.
213:2/15 Between Hen Fletcher vs Ric Kent & Eliz his wife; bail Ralph Bradshewe, Jn Phillips for response.
213:3/15 Pl. appoints Thos Hardwyck his attorney & presents suit in court; defs. appoint Ric Wryghte their attorney and request copy & day.
Actions of Qui Tam:
199:6/7 *Ve. fa.* between Jas Dissell vs Ryman return next court; court discharges, dismissed.
216:3/4 And said Will Page *morat in lege* on insufficiency of information.
Action unspecified:
186:10/10 Action between Paynter vs N Taylor compounded & finished. Discharged.
Action of assumpsit for debt:
212:4/4 Between Thos Browne vs Doe, granted discharge.

[f94]

Action of trespass on case:
180:11/16 Judgment between W Flie vs F Collingwood adjourned until next court.
Action of Dower/Debt; Fine:
213:4/15 & **218**:1/1 Elizabeth Kent examined alone by the mayor in court, responded and willingly confessed herself satisfied in respect of the Dower in any manner of claims in court in all that land whatsoever in the tenure of Roger Norwood gent . Fine.[67]
Action of debt:
219:1/7 Thomas Brown vs John Coles.

[f94v]

Portmoot court held at Guildhall on 15 January 1593 before Thomas Browne mayor.
Action of Qui Tam:
199:7/7 Discharged between Ryman def. and Dysell pl.
Action of trespass on case:
220:1/12 Henry Fetherston vs Syrack Okley, day to declare next court. Bail: T Duffild, Ric Wryt ; Mr Williams, Will Hix. Oklie essoined by Hen Redgat.

[67] Private examination of wife to confirm a fine that would, in this particular case, bar her dower claim, but not any kind of hereditary right.

Actions of debt:
213:5/15 R &E Kent have peremptory day till next court to respond to H Fletcher.
192:7/12 Sworn between Ric Wakfild pl. and Ric Fawdy def.[68]

[f95]

John Child is sworn and examined and says that Fawdry would just as well pay the said £4 as the 40s, and that plaintiff Wakfild would be paid in full, but asks the said promises, making a total for the payment of the six pounds willed his endowment, and he would seal it by sennight today. For the party of the defendant: Will Slaymaker sworn: at payment of the plaintiff heard not any promises; Troylus Butcher sworn; Thomas Busby sworn.
219:2/7 Thos Brown mayor essoined by Ric Wryte; bail for Coles: H Fletcher, Jn Heathe.
Action of trespass on case:
180:12/16 Court adjudges that W Flie should recover vs F Collingwood for damages 30s & 2d amercement, and for expenses of bringing suit to court 30s.
Action of Qui Tam:
216:4/4 *Morat in lege* for Page and copy of demurrer.
221 Child maintenance:
Ann Jeakes has promised to cause her father, with sufficient surety, to enter bond ('band') sufficient before Easter next that her child shall not hereafter be a charge to the borough.

[f95v]

Portmoot court held at Guildhall on 29 January 1593 before Thomas Browne mayor.
Actions of debt:
213:6/15 Day given Ric Kent to answer Hen Fletcher next court; and he produces letters of administration of all the goods etc. of John Phillips and is quit by virtue of having fully administered under the seal of the ordinary and (?) the acts of his office.
219:3/7 Thos Brown vs Jn Coles has day to declare next court.
Action of trespass on case:
220:2/12 H Fetherston appoints Ric Wryt vs S Ockley who has day & copy to respond in next court.
Action of Qui Tam:
222:1/3 James Dissell for Queen & himself vs Richard Mirry and has day to declare in next court.

[f96]

Actions of debt:
192:8/12 Court adjudges that R Wakfild should recover vs R Fawdry for his past debt of £6. 26s.[69]

68 All entry omitted in B77/1.
69 Rest of court omitted in B77/1.

225:1/2 Robert Ellis vs George Johnson; Jn Duber, Je White.
226:1/2 Thomas Tesdale vs Robert Sparrow.
Actions of Qui Tam:
223:1/3 James Dizel vs Raffe Malin, for Queen & himself in debt; T Bradshewe, Jer White.
224:1/2 William Harris for Queen & himself vs Geoffrey Pokins in debt; pledges Jn Heath, Hen Redgat.

Portmoot court held at Guildhall on 12 February 1593 before Thomas Browne mayor.
Action of debt:
213:7/15 Ric Kent has peremptory day to respond to Hen Fletcher in next court.
Actions of trespass on case:
220:3/12 S Okley responds to H Fetherston through Thos Hardwyck his attorney, & copy of declaration for response.
[f96v]
180:13/16 *Sci. fa.* for W Flye vs F Collingwood & surety.
Actions of debt:
192:9/12 *Sci. fa.* vs R Fadry & his pledges in suit of R Wakfield.
219:4/7 T Brown appoints Ric Wryte his attorney vs J Coles who is given day to respond next court.
Actions of Qui Tam:
222:2/3 Jas Dissell produces information vs Ric Merry, & day given to respond.
Permission granted for court to confer & compound with Merry on behalf of Dissell, so court responds with fine - 18d.
Action unspecified:
227:1/4 Richard Pyman has day to declare vs Robert Symons in next court.
[f97]
Portmoot court held at Guildhall on 26 February 1593 before Thomas Browne mayor.
Action of trespass on case:
180:14/16 *Fiat als. sci. fa.* vs F Collingwood & his surety, return next court; pl. W Flie.
Actions of debt:
192:10/12 *Fiat als. sci. fa.* vs surety of R Fawdry in suit of Wakefild, return next court.

213:8/15 Ric & E Kent respond to declaration of H Fletcher who replicates; Kents request copy & day in next court.
226:2/2 Continues in Thos Tesdale vs Sparowe, who comes in next court in own person.
Action of Qui Tam:
222:3/3 Court discharges between Jas Dissell vs Ric Merry.
Action unspecfied:
227:2/4 Ric Pyman appoints Ric Wryt his attorney vs Robt Symons.
Action continuing: **219**:5/7.

[f97v]

Actions of Qui Tam:
223:2/3 Jas Dissell requests permission of court to confer & compound with Ralph Malyn which is granted and fine for trespass paid to the chamberlains 7s.
223:3/3 Court discharges between Jas Dissell vs Malin.
224:2/2 Will Harris vs Geoff Pokis, requests permission to confer & compound, granted; fine paid to chamberlains 7s.
Action of debt:
225:2/2 Court discharges between Robt Ellis vs Geo Jonson by assent of Ellis because the debt of 40s. is paid.

Portmoot court held at Guildhall on 12 March 1593 before Thomas Browne mayor.

Actions of debt:
192:11/12 *Fiat executio* vs R Fawdry & pledge in suit of Wakfild.
213:9/15 *Ve. fa.* between H Fletcher vs R Kent, return next court.
Actions of trespass on case:
220:4/12 *Fiat ve. fa.* between H Fetherston vs S Okley, return next court.

[f98]

180:15/16 *Fiat executio* vs surety of F Collingwood in suit of W Flie.
Actions of debt:
229:1/3 Aloys Standard vs John Boutley; pledges for Bootly, Ralph Bradshewe, Jer Whit.
230:1/5 John Coles vs Zachary Shephard.
Actions unspecified:
227:3/4 R Pyman vs R Symons are agreed so that amercement & costs are paid in next court.
228:1/5 Michael Nursse appoints Thos Hardwyk his attorney vs Hercules Nashe who is essoined by Ric Wryt.
Action continuing: **219**:6/7.
Adjourned on 15 days, in next court.

[f98v]

Portmoot court held at Guildhall on 26 March 1593 before Thomas Browne mayor.

Action of trespass on case:

180:16/16 Sergeant-at-mace returns that judgment has been executed vs F Collingwood & surety in suit of W Fly, and debt with damages to value of £3. ld through attorney Thos Hardwyck, and Fly confesses himself satisfied.

Action of debt:

192:12/12 Sergeant-at-mace returns that judgment has been executed vs R Fawdry & surety for £7. 6s. which is similarly paid into court to the use of R Wakfild, and has been seized to the use of the borough, since Wakfild is suspected of being a felon, until he has been delivered.[70]

Actions of Qui Tam:

231:1/3 William Harris for Queen & himself vs William Hunt of Witney ('Wytney') for debt; information through T Hardwyk. Ric Wryte.

233:1/4 James Dissell vs Thomas Kent of Kidlington, for debt to Queen. Will Metcalf, Jn Williams.

Action of trespass:

232:1/3 William Harris vs Richard Pereman.

[f99]

Actions of debt:

213:10/15 *Ve. fa.* for H Fletcher vs R Kent because he has not yet delivered (the deed).

229:2/3 Jn Boutley requests day & copy to return as it stands in next court.

230:2/5 Jn Coles appoints Thos Hardwyck his attorney vs Zach. Shepard gent., & has day to declare next court; Shepard essoined by Ric Wryte attorney.

234:1/1 Richard Fawdry vs goods & chattels of Richard Wakfild; pledges to prosecute: Will Hix, Ralph Bradshewe.

Action of trespass on case:

220:5/12 *Fiat hab. corpora* for Fetherston vs Okley.

Actions unspecified:

227:4/4 Discharged between R Pyman vs R Symons since R Wryt attorney for Pyman confesses himself satisfied.

228:2/5 Mich Nursse vs Herc Nashe who through Ric Wryt attorney requests day & copy, granted.

Adjourned until 11th April.

[f99v]

Portmoot court held on 26 April 1593 before Thomas Browne mayor.[71]

[70] Conviction for felony, apart from the possibility of the death penalty, incurred forfeiture of lands and goods.

[71] This court date was a Thursday.

Actions of debt:
213:11/15 *Fiat hab. corpora* for H Fletcher to make jury between Fletcher vs Kent return in next court.
229:3/3 Discharged between Aloys Standart and John Boutley.
Action of conveyance:
235:1/1 Memo. that possession and seisin ('season') was had and taken by Margaret Prestman widow, of a tenement wherein William Rabon dwelleth the 26th April and by her delivered to the sergeant of the mace, and by him accordingly redelivered over to Richard Dubber and his heirs forever. In the presence of Thomas Brown mayor, John Williams, Ralph Bradshew, John Dubber chamberlains, Thomas Duffild, John Phillips, Richard Meade, Henry Redgat sergeant and many others.[72]
Actions continuing: **228**:3/5; **230**:3/5; **231**:2/3; **232**:2/3; **233**:2/4.

[f100]

Action of trespass on case:
220:6/12 Names of the jury between Henry Fetherston pl. and Sirac Okeley def.: Jn Phillips, Jn Rauson, Jerome White, Thos Blyth, Jn Bruce, Geo Fones, Hugh Hamon, Jn Heath, Mich Nursse, Jn Dissell, Mich Faux, & Jn Button: sworn. Witnesses sworn for the party of Fetherston: Phillipa Hands says that she promised her mother to lend to Syrack 20s. which she had of her mother, and delivered the same to Syrack to be repaid when she did demand the same, and further that Syrack did once or twice request her to do so. William Trevyse of the age of 53 years or there about says that, when the Queen's majesty was in the County on retreat,[73] he confessed he heard Syrack say he had not 20s. but a stack of 1 noble and 10 groats in money. And that the matter by consent of both parties was arbitrated by his self and one John Hands, & that in consideration of all matters as well of the money or other trifles they awarded Syrack to pay 25s. and that Syrack followed the parties to Woodstock to have an end, though.

[f100v]

John Hands deposed says that he was made acquainted with the matter first upon St. Matthew's Day last and that the award by his self and Will Trevyse was 25s. to be paid by Syrack Okley within a fortnight next.
The said Jury between Fetherston and Ockly assessed damages for plaintiff at 21s 1d, & for amercement & costs of suit.

Portmoot court held at Guildhall on 28 May 1593 before Thomas Brown mayor.

Action of debt:
230:4/5 Peremptory day for Z Shepard to respond to J Coles.

[72] This livery of seisin was a delivery of feudal possession, part of the process of feoffment (see also *VCH Oxon*. xii. 392i, n. 60).
[73] Elizabeth I came on progress through Oxfordshire in 1592, visiting Sir Henry Lee at Ditchley (Walters, 90).

Actions of Qui Tam
231:3/3 Discharged between W Harris vs W Hunt.
233:3/4 *Ve. fa.* between Jas Dissell vs Thos Kent, return next court.
Action of Trespass:
232:3/3 Discharged between Will Harris vs Ric Perman.
Action continuing: **228**:4/5.

[f101]

Action of debt:
213:12/15 Renewed *hab. corpora* for jury between H Fletcher vs Ric & E Kent for return the Wednesday after Pentecost next.
Actions of trespass on case:
220:7/12 Court adjudges that H Fetherston should recover vs S Okley in his action & for his damages 3ls 1d & for amercement & costs of bringing his suit 28s 4d, in total sum 49s 5d.
236:1/6 Peremptory day for John Coles to declare vs Richard Tredwell; defendant's pledges Fra Collingwood, Jn Heth.
Action of Qui Tam:
237:1/6 James Dissell in person informs on behalf of Queen & himself vs Richard Yatman; pledges J Dubber, R Walker; Ric Wryt for Yatman requests copy of information.
Action unspecified:
238:1/2 Peremptory day for John Coles to declare vs Richard Coles next court; pledges to respond Jn Williams, Jn Dubber.
239 Apprenticeship:
Robert Sear of Adstock in county Buckinghamshire, puts himself apprentice to John Dubber for the term of 7 years from 27 May 1593, 35 Eliz., in the art of shoemaker as bound for full indenture etc.

[f101v]

Trust Obligations:
240:1/2 Memo. that Mr Thomas Norwood gent executor to Mr Roger Norwood gent unto who certain obligations were committed of trust to be kept viz.: one of £80 for payment of £40, to one Jane Watson; the other of £80 for payment of £40 by Henry Whatson of Hethe ('heath') and Robert Payne of Nether Worton ('netherwort') to one Elizabeth Watson dated the 8th December 1586, of which last bond of £80 due to Elizabeth there was confessed in court by one Richard Bartleyt husband to the said Elizabeth Whatson that he has received upon the said bond £20 as parcel of the £40. And also he has promised that the other £20 shall remain in the hands of Henry Watson and the execution of Robert Payn to the use of John Mansell, Robert & Alice Mansell the children of the said Elizabeth; Which said obligation does as now remain in the Chamber of Woodstock of special trust to the children's use until further

order be taken. And so the said Mr Thomas Norwood is discharged, also Jane has received her obligation.
Adjourn for 15 days.

[f102]

Portmoot court held at Guildhall on 11 June 1593 before Thomas Browne mayor.

Actions of trespass on case:
220:8/12 *Scire facias* for Sirack Okley & surety.
236:2/6 Peremptory day for Jn Coles to declare vs Ric Tredwell.
Action of debt:
230:5/5 Discharged between Jn Coles vs Z Shepard as formerly cleared of charges.
Actions of Qui Tam:
233:4/4 *Ve. fa.* between Jas Dissell vs T Kent, return next court.
237:2/6 Ric Yatman requests day & copy to respond to Jas Dissell in next court.
Actions unspecified:
238:2/2 Discharged between Jn Coles vs Ric Coles.
241:1/1 Discharged between James Dissell vs Tredwell.

[f102v]

Action of debt:
213:13/15 Witnesses sworn for the party of Henry Fletcher p1.:Edward Sponer deposed affirms that the Inventory of Phillips' goods and things therein were favourably appraised and a good pennyworth. William James deposed says as the former deponent, affirms that the parcel or goods of the Inventory were favourably appraised and a good pennyworth.
For the party of the defendant:
William Clark deposed says that the horses and cattle were delivered as a debt to satisfy Mistress Clark of £21 16s 8d. upon a specialty due to ald Mr Clark and recovered before the mayor of Oxford being owed John Phillips his debt; 2 days before the death of Phillips.
Actions unspecified:
228:5/5 Continues between Mich Nursse vs Herc Nashe by assent of parties.
242:1/18 Richard Mede appoints Thos Hardwyck his attorney vs Thomas Bowle; pledges for Boll: Jn Pyman, Fras Collingwood; and Bowle requests day and copy.

[f103]

Action of debt:
213:14/15 Names of jury between Hen Fletcher p1. vs Ric Kent & Eliz his wife defs.:

RobtWalker,	Jn Dubber*,	Fra Collingwood,
Thos Blythe*,	Will Ball*,	Jn Tailor,

Ric Meede,	Nic Meade,	Robt Banting*,
Will Flie*,	Jn Heath*,	Jn Raunson*,
Thos Colegrove*,	Jer Whit*,	Mich Nurse*,
Geo Fones*,	Jn Tomlyn*,	Jn Bruce,
Jn Wilkinson,	Hugh Hamon,	Jn Dissell,
Jn Willis,	Robt Wynter	& Jas Dissell.

*sworn.

The aforesaid jurors say they find for the plaintiff and assess damages for him at 2d & amercement 2d.

Lease:

243:1/1 A lease of 60 years from the date to Mr Clark of a messuage and 2 yardlands, a cottage and 7 acres of free land, if John Phillips and Elizabeth so long live, from Walter Culpeper etc.:shewn in the court. The action begun 6 December 1592, 35 Eliz., and was taken further 16 January 1592/3.[74]

Court adjourned for 15 days.

[f103v]

Portmoot court held at Guildhall on 25 June 1593 before Thomas Browne mayor.

Action of debt:

213:15/15 Robert Clarke proffers royal writ of *hab. corpus cum causa* for Ric & Eliz Kent for return on the Tuesday next after the octave of Michaelmas.[75]

Actions of trespass on case:

220:9/12 Sergeant-at-mace returns *sci. fa.* for S Okly; *fiat als. sci. fa.* for surety of Okly for return next court.

236:3/6 Peremptory day for R Tredwell to respond to J Coles next court.

Actions of Qui Tam:

233:5/6 Imparlance granted for Jas Dysell and Thos Kent.

237:3/6 *Ve. fa.* for Jas Dissell, return & trial next court.

237:4/6 And Ric Yatman to the information against himself by Jas Dissell, maintains his word that in no manner is he guilty thereof, and he puts himself on the country.

Action unspecified:

242:2/18 Peremptory day for Thos Boll to respond to Ric Mead.

Adjourned for 15 days.

[f104]

Portmoot court held on 9 July 1593 before Thomas Browne mayor.

Actions of trespass on case:

220:10/12 *Als. sci. fa.* returned by sergeant for Fetherstone vs M Okley.

236:4/6 R Tredwell appoints Thos Duffild to respond to declaration of J Coles, & requests copy of Coles.

[74] Yardland: an area of land, usually of 30 acres. See Glossary.

[75] Removed to a Westminster court.

236:5/6 Arbitrament: Ric Tredwell assumes to Jn Coles in £20, Jn Coles to R Tredwell in £20 by giving each other 4d to stand and abide the order and award of James Apletre, Mr Phillip Bodwyn, Edward Baker and Edward Savage to end the cause in controversy in this court. The award to be put in writing and delivered to the parties within a month after this court. End.
Adjourned.
Actions of Qui Tam:
233:6/6 Discharged between Jas Dissell vs Thos Kent.
237:5/6 *Ve. fa.* for Jas Dissell vs R Yatman, trial next court.
Action unspecified:
242:3/18 Peremptory day for Boll to respond next court to Meade.

[f104v]

Portmoot court held at Guildhall on 30 July 1593 before Thomas Browne mayor.
Actions of trespass on case:
220:11/12 Sergeant returns body of S Okly to satisfy H Fetherstone for his damages of 21s 1d & amercement of 28s 4d, & his body is committed to sergeant for execution of judgment.
236:6/6 Memo. that the matter depending in court between J Coles and R Tredwell was by consent of both parties agreed before Mr Thomas Udall gent, and also Richard Wryt attorney confesses that the said Coles is pleased and contented as appears by a release sealed by Coles to Tredwell dated 27 July 1593. Discharged by the court.
Actions unspecified:
242:4/18 If Thos Boll comes to court and swears to respond truthfully, then the court will order judgment against him, unless this court is not able to maintain the plaint of Ric Mede's declaration before demurrer.
244:1/5 John Phillips appoints Thomas Hardwyck vs Richard Kent, and Kent appoints Richard Wryt his attorney and requests day & copy of imparlance in next court.

[f105]

Action of trespass on case:
220:12/12 Memo. that R Wryt attorney for H Fetherstone upon receipt of 49s 5d which by judgment & execution in this court the said Henry has received, and the said S Okly has satisfied the said debt & charges, and Wryt confesses satisfaction in court and said Syrack Okly is discharged.
Action of trespass:
245:1/9 John Heath requests day to declare vs John Coles in next court.
Action of Qui Tam:
237:6/6 Because Jas Dissell does not prosecute his action vs Ric Yatman but makes default, court discharges.

Trust obligations:
240:2/2 Memo. that this present day in court before the mayor and others, one obligation being dated 8 December 29 Eliz. (1586) of £80, wherein Henry Whatson of Hethe ('Heath') and Robert Payne of Nether Worton are bound to pay £40 at the feast of St. John the Baptist next, was delivered to Elizabeth the wife of Richard Bartlett of Wroxton ('Roxston') in county Oxon, and the court discharged the said writing.
246 Assize of Bread & Ale.
Fiat warrant to constables to present the assize of bread and ale on Wednesday next following.
To 15 days.

[f105v]

Action of debt:
219:7/7 John Brown vs John Coles, pledge to prosecute.[76]
Actions of trespass on case:
247:1/1 William Metcalf vs Hercules Nashe.
248:1/3 Thomas Bromryck vs Edward Huffer.
249:1/4 Between Thomas Bromrycke vs Edward Huffer & Mary his wife; pledges to prosecute: John Williams, Nicholas Tailor.

Portmoot court held at Guildhall on 13 August 1593 before Thomas Browne mayor.
Actions unspecified:
242:5/18 On behalf of Thos Boll either sufficient response in next court or judgment between attorneys.
244:2/5 Peremptory day for Ric Kent to respond to Jn Phillips in next court.
Action of trespass:
245:2/9 Jn Heath appoints Thomas Hardwyck his attorney vs Jn Coles, and Ric Wryt requests day & copy.

[f106]

Actions of trespass on case:
248:2/3 Thos Bromryk appoints Thos Hardwyck his attorney vs Edw Huffer.[77]
249:2/4 The same Bromryk appoints Thos Hardwyck his attorney (R Wryt, G Fones) vs Edw & Mary Huffer for goods & chattels; Jn Williams, Nic Tailor.
249a:1/2 The same Bromryck appoints Thos Hardwyck his attorney vs Edward & Mary Huffer.
250:1/3 George Audly gent vs Roger Cowper, and essoined by Ric Wryt, and said Cowper by James Boutley.

[76] John (*sic* Thomas) Brown.
[77] Rest of court omitted from B77/1.

Portmoot court held 27 August 1593 before Thomas Browne mayor.

Actions unspecified:

242:6/18 T Boll responds and plaintiff *morat in lege* and has day to replicate.

244:3/5 Jn Phillips vs Ric Kent who responds, and plaintiff requests copy of response & day to replicate next court.

Action of trespass:

245:3/9 Peremptory day for Jn Coles to respond to Jn Heath.

Action of trespass on case:

249:3/4 Peremptory day for Edw & Mary Huffer to respond.

[f106v]

Action of debt:

251:1/22 Edward Lee gent vs Thomas Bromryck.

Portmoot court held at Guildhall on 10 September 1593 before Thomas Browne mayor.

Actions unspecified:

242:7/18 Ric Mead replicates to response of Thos Boll, and Mead rejoinders on the demurrer. And said Mead and Boll have day to confer with their counsels and return the deeds to next court.

244:4/5 J Phillips replicates vs R Kent and puts himself on the country, and defendant similarly; *ve. fa.* for court for Phillips and Kent.

Action of trespass:

245:4/9 J Coles responds *non-assumpsit* to J Heath; *ve. fa.* for jury, for return next court.

[f107]

Actions of trespass on case:

248:3/3 Edw Huffer responds to Thos Bromryck.

249:4/4 Edw & Mary Huffer respond to Thos Bromryck.

249a:2/2 In further action vs Huffers, Edw &Mary respond, and request copy & day.

Action of trespass on case:

250:2/3 Continues between G Audley vs R Cowper next court.

Action of trover:

252:1/1 John Yemans of Deddington, of 50years and upwards, sworn, upon his knowledge concerning the mare arrested for Edward Huffers whose the mare is, says that Mr Edward Lee bought the said mare of Edw Huffers on St Peter's Day last for 26s 8d and still is the mare of Mr Lee and was at the time of the attachment the 7 August last; Whereupon the action of Trover against Edw Huffer is discharged. The charge of the arrest[78] is to be paid back. The court will advise.

Action unspecified:

253:1/1 Ralph Bradshewe & John Dubber vs goods & chattels of Thomas Coles.

[78] arrest = attachment.

[f107v]

Portmoot court held 17 September 1593 before Thomas Brown mayor.
(No other officers listed.)
Actions unspecified:
242:8/18 Demurrer delivered by Ric Wryt for Thos Boll for viewing and judgment, return next court.
244:5/5 Discharged between J Phillips vs R Kente, and confesses satisfaction through Thos Hardwyck.
Action of trespass:
245:5/9 *Fiat hab. corpora* between J Heath vs J Coles, return next court.
Action of debt:
251:2/22 Edw Lee appoints Ric Wryt vs Thos Bromryck in plaint of debt, and defendant through Thos Hardwyck requests day & copy. Peremptory day for Bromryck to replicate to 2 years arrears in next court. Jn Ruste?, Jn Coles prosecution.
Action continuing: **250**:3/3.
Adjourned for 15 days.[79]

[f108]

18 September 1593.
Actions of debt:
254:1/2 William Baker of North Aston vs Benet Roberts of Shipton upon Cherwell; pledge to prosecute.
255:1/1 Andrew Phippes husbandman of South Leigh vs Thomas Symons of same place; pledge to prosecute.

Portmoot court 1 October 1593 before John Williams mayor.
(Crossed through).
(No other officers listed.)
Action of trespass on case:
256:1/2 Thomas Rydge vs William Doyley; bailors for Doyley:
William Metcalf ald; John Coles.
Action of trespass:
257:1/2 John Symons & Susanne his wife vs Thomas Holland; pledge to prosecute; bailor for Holland: Humfrey James.

[f108v]

Portmoot court held 1 October 1593 before John Williams mayor.
(No other officers listed.)
Action of trespass:
245:6/9 William Herne sworn says that John Heth & John Coles came to his house on Ascension Eve and after divers speeches Jn Coles promised to pay

[79] B77/1 account of Portmoot ends here, apart from occasional notes. MS Bodl. d.47 'fair copy' starts at Portmoot 1 October 1593.

the money to Jn Heath:the 40s and the 44s on Monday in next Advent following.

Action of debt:

251:2/22 Peremptory day for Thos Bromryck to respond to Edw Lee in next court; copy requested.[80]

[f109]

Action of trespass:

245:7/9 Jury between Jn Heath vs Jn Coles; namely: Robt Walker, Hen Fletcher, Jn Dissell, Geo Fones, Will Flie, Jerome White, Jn Button, Robt Winter, Ric Lowe, Robt Giles, Lancelot Winter & Jas Dissell; all sworn.
The aforesaid jurors assess damages for the plaintiff at £4 and for costs of his suit at 2d.

[f109v]

Portmoot court held at Guildhall on 15 October 1593 before John Williams mayor.

Action unspecified:

242:9/18 R Meade vs T Bowle, defendant charged on demurrer.

Actions of trespass:

245:8/9 Court adjudges that J Heth should recover vs J Coles for his damages of £4 & for costs 2d & for further costs 26s 10d in toto £5:7s. *Fiat capias* vs J Cole in suit of J Heath.

201:1/1 Humphrey James in own person declares vs Jane Catt.

Action of debt:

251:3/22 T Brombrick responds to declaration of E Lee; both put themselves on country, therefore *ve. fa.* for jury.

[f110]

Action unspecified:

242:10/18 Court ordains that T Bowle to have good & sufficient response and foundation to declaration of R Meade, otherwise *nihil dicit*. (Entry crossed through.)
Memo. that both for plaintiff & defendant:plaintiff to mend his declaration and to deliver it up to 6 days before next court; and defendant to plead to it certainly at his peril at next court.

Action of trespass on case:

256:2/2 Thos Rydge requests day to declare in next court and conceded vs Will Doiley. William Springall & William Phippes to end the matter between this and the next court between Ridge and Doyley:charges assumptions each to other in £5 by 4d given to each other assumpsit, the end to be in writing to inform the court.

[80] Repeat entry; see f107v.

Action of trespass:
257:2/2 Thos Holland essoined by Humphrey Jemes in next court to respond to Jn Symons.

[f110v]

Action of Dower:
258:1/3 Ursula Weller widow claims her dower:namely one third of two thirds (excluding the dower of Ann Bulliphant) and order is given to summon the tenants of the lands to answer the said Ursula at the next court.
Conveyance:
259:1/5 Memo. that possession and seisin ('season') was had and taken by the said Richard Elliott & Alice his wife the 15th day of October and delivered by them to the sergeant-at-mace to be redelivered by him to Francis Collingwood and to his heirs[81] in perpetuity according to the custom of this borough, of all their parts of 2 tenements of this borough now in the use and possession of the said Francis and his assignees; in the presence of John Williams mayor, Will Ryley, Thos Brown & Will Metcalf, Hen Redgat sergeant, Thos Duffild, Will Rayer, Ric Wryt, Thos Norwood, Ann Brown, Ellen Brown, Edw Barnes, Phillip Blythe, Thos Metcalf, Hen Bradshewe and many others.

[f111]

259:2/5 Memo. also that Richard Elliot, cooper of Thatcham in county Berks. ('Barks.'), and Alice his wife being examined[82] alone of her self confessed before the mayor there that she freely yielded up her right and title whatsoever in these 2 messuages held in the tenure of Francis Collingwood or his wife to have and to hold to the said Francis and his heirs in perpetuity from the said Richard and Alice & their heirs and that the said Francis hath satisfied them fully for the same, and that this be recorded and a fine thereof duly levied according to the custom of this borough to the use of the said Francis & his heirs for ever. Richard Elliot;
X Alice her mark.
Conveyance:
260:1/6 Memo. that a possession and seisin ('season') was taken, by a letter of attorney from ald Thomas Norwood gent to Thomas Brown and Francis Collingwood first of November 1593, of the tenement[83] now in the occupation of Nicholas Taylor. And by them delivered to William Rayer of Weston-on-the-green and his heirs as also by the sergeant-of-the-mace, according to custom of this borough in the presence of John Williams mayor, Thos Duffild, Ric Wryt, Hen Redgat, Jn Tailor, Hen Thornton, Chris Batson & Thos Abotts.

[81] Livery of seisin: see Glossary 'Seisin'.
[82] Private examination of wife - see Glossary.
[83] For tenement see *VCH Oxon*. xii. 354, under The Bear Inn, and footnotes; also *WCA*, 36.

[f111v]

Portmoot court held at Guildhall on 5 November 1593 before John Williams mayor.

(Richard Wryt deputizing for Thomas Duffild; no other officers listed.)

Action of trespass:

245:9/9 *Fiat sci. fa.* vs surety of J Cole, return next court.

Actions unspecified:

242:11/18 Th Boll requests day & copy to respond to Ric Mead in next court, granted.

261:1/5 John Wells granted day to declare vs John Stiles next court.

Actions of debt:

251:4/22 *Ve. fa.* for Edw Lee vs T Bromryk.

254:2/2 Will Baker vs Benet Roberts, day to declare, Baker essoined.

Action of Dower

258:2/3 Ursula Weller seeks claim of her dower, day to declare in next court.

Action of Qui Tam:

262:1/4 William Harris for information vs Rancken, request for copy of information.

[f112]

Portmoot court held at Guildhall on 19 November 1593 before John Williams mayor.

(No other officers listed.)

Action of debt:

251:5/22 Return *ve. fa.* for Edw Lee vs Th Bromryck next court.

Action of Dower:

258:3/3 And Edward Bulliphant comes and claims to have and to hold a third part of all those lands and tenements which have been held by Justinian Weller, lately of Yarnton ('Yardington'), deceased, at time of his death in separate tenure or occupation by Robert Banting, Richard Smyth and John Pulcoe within the borough of New Woodstock, as the right of Anne lately wife of said Justin Weller; and it is ordered to summon the said tenants to be at the next court here etc. And because Hugh Weller, son & heir of said Justin Weller, and Jasper Weller present themselves in court to acknowledge not only the dower of the aforesaid Ursula but also of the aforesaid Anne and concede to both parties their dowers to be divided accordingly by unanimous assent of the court. (See also **427**)

Actions unspecified:

242:12/18 Th Bowle responds to declaration of Ric Meade through Ric Wryt attorney.

261:2/5 Jn Wells appoints Ric Wryte his attorney & declares vs Jn Stiles who appoints Thos Hardwyck his attorney & requests day & copy to respond in next court.

Action of Qui Tam:
262:2/4 Court grants permission for Will Harris to confer and compound with William Rancken, who confesses the action and himself to be guilty.

[f112v]

Portmoot court held on 10 December 1593 before John Williams mayor.

Action of debt:
251:6/22 *Ve. fa.* between Edw Le vs Th Bromryck.
Action on the case:
263:1/5 Henry Redgat vs William Harewood (Jn Ranson, Jn Hethe), essoins himself.
Actions unspecified:
242:13/18 Ric Mead vs Th Bowle put themselves on country therefore *ve. fa.* for return next court.
265:1/1 Because John Bruce does not prosecute his action vs Isabel Freman, therefore court adjudges that John should pay the said Isabel for amercement & costs 2s 6d.
Action of trespass on case:
264:1/6 Robert Strete appoints Humphrey James his attorney and requests day to declare vs John Knight, who appears in person, in next court.

[f113]

Action unspecified:
261:3/5 And the said Jn Stiles through Th Hardwyck attorney refuses to respond to declaration of Jn Wells unless first the particular deed in the declaration is specified and proffered in court, which will be granted at next court, with peremptory day to respond there.
Court adjourned until 17 December.
Action of assumpsit:
266:1/1 Hugh Hamon vs Richard Triplett of Hampton Gay.
Action of debt:
267:1/11 William Metcalf vs William Bowne; pledges to respond: John Pyman ald, Thomas Bradshewe gent .

[f113v]

Portmoot court held at Guildhall on 17 December 1593 before John Williams mayor.

Action of debt:
251:7/22 *Fiat hab. corpora* for Edw Lee vs Th Bromryck, next court.
Actions unspecified:
242:14/18 *Fiat hab. corpora* for jury for Ric Mead vs Th Bowle next court.
261:4/5 Court will advise at next court if response of Jn Stiles is sufficient to declaration of Jn Wells.

Action of case:
263:2/5 Hen Redgate appoints Humph James vs Will Horwood; three summonses with non-appearance, therefore warrant to be at court.
Action of trespass on case:
264:2/6 Robt Streat has day to amend declaration vs Jn Knight.

[f114]

Action of case:
263:3/5 *Fiat* writ of inquiry into damages for Hen Redgate vs Will Horwood for return next court.
Action of debt:
267:2/11 Will Metcalf requests & has day to declare vs Will Bowne who is essoined by Ric Wryte his attorney; Metcalf appoints Humph Jemes his attorney.
Action of conveyance:
269:1/1 Memo.:proclamation be made to begin at next court for John Dewe alias Sadlere for 2 tenements in The Common Green.
Actions unspecified:
268:1/1 Sir H Lee vs John Jason of Thrupp('-o-'), next court; bailors:Jer White, Hugh Hamon. (Entry crossed out.)[84]
270:1/1 Robert Banting for John Stiles, pledge vs John Davey.

[f114v]

Portmoot court held at Guildhall on 7 January 1594 before John Williams mayor.

Action of tenure:
271:1/1 Thomas Bolle pl. vs John Cowper def. . Witnesses Robert Symons & John Kent sworn.
John Cowper denies he has any lease or term of Thomas Bolle of either land, but so year to year and not so if Bowle lift not, and has had it so these two years.
Robert Symons knows well that John Cowper has occupied the land and the other premises for two years and upwards but knows not whether he has it by lease or otherwise. John Kent says that Jn Cowper has had the land and common in occupation two years and upwards but by what title or how he knows not.

[f115]

Actions unspecified:
242:15/18 Ric Mead solemnly charged does not come to receive judgment and therefore the court adjudges that he is in mercy for falsely claiming against said defendant Th Bowle who should recover amercement & costs of his suit; therefore *fiat* for writ of *fieri facias*.

[84] Actions **268** & **270** omitted from d. 47.

261:5/5 Court discharges between Jn Wells and Jn Stieles.
272:1/1 John Stiles appoints Thos Hardwyck his attorney vs John Wells; & copy & day.
Actions of debt:
251:8/22 Renewed *hab. corpora* for Edw Lee vs Th Bromryke.
267:3/11 Peremptory day for Wm Metcalf to declare in next court.
Actions of trespass on case:
264:3/6 Robt Streat appoints Humph Jemes his attorney vs Jn Knight, and copy.
273:1/6 John Wells pl; vs Thomas Stiles & Robert Stiles defs.
Action on case:
263:4/5 Continues between Hen Redgat vs Wm Horwood, writ for damages granted.

[f115v]

Saturday 12 January.
Actions of debt:
251:9/22 John Raunce & John Coles for Barlyke (*sic* Bromryck) to respond to Edw Lee.
274:1/1 John Phillips vs Nicholas Buckner.
Action of trespass on case:
273:2/6 For Thos Stiles bailors Robert Banting & John Bruce; for Robt Stiles of Rousham bailors George Fones & John Wells.
Action of assumpsit of debt:
275:1/1 Henry Fletcher vs Thomas Symons.

[f116]

Portmoot court held at Guildhall on 21 January 1594 before John Williams mayor.
(No other officers listed.)
Actions of debt:
251:10/22 Ann Cooke for the party of Edw Lee, sworn, says that she did deliver 6 bushels of pulses to the party of Mr Bromryk which was fetched viz. 4 bushels by a boy of his and 2 bushels by his maid.
251:11/22 Jury between Edward Lee gent pl. and Thomas Brombryck gent def. having been charged & tried, come and say that Lee has sustained damages in said action at 12s. & for expenses in his suit of 2d.
267:4/11 Declaration of Wm Metcalf vs Wm Bown; debt of 51s 10d.
Actions of trespass on case:
264:4/6 Peremptory day for Jn Knight to respond to Robert Steile (sic. Streat) in next court.

273:3/6 John Wells appoints Ric Wryt his attorney and responds. Court rules that there are to be not more than two attorneys in this court, namely Humphrey Jemes & Richard Wryte, henceforth in these causes.[85]

Action unspecified:

276:1/1 Fiat executio vs John Bruce for 2s 6d in suit of John Batt, return next court.

[f116v]

Actions of Qui Tam:

262:3/4 Permission granted for Wm Harris to confer & compound with Wm Rancke of Lechlade before next court, and to refer to Thos Duffild & Ralph Bradshewe on fine.

262:4/4 For the fine compounded from Wm Rancklen, 3s4d to chamberlains for Exchequer.[86]

Action of debt:

267:5/11 Peremptory day for Wm Bown to respond to Wm Metcalf in next court. (Crossed through.)

Court will consider over Wm Bown's debt and his response to this court to making no suit.

Actions of trespass on case:

273:4/6 Thos Stiles requests day & copy in next court to respond to Jn Wells; Wells appoints Ric Wryt his attorney vs Thos & Robt Stiles, and Thos Hardwyk attorney for Stiles to respond to the 2 actions against the Stiles; 2 copies.

277:1/1 George Fones vs John Batt.

278:1/1 George Fones vs Michael Wilsden alias Pulchoe.

Action unspecified:

242:16/18 Th Bowle vs Ric Mead discharged. (Crossed through.)

[f117]

Portmoot court held on 25 February 1594 before John Williams mayor.

Actions of debt:

251:12/22 Court adjudges that Thos Bromryck, defendant at last court in debt action by Edw Lee gent, putting himself on the country on jurors who recently having been heard, tried and charged to appear, and Bromryck similarly charged did not appear; which jury says for the plaintiff that he sustained damages of 12s, and 2d for costs, and for expenses & costs for bringing his suit 30s. In toto 41s 2d.

267:6/11 Peremptory day for Wm Bown to respond next court under peril.

[85] This ruling may have been directed particularly against Hardwyck (see Introduction), but for the general campaign on restricting attorney numbers at this period see Baker, 186.

[86] Presumably remittance of half the penal fine for delivery to the Court of the Exchequer, rather than transfer of the action to that court.

Action of trespass on case:
273:5/6 Continues between Jn Wells vs Jn Stiles & Thos Stiles to next court because it is committed to arbitrament by Thomas Brown & Thomas Duffild & Edulphus Dingley & Thomas Atwoode.
Action unspecified:
242:17/18 Court to advise on execution for Th Bowle vs Rc. Meade.

[f117v]

Action on the case:
263:5/5 Continues between Hen Redgat vs Will Harwood next court.
Action of trespass on case:
264:5/6 Because Jn Knight, after 3 solemn calls on charge to respond to Robt Streat, does not appear, therefore court adjudges to execute writ for inquiry into damages which said Robert sustained in said action, for return next court.
Actions of debt:
279:1/2 John Martin gent vs John Norwood gent.; pledge.
280:1/1 William Harwood of Banbury ('-bery') joiner vs William Kelinge, turner; pledge for prosecution: Ric Wryte.[87]

Portmoot court held on 11 March 1594 before John Williams mayor.
(No other officers listed.)
Action of debt:
251:13/22 *Scire facias* to summon tenant pledges for Th Bromrick:namely John Raunson & John Heath.
Action unspecified:
242:18/18 *Executio* granted to Thos Bolle vs Ric Meade.
Action of conveyance:
259:3/5 First proclamation concerning tenement of Francis Collingwood; and no one comes.[88]
Actions of trespass on case:
264:6/6 John Knight *assumpsit* with Robert Streete in £10 remaining on arbitrament of Will Metcalf & Jn Bentlye.
273:6/6 Agreement & award between Jn Styles and Jn Wells accepted in court.

[f118]

Actions of debt:
251:14/22 Renewed *scire facias* to summon counter pledges vs Thos Bromryck, namely Jn Browne & Jn Coles.
281:1/1 William Metcalf vs William Bowne gent (see also **267**)
282:1/1 Richard Merryck gent vs John Gurden yeoman for £12 debt.

[87] Change of handwriting here from that of town clerk Thomas Duffild to that of town clerk Edulphe Dingley.
[88] 'one' tenement here, but 'two' in **259**:5/5 and in d. 47.

283:1/1 Abraham Turner of Steeple Aston ('Aston Steeple') vs Richard Bowle alias Cook. pledges: H Standard, G Ivyto.
285:1/2 Edward Savage of Deddington vs John Coles of borough of New Woodstock for debt of 30s., and enters action through Gilbert Penley of Ascott by letter of attorney dated 26 March 36 Elizabeth on the surety of Francis Collingwood.
Action of conveyance:
260:2/6 First proclamation between William Rayer and Thomas Norwood for a tenement now in the tenure of Nicholas Taylor.
Action of assumpsit of debt:
284:1/1 William Bennett of Brackley in county Northants mercer vs Robert Crackloe of Aynho ('-noe') butcher.
Action of trespass:
286:1/2 John Coles vs Richard Meades.

[f118v]

Portmoot court held on 22 April 1594 before John Williams mayor.
(No other officers listed.)
Actions of debt:
267:7/11 Action continues between Will Metcalf vs Will Boone.
285:2/2 Jn Coles acknowledges debt vs Edward Savage.
288:1/11 John Gadbury of Kidlington vs John Pulchroe; pledges to respond: Jn Heath & Jn Bull.
Action of trespass:
286:2/2 Jn Coles vs Ric Meades.
Actions of trespass on case:
287:1/3 Henry Fletcher vs John Locke of Ledwell ('Lewd-') pledges to respond: Jn Pyman & Nich. Taylor.[89]
289:1/1 Christopher Bumar vs Edward Coff; Thos Rudge & Jn Bruce pledges to prosecute.
Actions of conveyance:
259:4/5 Second proclamation for Francis Collingwood; and no one comes etc.
260:3/6 Second proclamation between Rayer and Norwood for aforesaid tenement.
260:4/6 Memo. that a fine was acknowledged this day by Thomas Norwood & Mary his wife to William Rayer of Weston (-on-the-green) of a tenement lately in occupation of Nicholas Taylor.[90]

[89] See Gelling, 280.

[90] In d. 47 eleven lines given; including sole examination of Mary who 'confessed that she yielded up her title not for fear nor dread nor compulsion but merely of her free will & that a fine thereof should be duly levied to the use of the said Will Rayer & his heirs for ever according to the custom of this borough'.

[f119]

Portmoot court held on 13 May 1594 before John Williams mayor.
(No other officers listed.)
Actions of debt:
251:15/22 *Scire facias* against pledges of Thos Bromrick, namely Jn Raunce & Jn Coles, whilst Bromrick holds payment.
267:8/11 Wm Metcalf through Hen Redgate his attorney requests response from Wm Bowne, and granted through court.
279:2/2 Court discharges action between Jn Martin vs Jn Norwood.
Actions of debt:
288:2/11 Henry Redgate attorney for Jn Gadbury requests day to bring declaration against Jn Pulchroe; Ric Write essoins Pulchroe.
290:1/16 Margaret Yate of Deddington ('-edi-') widow vs John Coles of the borough of New Woodstock butcher for £8 4s. debt.
Action of trespass on case:
287:2/3 Henry Redgate attorney for Hen Fletcher requests day to bring declaration against Jn Lock; Ric Write essoins Lock.
Actions of conveyance:
259:5/5 Third proclamation concerning two tenements in tenure of Fras Collingwood lately given by Richard Eliot to the possession of the said Francis, and because no one comes to claim these tenements or contradict the claim therefore according to the custom of the borough: Fras Collingwood has and holds these tenements for himself & his heirs in perpetuity for the payment and proper use of Francis himself.[91]
260:5/6 Third proclamation between Rayer and Norwood and Wells etc.

[f119v]

Portmoot court held at Guildhall on 27 May 1594 before John Williams mayor.
Actions of debt:
251:16/22 Sergeant-at-mace returns *sci. fa.* between Th Bromrick and Edw Lee; and Ric Write attorney of Lee requests custom of court, *sicut alias* is granted for next court.
267:9/11 Ric Write attorney for Wm Boane requests copy of replication of Wm Metcalf.
288:3/11 Action continues between Jn Gadburye vs Jn Pulchoe to feast of St John the Baptist next.
290:2/16 Jn Coles in person requests advice before next court and therefore a privilege day; permission granted Margaret Yate to amend her declaration.
Action of trepass on case:
287:3/3 Court discharges between Hen Fletcher vs Jn Lock.

[91] Fuller account of conveyance in d. 47, ff. 12v, 13, giving the location in High Street.

[f120]

Actions of debt:
291:1/1 Thomas Gunn of Eynsham ('En-') vs John Coles of borough of New Woodstock.
292:1/1 Hartlye vs John Coles.
293:1/1 William Metcalf vs William Hutchins of Mickleton ('Michellton') (Glos.).
294:1/1 Thomas Norwood of Reading ('Red-') vs John Coles in debt of £5.
295:1/1 John Pyman ald vs John Coles in debt of 15s.
Action of conveyance:
296:1/4 Memo. that on 5th June possession and seisin were given by Henry Redgate sergeant-at-mace to John Pyman alderman for the possession and use of Robert Bicknell of Shipston-on-Stour ('Shipson super Le Stowre') in county Worcester baker, of one burgage messuage or tenement called Le Black Hall now in the tenure or occupation of foresaid Pyman; and said Hen Redgate attorney for this party of said Pyman handed over quiet and peaceful possession to hold to himself and his heirs in perpetuity of the chief lords of this fee.[92]

[f120v]

296:1/4 Before John Williams mayor of said borough; Humphrey Jeames, Robert Thomas, Robert Banting, Richard Write, William Hickes, Richard Dubber, William Noble, William Raunce, Thomas Medcalf and others.
Criminal Recognisance.
297:1/1 Sixth June Thomas Sheldon gent acknowledges his debt to Queen Elizabeth of £20, and Edward Court and Thomas Bradshewe each in £10, under condition that the said Sheldon shall appear at the next assize or gaol delivery etc.
Action of debt:
298:1/3 William Collins vs William Borman; pledges to prosecute: Will Metcalf & Jn Dissell.
Action of trespass on case:
299:1/24+ William Ball of borough of New Woodstock vs John Jarvis of Broughton.

[f121]

Portmoot court held at Guildhall on 10 June 1594 before John Williams mayor.
(No other officers listed.)
Actions of debt:
290:3/16 Jn Coles in person requests second day to respond to declaration of Marg Yate.

[92] Extended account in d. 47. Black Hall:see *VCH Oxon*. xii. 337, 349 and *WCA*, 33.

298:2/3 Will Collins appoints Hen Redgate his attorney vs Will Borman who is essoined by Ralph Bradshewe to next court.
Action of trespass on case:
299:2/24+ Will Ball appoints Ric Right his attorney & requests day to declare; Jarvis essoined by Hen Redgate; Robt Walker & Jerome White pledges to respond.
Arbitrament:
300:1/1 Arbitrament by the court between Anthony Noble clerk and William Ball cutler freeman, all causes and controversies dependant between the said parties from the first to the present times - Humphrey James & John Phillips on the part of Noble and Ralph Bradshew & John Bentlye for Ball and agreement is made.
Action of conveyance:
296:2/4 First proclamation for Robert Bicknell concerning the tenement lately of John Pyman called Black Hall and no one comes (to claim it.)
Action continuing: **251**:17/22.

[f121v]

Action of Qui Tam:
301:1/2 William Harris on behalf of the Queen & himself vs Clark in plaint of debt.
Action of trespass on case:
302:1/6 Ralph Bradshew vs John Browne.

[f122]

Portmoot court held on 24 June 1594 before John Williams mayor.
Actions of debt:
288:4/11 Jn Pulchoe through R Write granted copy of declaration.
290:4/16 Third day for Jn Coles to respond in next court.
298:3/3 Court discharges between Wm Collins and Wm Borman.
Actions of trespass on case:
299:3/24+ Continues between Wm Ball through attorney Ric Write vs Jn Jarvis through attorney Hen Redgate.
302:2/6 Jn Browne in person appears and is essoined firstly and pledged to respond by Jn Heath & Jn Janes in suit of Ralph Bradshawe.
Action of Qui Tam:
301:2/2 Court discharges between W Harris and Clarke.
Action of conveyance:
296:3/4 Second proclamation between Jn Pyman and Robt Bicknell concerning the tenement called Le Blackhall, and none comes etc.
Action continuing: **251**:18/22.

[f122v]

Actions of trepass on case:

303:1/1 William Hearne of Chelk(e)s ('de chelks') vs Thomas Trindall of Somerton.[93]

306:1/1 Nicholas Denton de Brucsyde vs Richard Charleton of Burford ('-foote').[94]

Actions of debt:

304:1/7 William Metcalf vs John Glover; pledges Ralph Bradshew & Michael Nurse.

305:1/1 Ralph Bradshew vs Henry Fletcher

308:1/1 Edmund White vs Francis Barnsdale.

8th July: Portmoot court adjourns to 15th of next month.

Actions of Qui Tam:

307:1/3 William Harris on behalf of the Queen & himself vs Thomas Smyth for selling certain leather contrary to the form of the statutes; pledges to respond: Jer White, Geo Fones.[95]

309:1/3 William Harris on behalf of the Queen & himself vs Henry Rowsham senior for offending the form of the statutes on brass-working; pledges to respond Lancelot Winter & Jerome White.[96]

[f123]

Portmoot court held on 15 July 1594 before John Williams mayor.

Actions of debt:

267:10/11 Boone confessed the action through attorney Ric Write.

288:5/11 Jn Pulchoe through attorney Ric Write responds to declaration of Jn Gadbury whose attorney Hen Redgate requests copy of response in next court.

290:5/16 Jn Coles in person requests copy of Mg Yate's declaration and granted response in next court; in peril, requests *in forma pauperis* but court will advise.[97]

Actions of trespass on case:

299:4/24+ W Ball through attorney Ric Write declares vs J Jarvis whose attorney Hen Redgate requests & is granted a copy.

302:3/6 Because Jn Browne does not appear, to respond, Ra Bradshew is granted execution of a writ of inquiry into damages.

93 'Chelk(e)s' or 'Thelk(e)s' not identified.

94 'Brucsyde' or Bryksyde (d. 47) not identified; possibly by the brook in Woodstock (cf. *WCA*, 213), or Brugeset alias St Clements, Oxford, 'Bridgsett' (Gelling, 20).

95 Penal statutes concerning the sale of leather goods included one regarding the area of sale (24 Henry VIII, c. 1. sect. 2. ; Holdsworth iv, 321) and another relating to honest goods (5 Eliz. c. 8; see also B78/2 ff49v/50).

96 The penal statute concerning working in brass might relate to being licensed to the trade, or to the sale of defective brass which would be forfeit. (Jacob's *Dictionary*: Brass, defective; statute 19. Henry VII, c. 6).

97 *forma pauperis*: poor persons with total possessions worth less than £5 were admitted to sue or defend without fees or costs.

Action continuing: **251**:19/22.

[f123v]

Action of debt:
304:2/7 Will Metcalf through attorney Hen Redgate vs Jn Glover requests day to declare; Glover essoined by Ric Write; pledges to respond: Ralph Bradshew, Michael Nurse.
Actions of conveyance:
260:6/6 Memo. that a fine with the proclamation annexed thereunto was sealed to William Rayer acknowledged by Thomas Norwood & Mary his wife the 22nd day of April 1594.[98]
296:4/4 Third proclamation between Jn Pyman and for Robt Bicknell plaintiff concerning the tenement called the Blackhall, and no-one comes to oppose this claim. Therefore according to the custom of this borough it is advised that Robt Bicknell has enjoys and possesses the said tenement with all and every-one of its appurtenances to himself & his heirs in perpetuity.
Actions of Qui Tam:
307:2/3 Permission given Will Harris to confer with Thos Smyth.
309:2/3 Given also to said Harris to confer with Hen Rowsham.
311:1/4 William Harris both for Queen & for himself vs Raphael Narrowey in trespass against the form of the statutes.

[f124]

Action of Qui Tam:
312:1/1 William Harris both for Queen & himself vs Humphrey Jukes against the form of the statutes.
Actions of debt:
313:1/1 Thomas Collins vs Edmund Cooper; pledges to prosecute: Jn Heath & Jn Janes.
316:1/1 Jone Marshall widow vs Thomas Thruston.
Actions of trespass on case:
314:1/1 William Ryley alderman vs Thomas Blythe.
315:1/1 Thomas Blythe vs William Ryley ald.

[f124v]

317. The Assize set down of Bread and Ale the 17 July, by John Williams mayor, William Ryley and William Metcalf assistants.
Jury: John Phillips, Robard Walker, William Rayer, John Wilkinson, Hugh Hamon, John Heath, John Bruse, William Hickes, John Wells, Abraham Danter, William Wells, John Janes & Lancelot Winter.
The said jury presents:
Firstly, the best wheat at 40s. the quarter.
Item the second, price the quarter at 25s.

98 A fuller version of the conveyance fine dated 22 April 36Eliz. is given in d. 47, ffl6r&v.

The assize given by the mayor and his assistants aforesaid:

Item the half penny white loaf to weigh	6½ ounces.
The penny white loaf to weigh	13 ounces.
The half penny wheaten loaf	9 ounces 3 quarters.
The penny wheaten loaf -	19½ ounces.
The penny household loaf -	36 ounces.

Item, the best ale and beer to be sold within the house and without, the quart 1d.
Item, the small drink the gallon - 1d.

[f125]

Actions of trespass on case:
318:1/5 William Wise vs Richard Kent alias Essex; pledges to prosecute: Jerome White & Humph Jeames ('J. W & H J').
320:1/14 Edmund White of Hampton Poyle vs William East; pledges to prosecute: Jn Raunce & Hugh Hamon.
321:1/1 Edmund White vs William Heynes of Bladon.
322:1/3 Henry Redgate vs William Parsons.
323:1/1 Henry Redgate vs William Parsons.
Action of debt:
319:1/1 Zachary ('Sacrye') Pen of Middle Aston ('Asson') vs Hankes.

[f125v]

Actions of debt:
324:1/5 Edmund Hiorne vs John Boucher of Cleveley ('-lye'); Boucher essoined.
325:1/1 Nicholas Launce of Eynsham ('En-') vs Robert Walker; pledges to prosecute: Humph. Jeames & Henry Redgate ('HJ&HR').

[f126]

Portmoot court held at Guildhall on 29 July 1594 before John Williams mayor.
Action of debt:
267:11/11 Memo. that Symon Symons of Burford ('-foote') in county Oxon clothier pays and satisfies William Boone through attorney Humphrey Jeames of 51s 10d and for said 50s same Will Boone delivers to discharge of all causes and controversies from the beginning of the world up to this day pending between the said persons as much as the sum of 50s aforesaid. Said Boone delivers in open court through attorney Richard Write to William Metcalf as he owes the same Will Metcalf for himself to recover in court as is clear for the said Metcalf is acknowledged satisfied and the court discharges from the said action.
Action continuing: **251**:20/22.

[f126v]

Actions of debt:

288:6/11 Court grants that *venire facias* be issued for jury between Jn Gadburye vs Jn Pulchoe.

290:6/16 Court grants *venire facias* to be issued between Jn Coles def. and Marg Yate pl.

Actions of trespass on case:

299:5/24+ Imparlance granted for Jn Jarvis to next court under peril.

302:4/6 Because Jn Browne, solemnly three times charged, does not appear, to respond to Ra Bradshaw, then execution of writ of inquiry into damages.

318:2/5 Permission to imparl for William Wise to declare vs Richard Kent, and Kent essoined by Ric Wright; Hen Redgate attorney for Wise has peremptory day; Thos Browne pledge to prosecute.

320:2/14 Edmund White appoints Hen Redgate his attorney and requests day to amend his declaration vs East; & East essoined by Ric Writ his attorney; pledges to respond: Jer White, Will Rathbone.

322:2/3 Henry Redgate refers himself to the court on action pending between himself and W Parsons, therefore it continues.

Actions of Qui Tam:

307:3/3 Thomas Smyth appears in person and pays his fine of 3s. and pays and satisfies the court so that it discharges the said 3s delivered to John Dubber conveyed to the use of the Queen.

311:2/4 Permission given for Will Harris with his information to imparl with Raphael Narrowey.

Action continuing: **304**:3/7.

[f127]

Actions of Qui Tam:

309:3/3 Memo. that Hen Rowsham gave his fine of 12d and court discharges him of it.

326:1/2 William Harris both for Queen & himself vs Hugh Turner in plaint against the form of the statutes.

Action of debt:

324:2/5 Edmund Hiorne appoints Henry Redgate his attorney and requests day to declare vs John Boucher, who is essoined by Richard Write his attorney; pledges to prosecute: Jn Heath & Will Hickes.

Actions of trespass on case:

329:1/4 Thomas Bowle vs Francis Doltman.

330:1/4 John Batt vs Roger Deye.

Actions of debt on account:

327:1/1 John Coles vs Nicholas Tayler.

328:1/1 John Coles vs Roger Powell.[99]

[99] '...debt of account on arrearages...' in d.47.

[f127v]

Portmoot court held on 12 August 1594 before John Williams mayor.

Actions of debt:

288:7/11 *Fiat hab. corpora* for jury between Gadburye vs Pulchoe.

290:7/16 *Fiat hab. corpora* for jury between Ma Yate vs Jn Coles.

Action continuing: **251**:21/22.

Actions of trespass on case:

302:5/6 Jury between Ralph Bradshew pl. and John Browne def.:
Henry Fletcher, Robard Walker, John Raunson, Nicholas Tayler, John Tayler, Thomas Blythe, William Hickes, John Bull, William Rathbone, Hugh Hamon, John Wilkinson & John Dissell. Who assess damages at 5s 4d and amercement at 2d, therefore they give judgment that Bradshew should recover said damages & amercement, with costs of bringing his suit 16s 8d.

[f128]

Sci. fa. granted for the pledges of John Browne, viz. Jn Heath & Jn Janes.

299:6/24+ Jn Jarvis appoints Hen Redgate attorney & responds to Wm Ball and requests to imparl & copy, granted next court.

318:3/5 Wm Wise appoints Hen Redgate vs Ric Kent (alias Essex) and declares, & Kent appoints Ric Write his attorney and requests imparl & copy at next court, granted.

320:3/14 Edm White appoints Hen Redgate vs Wm East & declares; East appoints Ric Write his attorney & requests copy & imparl at next court.

329:2/4 Thos Bowle appoints Hen Redgate his attorney vs Fras Doltman and requests day to declare; Doltman essoined by Ric Write. Ric Meades & Geo Fones pledges to respond.

Actions of Qui Tam:

311:3/4 Court will advise on judgment between Wm Harris vs Ralph Narrowey at next court.

326:2/2 Hugh Turner gives his fine of 12d to Ralph Bradshew to satisfy the informer; therefore court discharges him.

Actions continuing: **304**:4/7; **322**:3/3; **324**:3/5.

[f128v]

Actions of trespass on case:

331:1/2 Thomas Blythe vs. William Ryley.

336:1/4 William Ryley vs Thomas Blythe.

Actions of debt:

334:1/1 William Metcalf vs John Coles.

335:1/1 William Metcalf vs Richard Coles.

Action of detinue:

332:1/1 Thomas Blythe vs Michael Nurse.

Action of Qui Tam:
333:1/4 William Harris for Queen & himself vs Richard Widowes in plaint of breaking the penal statutes.

[f129]

Portmoot court held on 26 August 1594 before John Williams mayor.
Action continuing: 251:22/22.
Action of debt:
288:8/11 Witnesses sworn between John Gadburye pl. and John Pulchoe def.
On part of plaintiff:
Mistress Gadburye says that the aforesaid Jn Pulchoe did work at the house of Jn Gadburye and received a cloak price 12s. promising to pay the said 12s. to Jn Gadburye. John Turner says that he met with Jn Pulchoe at Woodstock above said and he told him that he, Pulchoe, received a cloak of Gadburye but not to pay 12s. for it but 11s.

[f129v]

288:8/11 Jury between John Gadburye vs John Pulchoe: Henry Fletcher, John Raunson, Jerome White, Thomas Colgrave, George Fones, John Bruse, John Dissell, John Wells, John Janes, Michael Faux, Lancelot Winter, William Wells, William Hickes (crossed out).
Who swear on their oath that they find Jn Pulchoe owes the said 12s. in the manner said and assess damages at 12s 6d and amercement & costs at 2d.
Action of debt:
290:8/16 Witnesses sworn between Margaret Yate pl. vs John Coles defendant.
Witnesses on part of plaintiff:
William Mase says that being at the house of John Yate there was an even reckoning made between the said Yate and John Coles, and Coles put his hand to a certain writing wherein he confessed himself to owe £7 to the said Jn Yate. Phillip Lodwing says that Margaret Yate is sole executrix of the goods of her husband John Yate.

[f130]

290:9/16 Jury between Marg Yate pl. and Jn Coles def. .

John Phillips,	Robard Walker,	Thomas Blythe,
Nicholas Tayler,	John Heath,	Michael Nurse,
William Hickes,	John Bull,	John Button,
Hugh Hamon,	James Dissell	& John Wilkinson.

Who, having been tried and charged, swear on oath that they find that said Jn Coles owes the said £7 to Marg Yate and assess damages at £7:6d and amercement & costs at 2d.
Actions of trespass on case:
299:7/24+ Jn Jarvis to respond in next court.
302:6/6 Jn Browne delivers his body in open court because etc.

318:4/5 Ric Kent peremptory response in next court.
320:4/14 Will East peremptory response in next court.
320:5/14 *Executio* for Will East to respond to Edm White.
329:3/4 Thos Bowle appoints Hen Redgate his attorney & declares vs Christopher (sic. ? Francis) Doltman who through Ric Write his attorney requests copy and day to imparl in next court.
Actions continuing: **304**:5/7; **324**:4/5.

[f130v]

Action of trespass on case:
330:2/4 Jn Batt appoints Hen Redgate his attorney & requests day to declare vs Rog Daye who is essoined by Ric Write, with pledges to respond John Raunson & Nicholas Tayler.
Action of Qui Tam:
333:2/4 Permission granted for Will Harris to imparl till next court; pledges to respond John Phillips & John Dubber.
Actions of debt:
337:1/1 Gyles Preston alias Fowler vs Leonard Yate gent.
338:1/1 William Harris vs Thomas Bodye.
339:1/1 John Rathbone vs Richard Coles.
340:1/1 Robard Parren vs Nicholas Hickes.
Actions continuing: **331**:2/2; **336**:2/4.

[f131]

Action of debt:
341:1/1 Robard Bynckes vs Richard Coles.
Portmoot court held on 9 September 1594 before John Williams mayor.
(No other officers listed.)
Actions of debt:
288:9/11 Court adjudges that Jn Gadburye should recover vs Jn Pulchoe def. the debt for 12s together with damages and also 30s 1d for amercement & costs of suit. *Fiat sci. fa.* against pledges Jn Heath & Jn Bull.
290:10/16 Court adjudges that Marg Yate should recover vs Jn Coles def. the debt for £7 together with aforesaid damages and also for amercement & costs of suit at 29s 8d.
324:5/5 Discharged between Edm Hiorne vs Jn Boucher.
Actions of trespass on case:
299:8/24+ *Fiat ven. fac.* for jury between Will Ball vs Jn Jarvis.
318:5/5 Discharged between Wm Wise vs Ric Kent.
320:6/14 Wm East through attorney Hen Redgate responds to Edm White who requests copy.
Action continuing: **304**:6/7.

[f131v]

Actions of trespass on case:

149:15/19 *Fiat executio* vs John Browne in suit of Robert Symons (see *f84v).*

320:7/14 Copy of response granted to Edm White next court.

329:4/4 Because Francis Doltman does not respond to Thomas Bowle, therefore *nihil dicit.*

336:3/4 Will Ryley appoints Hen Redgate vs Thos Blythe & declares; Blythe essoined by his attorney Ric Write.

343:1/1 John Bryan of Bicester ('Burcester alias Byssiter') vs Henry Brooke of the same town.

Actions of debt:

342:1/1 Henry Whing of Islip ('Iseleepe') vs Edward Hanckes of Tackley ('-ye').

344:1/2 John Bryan abovesaid vs Thomas Gylberd of Bicester ('Bisseter').

Actions continuing: **330**:3/4; **333**:3/4.

[f132]

Actions of trespass on case:

345:1/3 Thomas Daniell of Burford ('Burfoote') vs Giles Pratte of Witney; pledges to respond John Phillips & Robert Banting.

348:1/1 George Fones vs Thomas Freeman.

Actions of debt:

346:1/1 James Foster of Hailey ('Haylye') vs Ambrose Lardener & Henry Lardener his son of Ramsden ('-don').

347:1/1 John Coles of Chipping Norton vs William Heynes of Bladon for debt of £9 7s 7d.

Action of Qui Tam:

349:1/8 William Harris on behalf of Queen & himself vs Thomas Daniell in plaint of transgression of penal statutes; pledges to respond: John Dubber & John Phillips.

[f132v]

Portmoot court held on 23 September 1594 before John Williams mayor.
(No other officers listed.)

Actions of trespass on case:

149:16/19 Renewed execution between Robt Symons vs Jn Browne.

299:9/24+ *Fiat ve. fa.* for jury between Wm Ball vs Jn Jarvis, return next court.

320:8/14 *Fiat ve. fa.* between Edm White vs Wm East.

330:4/4 Discharged between Jn Batt vs Rog Daye.

345:2/3 Gyles Pratt confesses action between himself and Thos Daniell pl.; therefore *fiat* writ of inquiry into damages.

Action of debt:

288:10/11 Continues *sci. fa.* between Jn Gadburye vs Jn Pulchoe.

Action of Qui Tam:
311:4/4 Discharged between Wm Harris vs Ral Narrowey who gives his fine of 2s 6d to Ralph Bradshew and received by court.
Actions continuing: **304**:7/7 by assent; **336**:4/4.

[f133]

Actions of Qui Tam:
333:4/4 Ric Widowes pays fine of 2s. to Ralph Bradshew & satisfies court, therefore he is discharged.
349:2/8 Copy granted to Thos Daniell of information of W Harris.
352:1/15 William Harris for Queen & himself vs Michael Puddell in plaint of offence against form of the statutes.
Actions of debt:
344:2/2 Court discharges between Jn Bryan vs Thos Gylberd.
355:1/3 Thomas Collins vs Edmund Cupper (see **350**).
Action unspecified:
350:1/1 Because Thomas Collins does not come to prosecute vs Edmund Cooper, therefore in false claim (see **355**).
Actions of trespass on case:
351:1/1 Francis Barnesley of Bletchingdon ('Blechesdon') vs Edmund White of Hampton Poyle.[100]
353:1/6 Thomas Maunde vs John Norwood; pledges to prosecute: Richard Write & George Fones (see f139v).
354:1/6 Richard Bennett of Bicester ('Bisseter alias Burcester') vs John Bryan and his goods.

[f133v]

Action of debt:
356:1/1 Ralph Bradshew vs John Button that he should pay 14s 5d of his debt and unjustly does not give it.

Portmoot court held on 7 October 1594 before John Williams mayor.

Action of debt:
288:11/11 Continue *sci. fa.* between Jn Gadbury vs Jn Pulchoe to next court.
Actions of trespass on case:
299:10/24+ *Fiat hab. corpora* for jury between Wm Ball vs Jn Jarvis, return next court.
320:9/14 *Fiat ven. fa.* for jury between Edm White vs Wm East, return next court.
Action of Qui Tam:
349:3/8 Thos Daniell through attorney Hen Redgate requests day to respond to both Queen & Will Harris, & has day.

100 See Gelling, 201: Blechesdoun to 1428.

[f134]

Actions of trespass on case:
149:17/19 Renewed execution for R Symons vs J Browne (see *f151*).
345:3/3 Discharged between Thos Daniell vs Gyles Pratt.
354:2/6 Ric Bennett appoints Ric Write his attorney vs Jn Bryan & requests day to declare & is essoined by Hen Redgate.
358:1/1 James Morris of Deddington ('-edi-') in county Oxon. vs John Button (see **388**).
359:1/1 Henry Redgate vs John Saunders.
Action of Qui Tam:
352:2/15 William Harris for Queen & himself puts information vs Michael Puddell, who requests copy at next court through his attorney Ric Write.
Actions of debt:
355:2/3 Court will advise over adjourning judgment vs Thos Collins in suit vs Edm. Cupper in next court.
356:2/2 Court discharges proceedings between Ralph Bradshew vs John Button.
Action of trespass:
357:1/9 Richard Richardson of Hanborough ('-boughrough') vs Richard Stutter of same place junior (see *f141v*).

[f134v]

Portmoot court held on 21 October 1594 before John Williams mayor.
Action of trespass on case:
299:11/24+ Witnesses sworn between William Ball pl. vs John Jarvis def.
On part of plaintiff Briget Spittell says that John Jarvis did send her to go to William Ball for iron nails ('yron clouts') and other kind of ironmonger ('Iaramonger') wares that she went and received them.
On part of plaintiff: Dorritye Ball says she delivered to Briget Spittell ironware so much as come to 3s 1d to the use of John Jarvis.

[f135]

Also the said Dorritye Ball says that she demanded the said 3s 1d of the said Jn Jarvis and he promised payment thereof. Names of the jury between Will Ball pl. vs Jn Jarvis def.:

Henry Fletcher,	Thomas Blythe,	William Rayer,
Nicholas Tayler,	Jerome White,	John Heath,
John Wells senior,	Thomas Colgrave,	Michael Faux,
John Bruse,	John Dissell	& Hugh Hamon,

George Fones (crossed out).
Who after having been tried and charged upon their oath, find against Jn Jarvis for *assumpsit* in the manner & form as claimed, and assess damages for plaintiff at 4s. with expenses & costs 2d.

320:10/14 *Fiat hab.corpora* for jury next court between Edm White vs.Wm East.

[f135v]

Actions of Qui Tam:
349:4/8 *Fiat ve. fa.* for jury between Queen & Will Harris vs Thos Daniell, return next court.
352:3/15 Peremptory day for Mich Puddell to respond to Queen & Will Harris at next court; bailors for Puddell:John Bruse & Abraham Danter.
Actions of debt:
290:11/16 *Fiat executio* vs Jn Coles in suit of Marg Yate.
360:1/1 Richard Meshborne of Chipping Norton vs Thomas Freeman of Kiddington.[101]
Actions of trespass on case:
354:3/6 Ric Bennett appoints Ric Write his attorney & declares vs Jn Bryan who through attorney Hen Redgate requests to imparl and copy for return next court.
359:2/2 Discharged between Hen Redgate vs Jn Saunders.
361:1/1 John Coles vs William Mace.
362:1/1 John Hemming of Coventry ('-ye') vs Robert Smith of Banbury ('Bamburye').

[f136]

363:1/1 John Yardlye of Brackley ('-lye') vs William Adams.

Portmoot court held on 4 November 1594 before John Williams mayor.
Action of trespass on case:
320:11/14 Witnesses sworn between Edmund White pl. vs William East def. On part of plaintiff: John White deposed says that William East did promise to pay the £3 6s 8d to Edm White if William Hampton did not.

[f136v]

William Moulder deposed says that a boy of Will East's did fetch the 2 kyne of Edm White, and further says that East promised to pay for the kine if Hampton did not. William Teaslear deposed says that Edm White demanded the money for the 2 kine of William Hampton and said that he would arrest his surety Will East for the aforesaid money for the kine and said Hampton answered that he could not remedy it but he must pay it.
Jane Tredwell deposed says that Will East came to the house of one Fleming and said that he had given his word for 2 kine and that he thought he should pay for them.

101 Actions **360** to **363** omitted from d. 47.

On part of defendant: George Cobwell deposed says that Edm White asked him whether he knew of the matter between East and himself and whether he knew that East gave his word for the payment of the money aforesaid.

[f137]

Names of the jury between Edmund White pl. vs William East def.:

John Phillips,	Ralph Bradshew,	John Raunson,
William Flye,	Michael Nurse,	John Wilkinson,
John Dissell,	John Janes,	William Wells,
John Bruse,	George Fones	& John Heath.

Who, having been tried, find on their oath they declare against the defendant for *assumpsit* in the manner & form declared, and assess damages for plaintiff at £3 7s. & amercement at 1d.

299:12/24+ The court adjudges that Will Ball should recover vs Jn Jarvis for damages 4s. with amercement 2d and further amercement & costs of bringing the suit 30s.

[f137v]

Actions of debt:

290:12/16 Renewed execution vs Jn Coles in suit of Marg Yate.[102]

355:3/3 Proceedings discharged between Th Collins vs Ed Cooper.

Actions of Qui Tam:

349:5/8 Permission granted for Wm Harris to imparl & compound with Thos Daniell, for return next court.

352:4/15 Permission granted for Wm Harris to imparl & compound with Mich Puddell, for return next court.

Action of trespass on case:

354:4/6 Peremptory summons for Jn Bryan to respond to Ric Bennet in next court.

[f138]

Portmoot court held on 18 November 1594 before John Williams mayor.

Action of trespass on case:

320:12/14 Court adjudges that Edm White should recover vs Will East for damages £3 7s and for amercement 1d and also 30s 4d for costs of bringing suit to court (see *f149v*).

Action of Qui Tam:

352:5/15 *Fiat hab. corpora* for jury between Queen & W Harris vs Mich Puddell, return next court.

Actions continuing: **349**:6/8; **354**:5/6.

[f138v]

Action of debt:

290:13/16 Renewed *executio* vs Jn Coles in suit of Marg Yate.

102 'Renewed writ of *capias ad satisfact.* vs Jn Coles' in d. 47.

Actions of trespass on case:
299:13/24+ *Sci. fa.* vs Jn Jarvis in suit of Wm Ball, till next court.
364:1/1 William Metcalf vs Richard Morris. (Crossed through.)
365:1/3 John Hill vs Richard Morris.
366:1/1 William Rathbone vs Gryffin Lyn.

[f139]

Portmoot court held on 2 December 1594 before John Williams mayor.[103]
(No other officers listed.)
Action of debt:
290:14/16 Renewed *executio* for Marg Yate vs Jn Coles; next court.
Actions of trespass on case:
299:14/24+ *Fiat sci. fa.* for pledges of Jn Jarvis in suit of Wm Ball; return next court.
354:6/6 Discharged by court between Ric Bennet vs Jn Bryan.
365:2/3 Jn Hill appoints Hen Redgate attorney & requests day to declare in next court vs Ric Morris, who appoints Ric Write attorney; pledges to respond Jn Phillips & Fras Collingwood.
Action of Qui Tam:
352:6/15 Renewed *hab. corpora* between Queen & Wm Harris vs Mich Puddell, return next court.
Action continuing: **349**:7/8.

[f139v]

Actions of trespass on case:
353:2/6 Thomas Maunde appoints Ric Write attorney vs John Norwood and has day to next court to declare; Norwood essoined by attorney Hen Redgate to same day; pledges to respond John Heath & William Hickes (see *f133*).
367:1/2 Gregory Jakeman of Westbury ('-rye') in county Northampton[104] woolwinder vs Humphrey Jukes for his goods.
369:1/3 George Fones vs Peter Pierson.
370:1/2 William Ball vs Richard Coles.
Action of Qui Tam:
368:1/4 William Harris for Queen & himself vs John Carter for breaking the form of the statutes.

[f140]

Portmoot court held on 16 December 1594 before John Williams mayor.
(No other officers listed.)
Action of debt:
290:15/16 Renewed *executio* vs Jn Coles in suit of Marg Yate.

103 Portmoot officers listed in d. 47.

104 Westbury is within Buckinghamshire, 2 miles east of Brackley, next to Northants & Oxon: on John Speed's map of 1610 & on modern maps. Actions **367** to **370** omitted from d. 47.

Actions of trespass on case:
299:15/24+ Court will advise on Will Ball having writ *de capias ad satisfaciendum* vs pledges of Jn Jarvis in next court.
353:3/6 Thos Maunde appoints Ric Write attorney and declares vs Jn Norwood who, through attorney Hen Redgate requests imparlance and copy in next court.
Actions of Qui Tam:
349:8/8 Discharged between Will Harris vs Thos Daniell.
352:7/15 Renewed *hab. corpora* between Will Harris vs Mich Puddell to next court.

[f140v]

Action of Qui Tam:
368:2/4 Imparlance and copy granted to Jn Carter to respond to Queen & Wm Harris next court; pledge to respond John Bull. Discharged.
Action of conveyance:
371:1/5 First proclamation between William Metcalf and John Garlick concerning two tenements within the borough and none comes here to object.[105]
Actions of trespass on case:
365:3/3 Jn Hill appoints Hen Redgate attorney and declares vs Ric Morris who, through attorney Ric Write, requests imparlance and copy in next court. Discharged.
367:2/2 Proceedings by Greg Jakeman vs Humph Jukes discharged.
372:1/1 George Kemp of Witney vs William Handes of Ramsden ('-don').[106]

[f141]

Action of account:
373:1/2 Thomas Browne ald vs John Woodroff.
Actions of trespass on case:
379:1/1 Thomas Goles vs Robert Wynter.
380:1/1 Thomas Coles vs Thomas Osborne of Hensington.
Actions of debt:
374:1/1 John Phillippes vs Richard Swyft. Discharged.
375:1/1 John Hall of South Leigh ('Southlie') vs Richard Coles. Discharged.
377:1/3 John Phillippes vs Richard Stutter.
378:1/1 Thomas Coles vs Robert Wynter.
382:1/1 John Phillippes vs Edward Hanckes (of Nethercott). Discharged.
Action of trespass:
383:1/1 John King vs William Haynes.

105 For these tenements see *VCH Oxon*. xii. 349ii.
106 Actions **372** to **383** omitted from d. 47.

Action of Qui Tam:
376:1/4 William Harris for Queen & himself vs Richard Buller of Sandford for the purchasing of barley for re-selling at prices contrary to the form of the statutes.[107]
Action unspecified:
381:1/1 John Phillippes vs Edward Hanckes alias Warr of Nethercott ('Neather Cott') for his goods & chattels. Discharged.[108]

[f141v]

Portmoot court held on 13 January 1595 before John Williams mayor.
Actions of debt:
290:16/16 Satisfaction confessed by Hen Redgate attorney for Marg Yate vs Jn Coles.
377:2/3 Richard Stutter brings bailors Richard Mead & Hugh Hamon in suit of Jn Phillips; and Stutter requests copy of declaration in next court, granted.
Action of trespass:
357:2/9 Ric Richardson appoints Ric Wright his attorney vs Ric Stutter who brings bailors Ra Bradshaw & Jn Heath; & plaintiff requests day to declare next court; granted (see *f134*).
Actions of trespass on case:
299:16/24+ Court will advise on Wm Ball having writ of *capias ad satisfaciendum* vs pledge Wm Metcalf; Jn Jarvis return in next court.
353:4/6 Day given Jn Norwood to respond to declaration of Thos Maunde next court.
370:2/2 Ric Coles confesses to action of Wm Ball. Therefore, etc.
Actions of Qui Tam:
352:8/15 Renewed *hab. corpora* between Wm Harrys vs Mich Puddell.
368:3/4 Proceedings between Wm Harris vs Jn Carter discharged.
368:4/4 Memo. that the matter between Wm Harris and Jn Carter being agreed between them it was referred by order of Mr mayor in this court to Edulphus Dingley and William Rayer to consider what said Carter should give the town on consideration of said agreement and for as much as Carter did shew a bill of covenant by which it did appear to them that he did serve in the trade of shoemaker; they have notwithstanding awarded him to pay 2s. to the use of the town. To Jn Dubber:2s.[109]
376:2/4 Imparlance between Wm Harrys vs Ric Buller granted.
Actions of conveyance:
371:2/5 Second proclamation between William Metcalf and John Garlick concerning two tenements etc. .

107 Barley purchase for profit:see 'engrossing' in Glossary.
108 Nethercott in Tackley; see Gelling, 285 & B78/2, f 59.
109 Action presumably under Statute of Artificers 1563(5Eliz. c. 4) requiring apprenticeship of 7 years, or under borough orders of 1580(WBM 82, clauses 20, 21) limiting trade of non-freemen.

384:1/6 First proclamation between Edmund Copland and John Glover concerning one tenement in the said borough.

Action of account:

373:2/2 Jn Woodroff brought bail by John Raunce & John Heath, and requests copy of declaration of Thos Browne aldm. and this is granted. Discharged.[110]

[f142]

385 (Assize of Bread & Ale.)

Court of the Clerk of the market of the borough held 18 January 1595 before John Williams mayor, Wiliam Rylie and William Metcalf aldermen assistants.

Jury:

Henry Fletcher,	Francis Collingwood,	John Taylor,
Ralph Bradshawe,	John Raunce,	Robert Walker,
William Ball,	Hugh Hamon,	William Hickes,
John Wells senior,	Abraham Danter	& William Wells:

sworn.

The jury present that:
Firstly, the best wheat at 40s. the quarter.
Item the second wheat 37s 4d the quarter.
Item malt the bushel 3s.
The assize given and set down by the mayor and his assistants:
Item the halfpenny white loaf to weigh 6 ounces.[111]
Item the penny white loaf to weigh 12 ounces.
Item the halfpenny wheaten loaf to weigh 8 ounces.
Item the penny wheaten loaf to weigh 16 ounces.
Item the penny household loaf to weigh 22½ ounces.
Item the best beer and ale to be sold within the house and without to good and stale a quart 1d,
Item small drink a gallon for 1d.

[f142v]

Action of Detinue

386:1/4 William Shad of North Leigh ('Northlie') vs Leonard Morrell; pledges (R.) Banting & R(alph) Bradshaw.

Action of debt:

387:1/6 Henry Billingham vs William Teslar; pledges Jn Heath & George Fones.

Action of trespass on case:

388:1/1 John Button vs James Morrys (see **358**).

110 Copy d. 47 goes straight to Portmoot 3 February 1595.

111 The minims of 'vi and xii ounces' are extremely smudged, but by comparison with the best-wheat and white-loaf prices of July 1594 the values are taken to be 6 and 12.

389 (Grain Dearth Survey.)
Names of jury for Wheat and Other Grains:

Robert Bantinge,	Robert Walker,	William Flye,
Hugh Hamon,	John Heathe,	John Bruse,
John Yanes,	John Wilkinson,	Robert Wynter,
James Dyssell,	John Welles senior,	William Wells junior
& William Hickes:		

sworn.[112]

[f143]

Portmoot court held on 3 February 1595 before John Williams mayor.
(No other officers listed.)
Actions of trespass on case:
299:17/24+ *Als. fiat sci. fa.* vs surety of Jn Jervys in suit of Wm Ball.
353:5/6 *Morat in lege* by Jn Norwood to declaration of Th Maunde.
Action of trespass:
357:3/9 Peremptory day for Ric Stutter to respond to declaration of Ric Richardson next court on his peril.
Actions of debt:
377:3/3 Peremptory day given Ric Stutter to respond to Jn Phillips.
387:2/6 Peremptory day for Hen Billingham vs Wm Teasler next court; Teasler essoined by Ric Wright.
390:1/1 Thomas Tysdale of Glympton vs Richard Coles.
Action of detinue:
386:2/4 Peremptory day for Wm Shad to declare vs Leo Morrell.
Actions continuing: **352**:9/14; **376**:3/4.

[f143v]

Portmoot court held on 17 February 1595 before John Williams mayor.
Actions of trespass on case:
299:18/24+ Renewed *sci. fa.* vs surety of Jn Jarvis.
353:6/6 Court will advise on writ *corpora cum causa* for Jn Norwood until next court.[113]
Action of Qui Tam:
376:4/4 Permission granted to Wm Harrys vs Ric Buller to imparl & compound in next court.
Action of conveyance:
384:2/6 The Fine has been recognised at this court for John Glover to work and use the tenement of Edmund Copland in the Woolmarket Street with John Button.

112 A book of dearth orders was re-issued in 1594 describing the organisation of local searches for grain and the compulsory provision of markets. See also p. xl.
113 Removal to a Westminster court.

Actions continuing: **352**:10/15; **386**:3/4; **387**:3/6.
Actions of trespass:
357:4/9 Ric Stutter through Hen Redgate his attorney responds to declaration of Ric Richardson.
392:1/6 Thomas Boddy vs Nicholas Bridges.[114]
395:1/2 Thomas Blith vs (blank)
Actions of debt:
393:1/1 Anthony Noble vs Richard Pymont. Discharged.
394:1/1 George Nurse vs William Boreman.

[f144]

Portmoot court held on 3 March 1595 before John Williams mayor.
Action of trespass on case:
299:19/24+ *Sci. fa.* vs surety of Jn Jarvis next court in suit of Wm Ball.
Action of detinue:
386:4/4 Court discharges between Will Shad vs Leonard Morrell.
Actions of trespass:
357:5/9 *Ve. fa.* between Ric Richardson vs Ric Stutter, next court.
392:2/5 Thos Boddie appoints Ric Wright attorney vs Nich Bridges and granted day to declare; pledges to respond Jn Heath & Nich Taylor.
Actions continuing: **352**:11/14; **387**:4/6.

[f144v]

Actions of conveyance:
371:3/5 First proclamation for William Metcalf concerning two messuages purchased from John Garlick (as for **371**:1/5).
384:3/6 First proclamation for Edmund Copland concerning one messuage purchased from John Glover (as for **384**:1/6).
Action of trespass:
395:2/2 Proceedings continue between Blith.......Discharged.
Action of debt:
396:1/2 William Metcalf appoints Hen Redgate attorney vs Richard Coles; pledges to respond Francis Collingwood & John Yanes.

Portmoot court held on 17 March 1595 before John Williams mayor.
(No other officers listed.)
Action of trespass on case:
299:20/24+ Proceedings renewed against surety of Jn Jervis on behalf of Will Ball.
Actions continuing: **352**:12/15; **387**:5/6.

114 Actions **392** to **395** omitted from d. 47.

[f145]

Actions of conveyance:
371:4/5 Second proclamation for William Metcalf concerning two messuages, and no one comes etc. (as for **371**:2/5).
384:4/6 Second proclamation for Edmund Copland concerning one tenement in the Woolmarket Street, and no one comes etc.
Action continuing: **396**:2/2.
Actions of trespass:
357:6/9 *Fiat hab. corpora* for jury between Ric Richardson vs Ric Stutter.[115]
392:3/6 Thos Boddie declares vs Nich Bridges, copy granted.
399:1/1 Francis Collingwood vs Richard Keene. Discharged.
Actions of trespass on case:
369:2/3 George Fones vs Peter Peirson; pledges Nic Tailer & Jn Wilkinson.
397:1/6 John Scott vs Alice Pickyver; pledges Je White & Jn Heath.
398:1/3 Richard Stutter vs Justinian Weller; pledges Jn Dubber & Jerome White.

[f145v]

Actions of debt:
400:1/1 John Sale vs John Carpenter.
401:1/1 Nicholas Weekes vs William Boreman.
402:1/2 William Brushe vs John Hall for debt of 27s.
404:1/1 William Durley vs John Pope. Discharged.
405:1/3 Richard Clempson vs John Lane; pledges Jer White & Robt Walker.
Actions of trespass:
403:1/1 John Bingston vs Thomas Blakeman.
406:1/5 Thomas Collyns vs Thomas Disling; pledges Jer White & Thos Rathbone.
407:1/3 Richard Stutter vs Richard Richardson; pledges Hen Fletcher & Robt Walker (see *f150v*).
Action of detinue:
408:1/3 Richard Richardson vs Richard Stutter on detinue of inventory.[116]

[f146]

Portmoot court held on 31 March 1595 before John Williams mayor.
Action of debt:
387:6/6 Proceedings continue between Hen Billingham vs Wm Teasler. Discharged.
Action of trespass:
392:4/6 Peremptory day for Nic Bridges to respond to declaration of Thos Boddy.

115 Rest of this court omitted from d. 47.
116 See Jacob, 'Detinue of deeds & charters' with regard to land.

Action continuing: **352**:13/15.[117]
Action of trespass:
357:7/9 Names of jury between Richard Richardson pl. vs Richard Stutter def.:

Henry Fletcher,	Robert Walker,	Thomas Blith,
William Flye,	John Dissell,	Michael Nursse,
William Hickes,	Hugh Hamon,	John Bull,
John Bruce,	John Yanes	& John Welles senior.

Who having been charged and tried, say that we find for the plaintiff and assess damages at 20s. with 2d. to the court.[118]

[f146v]

On part of the plaintiff: John Wildgoose, sworn, says that coming into a piece of ground belonging to the defendant, being then his master, and having a bitch of his said master there with him, he did cry "hoye hoye" to certain hogs that were at that instant in the same grounds and therewithal the bitch did presently run upon the same hoggs and did shake one of them and being off from the same hog the same bitch would have run upon the same hogs again. And says that his master at Michaelmas when he went away from his sheep did stop 10s. of his wages to satisfy the plaintiff for his hog which died of (blank).
On part of the plaintiff: James Rosse, sworn, says that being tenant to the defendant he had liberty by his lease to keep a hog which going up and down the yard there, a bitch of the defendant did usually fall upon his hog and shake him, and he told the defendant divers times that if he would not make away his bitch he would hang her and further says that often times his hog being sore and swelled with these shakings he did use to wash it and to dress it and so do to recover it again. On part of the plaintiff (*sic* ?): Richard Stutter sworn says that saving some judgments to cut and help beasts that were swollen or hurt the plaintiff showed him a hog which was bitten under the shoulder and required him to lance ('launche') it but he refused, telling him the hog would die of that hurt which afterwards came to pass but how he came of that hurt he knows not.
On part of the plaintiff: Annable Reade sworn says she saw John Wyldgoose then servant with the defendant take of a bitch of his master's which was shaking of a hog but whether the hog died of that shaking she knows not.
409:1/1 Michael Vaux vs Dryver Jepherson. Discharged.

[f147]

Actions of trespass on case:
397:2/6 Peremptory day for Jn Scott to declare vs Alice Pickyver next court.
398:2/3 Justinian Weller essoined by Richard Wright.
412:1/1 William Browne of Great Tew ('Tewe magna') vs Edmund Fletcher. Discharged.

117 Most items in the rest of this court omitted from d.47.
118 Referred to in *VCH Oxon*. xii. 392ii, n. 73.

Actions of debt:
402:2/2 It is ordered by the court that if John Hall before next court produces sufficient pledge to respond to the proceedings of William Brushe of which 27s. then remains in the hands of Edulphus Dingley for pledge of the said Jn Hall to be delivered to aforesaid Will Brushe.
405:2/3 John Lane essoined by Hen Rudgate.
410:1/1 Thomas Brown vs Edward Jeffes. Discharged.
Action of Qui Tam:
411:1/4 Information by William Harris vs Leonard Guy; pledges Robt Banting & Jas Dissell.
Action of trespass:
406:2/5 Thomas Disling essoined by Hen Rudgate; pledges Jer White & Thos Rathbone.
Action continuing: **369**:3/3.
Actions of conveyance:
371:5/5 Third proclamation for two tenements recently purchased by William Metcalf from John Garlick, and no one comes to claim, therefore it is adjudged that the said tenements are the right of the said William.
384:5/6 Third proclamation for one tenement recently purchased by Edmund Copland pl. from John Glover def., and no one comes to claim,therefore it is adjudged that the said tenement is the right of the said Edmund.

[f147v]

384:6/6 This is the final concord made in the Portmoot court of the said lady Queen of the said borough on 17 February in the thirty-seventh year of the reign of our Lady Elizabeth, in accordance with the custom of the same borough from time out of mind till now and approved in accordance with the liberties conceded to the mayor and community of the same borough by the charters of the said lady Queen and of her various progenitors late kings and queens of England before John Williams mayor, William Metcalf alderman & others the lieges of the said present queen then present, Between Edmund Copland pl. through Edulphus Dingley his attorney with power to win or lose, (Marginal note: Paid Mr Dubber by Copland 3s.)
And John Glover deforciant of one messuage, burgage or tenement situate, lying and existing in the borough of New Woodstock in the street called the Woolmarket ('Wollmarket') Street between the tenement which John Heath now inhabits on the west side, and the tenement which Thomas Rathbone in the manner inhabits on the east side. The tenement of James Dissell is on the south side. And the said Woolmarket St. is on the north side recently in the tenure of John Button with all and singular appurtenances.
Which same premises Edm Copland has as the gift of Jn Glover and which are handed over in this same court to have and to hold by Copland & his heirs of the chief lords of that fee which belongs to these tenements. And moreover Jn

Glover grants that he himself & his heirs will warrant to Edm Copland & his heirs to hold the said appurtenances against Jn Glover & his heirs in perpetuity. And for this fine the said John witnesses the sealed writings for the Commonalty appended. And further, because the said Edmund comes to this Portmoot court and claims to hold for himself & his heirs in perpetuity the said tenement & appurtenances described above and makes claim in accordance with the custom of the borough in open court solemnly proclaimed and recorded and so proclaimed and recorded for the first time. And on this he comes through his attorney to this Court held 17 March, Year abovesaid to proclaim & record in the manner & form as above in open court proclaimed the second time. And further to the next court following held last day of March the year abovesaid the said Edm Copland seeks through his attorney to make his claim by the third oral proclamation.

[f148]

And thus three oral proclamations are made for the Claim as above. And because no one comes to this or other sittings of the court to contradict or challenge the claim. Therefore in accordance with the custom of the said borough since time out of mind it was approved and attested by John Williams then & there mayor of the said borough, & William Medcalf aldm. & others present then & there present.

For which proclamation and enrolment the said Edm Copland gives a fine of 4s. And thus also by the said Jn Williams mayor & several of his aldermen in accordance with the custom of the borough it is adjudged that the said Edm Copland shall have, enjoy and possess the aforesaid tenement with appurtenances. And holds them for himself & his heirs in perpetuity. In testimony of this matter the common seal is attached to this present writing. Completed and seal affixed as above 14 April 37 Eliz., witnessed by John Williams mayor, William Rylie aldm., Thomas Browne aldm., John Dubber chamb., Edulphus Dingley clerk; William Rayer, John Dissell constables; Richard Wright; Henry Rudgate attorney of the court, and others.

Action of Qui Tam:

411:2/4 Will Harris for Queen & himself vs Leo. Guy for debt.[119]

[f148v]

Portmoot court held at Guildhall on 14 April 1595 before John Williams mayor.

(No other officers listed.)

Actions of trespass on case:

299:21/24+ *Fiat alias sci. fa.* vs surety of Jn Jarvis in suit of Wm Ball, return next court.

397:3/6 Jn Scott appoints Ric Wright vs Alice Pickiver and declares; defendant through Hen Redgate requests day & copy.

[119] *Qui Tam*: see footnote 58.

398:3/3 Continues between Ric Stutter vs Just Weller. Discharged.
Action of trespass:
392:5/6 Since Nich Bridges does not appear after peremptory summons and *nihil dicit* to declaration of Thos Boddy in plaint of *assumpsit,* therefore adjudged that Bridges should bring a writ for next court.
Action of debt:
405:3/3 Since Jn Lane does not appear after peremptory summons and *nihil dicit* to declaration of Ric Clempson (see *f145v*) therefore adjudged by court that Clempson should recover said £9 12s. specified in declaration and (blank) for amercement & cost of suit. Discharged.
Action continued: **352**:14/15.

[f149]

Action of Qui Tam:
411:3/4 Wm Harrys granted imparlance & compounding with Leo Guy, return next court.
Action of trespass:
406:3/5 Thos Collyns appoints Hen Rudgate vs Thos Dislinge and declares and requests day & copy.
Actions of trespass & detinue:
357:8/9; **407**:2/3; **408**:2/3 Memo. that at this court all actions whatsoever depending between Richard Stutter and Richard Richardson are by consent referred to the arbitrament and end of George Whitton esquire and John Rathbone gent.,[120] and if they can not agree then to be over-ruled and umpired by Walter Culpeper[121] esquire this to be concluded at or before the 13th day of May next in writing and for the performance hereof either of the said parties have affirmed in £10 apiece to stand to the same arbitrament by giving 6d apiece either to other.[122]
Actions of trespass:
413:1/1 Thomas Browne vs Michael Vaux; pledge Glover. Discharged.
414:1/2 Thomas Brown vs George Fones; pledges Jn Heath & Jn Rylie.
416:1/2 William Browne vs Hugh Hancocks; pledges Hen Fletcher & Thos Colgrave.
Action of trespass on case:
415:1/16 Richard Meade vs Thomas Bowle; pledges Fras Collingwood & Geo Fones.

[f149v]

Portmoot court held on 28 April 1595 before John Williams mayor.
(No other officers listed.)

120 John Rathbone landowner in Bletchingdon and juryman at trial on Oxfordshire Uprising of 1596 (Walter, 112).

121 Walter Culpeper of the Commission of the Peace, Oxfordshire 1609 (Gleason, 256).

122 Rest of this court omitted from d. 47.

Actions of trespass on case:
299:22/24+ Court adjudges that Jn Jarvis does not provide the recovery adjudged in the suit of Wm Ball (see **299**:12/24+), so a *fiat executio* is given against his surety.
320:13/14 *Sci. fa.* granted vs surety of Wm East in suit of Edm White (see *f138*).
397:4/6 Response by Al Pickiver who comes to court, granted for return next court in suit of Jn Scott.
Actions of trespass:
406:4/5 Peremptory day for Th Disling to respond to Th Collyns' declaration in next court under peril.
416:2/2 Wm Browne appoints Hen Rudgate attorney & declares vs Hugh Hancocks who, through Ric Wright, requests day & copy.
Actions continuing: **352**:15/15**;** **392**:6/6; **414**:2/2.

[f150]

Actions of trespass & detinue:
357:9/9 & **408**:3/3 Court adjudges that Ric Richardson should recover 20s damages and 39s 8d for costs of suit vs Ric Stutter.
Action continuing: **411**:4/4.[123]
Actions of debt:
417:1/1 William Metcalf vs Robert Symons.
421:1/1 Richard Kenche vs Simon Rilie. Discharged.
422:1/1 John Gobbett vs John Allen. Discharged.
423:1/1 Richard Parratt vs William Bowlter; pledges Jn Heath & Abram Daunter.
424:1/1 John Clark vs Robert Wynter. Discharged.
425:1/12 Robert Binckes vs Richard Coles; pledges Hugh Hamond & Will Wells.
Actions of trespass on case:
418:1/1Thomas Hollycombe vs Francis Millway. Discharged.
419:1/1 John Rolright vs John Phips.
420:1/1 Thomas Boddy vs John Seely (see **494**).

[f150v]

Portmoot court held on 26 May 1595 before John Williams mayor.
(No other officers listed.)
Actions of trespass on case:
299:23/24+ *Writ of error* for Jn Jarvis in the suit of Wm Ball for return on day in Trinity quindene, & court will advise[124] (see *f161v*).
149:18/19 *Fiat writ of executio* vs Jn Brown in suit of Robt Symons (see *f134*).

123 Actions **417** to **425** omitted from d. 47.
124 Action removed to Queen's Bench and returned to Portmoot.

320:14/14 *Fiat alias sci. fa.* vs surety of Edm White (*sic* ?Will. East? see 13/14) for return next court. Discharged.
397:5/6 *Fiat writ hab. corpora* for jury for Jn Scott vs Al Pickiver in next court.
415:2/16 Ric Meades appoints Ric Wright vs Thos Bowle & imparls & declaration in next court; Bowle essoined by Hen Rudgate.
Actions of trespass:
407:3/3 Since Ric Stutter does not prosecute suit vs Ric Richardson therefore non-suit and court adjudges recovery for costs (see *f145v*).
406:5/5 Imparlance & copy for Thos Collins to replicate to Thos Disling next court. Discharged.
Action of debt:
425:2/12 Robt Binckes appoints Hen Rudgate attorney vs Ric Coles to imparl on declaration in next court; Coles essoined by Ric Wright.
Action unspecified:
426:1/8 Ric Richardson declares vs Ric Stutter and imparls & copy & day in next court.

[f151]

Action of dower & conveyance:
427:1/5+ There are to be separate partitions/divisions for Edward Bulliphant & his wife Anna and Edmund Oven & his wife Ursula for their dower shares of the tenements in the several tenure of Robert Banting and Richard Smyth and John Pulco within the borough provided that the said Edward Bullyphant claims said dower at the next court; and the same day is given etc.[125] (See also **258**).
Action of trespass on case:
428:1/1 Humphrey Salmons vs Thomas Baslie. Discharged.
Action of account:
429:1/9+ Thomas Barton & Mary his wife vs John Crost.
Action of debt:
430:1/1 Henry Dodwell vs Nicholas Taylor.

Portmoot court held on 16 June 1595 before John Williams.
(No other officers listed.)
Action of trespass on case:
415:3/16 Ric Meades declares vs Thos Bowle and appoints Hen Rudgate attorney and granted imparlance & copy.
Actions unspecified:
426:2/8+ Peremptory day for Ric Stutter to respond to Ric Richardson.
431:1/1 Discharged between Colgrove vs Ric Pickiver.

[125] Rest of this court omitted from d. 47.

Action continuing: **425**:3/12+.

[f151v]

Action of trespass on case:
149:19/19 Sergeant-at-mace returns *cepi corpus* of Jn Browne on writ of *executio* in suit of Rob Symons (same entry on *f152*).
Action of account:
429:2/9+ Thos Barton & Mary his wife declare through attorney Hen Rudgate vs Jn Crost who is granted copy through attorney Ric Wright.
Actions of trespass on case:
397:6/6 Names of jury between John Scott pl. vs Alice Pickiver def.:

John Phillips,	Robert Walker,	Thomas Blith,
William Flie,	William Raier,	William Hickes,
Hugh Hamon,	John Wilkinson,	George Phones,
John Bull,	William Wells	& John Button:

sworn.
Which jury, having been tried and charged, say, we find that Alice Pickyver did not use those slanderous words in the manner and form as the plaintiff has declared.[126, 127]
Thomas Parkyns alias Cowper, sworn, says that Jn Scott had a sow and certain pigs and so likewise had the goodwife Pickyver, whose daughter Alice came to Scott and called him arrant thereof saying he had stolen her mother's pig and so took up and used Scott's pig and carried it away.
John Johnson of Adderbury affirmed the like.
432:1/13+ John Scott vs Alice Pickiver; pledges Jerome White & John Heath. Court adjourns for 16 days (see **397**:6/6 above).

[f152]

Portmoot court held at Guildhall on 16 June 1595 before John Williams mayor.[128]
Action continuing: **425**:3/12+ (repeat entry).
Action unspecified:
426:3/8+ Day given to Ric Stutter to respond next court. By royal *mandamus* a writ of error for the suit to recover between Ric Richardson pl. and Stutter def. for return on day in Trinity three weeks.[129]
431:1/1 Day given Thomas Colgrove to declare vs Pickiver (repeat entry).
Action of trespass on case:
149:19/19 Sergeant-at-mace returns *cepi corpus* of Jn Browne on writ of *executio* in suit of Rob Symons (repeat entry).

[126] This sentence is also included on a loose quarter-sheet of paper pinned to f142.
[127] The rest of this court is omitted from d. 47.
[128] This section of Portmoot court up to next court is crossed through in B78/1.
[129] Case referred to a Westminster court, then returned to Portmoot.

Portmoot court held at Guildhall on last day (30) June 1595 before John Williams mayor.
(No other officers listed.)
Action unspecified:
426:4/8+ *Morat in lege* by Ric Stutter in suit of Ric Richardson.
Actions of trespass on case:
415:4/16 Peremptory day for Thos Bowle to respond next court.
432:2/13+ Peremptory day for Jn Scott to declare vs Al Pickiver in next court.
Action continuing: **425**:4/12+.

[f152v]

Action of account:
429:3/9+ Thos & Mary Barton declare vs Jn Crost, imparlance & copy granted.
Actions of dower & conveyance:
427:2/5+ Edmund Oven & Ursula his wife in person claim her dower of her right to the three tenements in the borough, namely those in the tenure of Robt Banting, Ric Smyth & Jn Pulco; and Edward Bulliphant through their attorney Ric Wright makes similar lawful claim of part of the third part of the premises of the dower of Anne (Bulliphant?).
Action of debt:
433:1/2 John Sherley vs John Coles.

Portmoot court held on 14 July 1595.
(No presiding or other officers listed.)
Action of trespass on case:
415:5/16 Response for Th Bowle & *ven. fac.* granted.
Action of account:
429:4/9+ Peremptory day for Jn Crost to respond to T & M Barton.
Action unspecified:
426:5/8+ Replication by Ric Richardson.
Action of dower & conveyance:
427:3/5+ Edmund Oven & Ursula his wife through Hen Rudgate their attorney produce a writ of partition/division referring to the premises abovesaid and similarly is produced for Edward Bulliphant through his attorney Ric Wright.
Actions continuing: **425**:5/12+; **433**:2/2.

[f153]

Actions of debt:
434:1/1 Richard Clarke vs Thomas Turner.[130]
435:1/1 John Asshebe vs George Howbrooke.
436:1/5 John Ashbe vs James Tasker.
437:1/1 William Nicoll vs John Clarke.

130 Rest of this court omitted from d. 47.

438:1/1 Gregorie Peter vs Thomas Symonds, chapman. Discharged.
439:1/1 Thomas Rogers vs Thomas Turner. Discharged.
Action of trespass:
440:1/12 Magdalen Bruce vs Robert Banting; pledges Nich Tailor & Jn Wilkinson.

Portmoot court held on 28 July 1595.
(No presiding or other officers listed.)
Action of trespass on case:
415:6/16 *Hab. corpora* for witnesses between Ric Meades vs Thos Bowle for return next court.
Action of account:
429:5/9+ Queen commands *writ of certiorari* to proceed between T & M Barton vs J Crost[131] (see *f159v*).
Action unspecified:
426:6/8+ Day given Ric Stutter to *rejoinder.*
Action continuing: **425**:6/12+.

[f153v]

Actions of trespass on case:
432:3/13+ Day given Alice Pickiver to respond next court.[132]
441:1/1 Justinian Weller vs Thomas Maltman; pledges Jer White & Jn Raunson. Discharged.
Action of trespass:
440:2/12 Magd Bruce appoints Ric Wright attorney vs Robt Banting who appoints Hen Redgate attorney and bailed to Nich Tailor & Jn Wilkinson and is essoined by Redgate; Bruce requests day to declare next court.
Action of dower & conveyance:
427:4/5+ A writ of partition/division is granted to Edward Bulliphant here in person returnable to the next court for the assignment of the whole one third of various tenements in the tenure of Richard Banting, Richard Smyth and John Pulcoe (see *f163v*).
Actions of debt:
436:2/5 John Asshebe appoints Hen Rudgate attorney vs James Tasker and declares, and Tasker appoints Ric Wright attorney and requests copy which is granted.
442:1/1 John Golding of Dean ('de Denne') vs Henry Allis for debt of £3.[133]
443:1/5+ John Gobett of Hanborough ('Hanbrow') vs Thomas Martyn; pledges Thos Browne & Jn Dubber. Will Rayer.
444:1/1 Thomas Brown vs John Kent.

[131] Action removed to Westminster court & returned to Portmoot.
[132] Actions **441** to **446** omitted from d. 47.
[133] Dean:probably in Spelsbury (Gelling, 379), possibly in Steeple Aston (Emery, 134).

445:1/1 Thomas Brown vs John Heath & John Yanes.
446:1/1 Thomas Brown vs Richard Smyth.

[f154]

Portmoot held at Guildhall on 18 August 1595 before John Williams mayor.

Actions of trespass on case:
415:7/16 All matters between R Meades and T Bowle are referred to the arbitrament of Vincent Coventrie and Edmund Meese and their findings to be put in writing before 13 October next.
432:4/13+ Alice Pickiver responds and a copy is granted.
Action unspecified:
426:7/8+ All matters between R Stutter and R Richardson are compromitted to John Raunson & William Rayer arbitrators and to Thomas Brown umpire to be given up before 13 October on pain of a written bond for £40.
Action of trespass:
440:3/12 Declaration of Magd Bruce and copy granted.
Actions of debt:
436:3/5 Peremptory day for J Tasker to respond to declaration of J Asshebe by next court.
443:2/5+ Jn Gobett appoints Ric Wright attorney vs Thos Martyn
who appoints Hen Rudgate his attorney.
Action continuing: **425**:7/12+.

[f154v]

Portmoot court held on 1 September 1595 before John Williams mayor.

(No other officers listed.)
Actions of debt:
425:8/12+ R Bincks declares vs R Coles who requests imparlance and is granted copy.
436:4/5 J Tasker responds in suit of J Ashbie.
443:3/5+ Since Jn Gobbett does not prosecute his suit vs Thos Martyn therefore he is in mercy.
Action of trespass:
440:4/12 Peremptory day for Rob Banting to respond next court.
Actions continuing: **415**:8/16; **426**:8/8; **432**:5/13+.

[f155]

Portmoot court held on 15 September 1595.

(No presiding or other officers listed.)
Actions of debt:
425:9/12+ Peremptory day for R Coles to respond next court.
443:4/5+ Court adjudges that Thos Martyn should recover 5s 2d vs Jn. Gobbett.

448:1/1 Abraham Mylling vs William Mowlder. Discharged.[134]
449:1/1 Hercules Raynford vs Arthur Osbaston.
454:1/1 William Metcalf vs John Coles.
Actions of trespass on case:
432:6/13+ *Venire facias* for Jn Scott for return next court.
447:1/8+ Edmund White appoints Hen Redgate attorney vs Bartholomew Stere who draws bail from Thos Browne & Jn Heath.
Actions continuing: **415**:9/16; **436**:5/5.
Actions of trespass:
440:5/12 *Ve. fa.* for Magd Bruce for return next court.
450:1/2 William Flaxney vs William Wyse; pledge Jerome White.
451:1/1 William Wyse vs William Flaxney.
452:1/7+ Richard Brown vs Richard Gonne; Mr Thos Browne.
453:1/1 Henry Terry vs William Cox.

[f155v]

Portmoot court held on 29 September (1595).
(No presiding nor other officers listed.)
Actions of debt:
425:10/12+ Ric Coles responds to declaration of Rob Bincks.
443:5/5 Jn Gobet through attorney Ric Wright seeks full payment of 5s 2d for costs against Th Martyn, court to adjudge on the recovery.
Actions of trespass on case:
432:7/13+ *Hab. corpora* for Jn Scott vs Alc Pickiver next court.
447:2/8+ Edmund White appoints Hen Rudgate attorney vs Barth Steere, and granted day to declare in next court.
Action continuing: **415**:10/16.
Actions of trespass:
440:6/12 *Hab. corpora* for Magd Bruce vs Robt Banting next court.
450:2/2 Wm Flaxney appoints Ric Wright attorney vs Wm Wyse and requests day to declare next court; Wise essoined by Hen Redgate attorney and draws bail from Ralph Bradshawe & Jn Heath. Discharged.
452:2/7+ Ric Browne appoints Ric Wright attorney vs Ric Gonne and granted day to declare next court; Gonne essoined by Hen Rudgat, and draws bail from Jerome White & Jn Bruce.

[f156]

Actions of debt:
455:1/6+ Richard Cowper vs Thomas Turner; pledge by written bond in hand of Mr mayor.[135]
458:1/1 John Hamon vs John Lawrence; pledge Hugh Hamon. Discharged.

134 These entries on actions **448** to **454** omitted from d. 47.

135 These entries on actions **455** to **459** are omitted from d. 47.

Actions of trespass:
456:1/1 Nicholas Buckner vs Richard Ibell. Discharged.
457:1/1 Richard Deane vs Francis Collingwood; pledge Jn Phillips. Discharged.
459. Election of Mayor.
William Metcalf clerk is mayor of the aforesaid borough by agreement of the commonalty of the said borough.
Court held on 13 October (1595) before William Metcalf mayor.
Action of debt:
425:11/12+ *Ve. fa.* for Rob Bincks vs Ric Coles.
Action of trespass:
452:3/7+ Ric Browne appoints Ric Wright attorney vs Ric Gonne and draws bail from Jer White & Jn Bruce; Browne declares & grants Gonne a copy.
Actions of trespass on case:
447:3/8+ *Ve. fa.* for Edm White vs Bart Steere.

[f156v]

415:11/16 Renewed *hab. corpora* between Ric Meades vs Thos Bowle for return next court.
Action of debt:
455:2/6+ Ric Cowper appoints Hen Redgate attorney vs Thos Turner who draws bail from Jn Raunson & Rob Walker & is granted copy of declaration.
Action of trespass:
440:7/12 Names of jury between Magdalen Bruce pl. vs Robert Banting def.:

Ralph Bradshawe,	Michael Nursse,	Michael Vaxe,
Jerome White,	William Rayer,	John Heath,
John Bull,	George Phones,	John Wells,
John Janes,	Robert Wynter	& John Button.

Who having been tried and charged say we find for the plaintiff and assess damages at 20s. and costs at 2d.
Action continuing: **432**:8/13+.

[f157]

Actions of trespass:
460:1/5+ Dorothy Norwood vs Benedict Norwood for his goods.[136]
462:1/3+ Ralph Bradshaw vs William Parsons.
Action of ejectment:
466:1/6+ Ethelbert Doa vs Robert Banting in plaint of trespass and *ejectione firma.*
Actions of debt:
461:1/1 William Smyth vs Thomas Talbot.
463:1/1 Julian Davies (spinster) vs Benedict Norwood.

136 These entries on actions **460** to **469** are omitted from d. 47.

464:1/1 John Norwood vs Benedict Norwood.
465:1/1 William Metcalf vs Benedict Norwood.
467:1/6+ William Rilie vs Richard Coles.
468:1/1 Thomas Gonn vs John Coles.
Action of assumpsit:
469:1/4 Richard Deane vs Francis Collingwood.

[f157v]

Portmoot court held on 27 October 1595 before William Metcalf mayor.
(No other officers listed.)
Actions of trespass:
452:4/7+ Peremptory day for Ric Gunne to respond in next court.
460:2/5+ Dorothy Norwood appoints Hen Rudgate attorney vs Bene Norwood to attach his goods, and she declares.
Action of trespass on case:
447:4/8+ *Ve. fa.* for Edm White vs Bart Steere.
Actions of debt:
455:3/6+ Peremptory day for Thos Turner to respond next court.
467:2/6+ Wm Rilie appoints Hen Rudgate attorney vs Ric Coles, who is essoined by Ric Wright.
Action of ejectment:
466:2/6+ First privilege day for Rob Banting in suit of Eth Doa, and he requests copy of declaration.
Action unspecified:
470:1/2 Alice Phips appoints Hen Rudgate attorney vs John Bruce, Richard Smyth & Magdalen Bruce, and they are essoined by the said John.
Action continuing: **425**:12/12.

[f158]

Actions of trespass on case:
415:12/16 Names of jury between Richard Meade p1. and Thomas Bowle def.:

John Raunson,	William Ball,	Robert Walker,
Thomas Blithe,	Nicholas Taylor,	John Bruce,
John Wilkynson,	Hugh Hamon,	William Hickes,
John Janes,	John Wells senior	& William Wells

sworn: Who having been tried and charged say we find for the plaintiff and assess damages at 12d and for costs of the suit 2d.
432:9/13+ Names of the jury between John Scott p1. vs Alice Pickiver def.: John Phillips, Richard Meade, William Ball, Thomas Blith, John Raunson, Nicholas Taylor, William Flye, Hugh Hamon, George Fones, John Bull, Robert Wynter & John Button; sworn: Who having been tried and charged say we find for the plaintiff and assess damages at 6d. and costs of the suit 1d.

Action of trespass:
440:8/12 Court adjudges that Magd Bruce should recover vs Robert Banting 20s. for damages and 24s 8d for costs of bringing suit.
Action of assumpsit:
469:2/4 Ric Deane appoints Henry Wright (*sic* ?Redgate?) his attorney vs Fras Collingwood and requests day to declare next court; and Collingwood is essoined by Ric Wright his attorney.

[f158v]

Actions of trespass:
462:2/3+ Ral Bradshawe appoints Hen Rudgate attorney vs Wm Parsons, who is essoined by John Janes.
471:1/1 John Scot vs Alice Pickiver. Discharged.[137]
477:1/1 Adrian Whiscker vs William Kilby.
Actions of debt:
473:1/1 Richard Neale vs Richard Coles. Discharged.
474:1/1 William Barber vs Walter Robynson. Discharged.
475:1/1 Robert Symons vs John Bull. Discharged.
476:1/1 John Harrys vs John Hedges.
478:1/1 John Selwood vs Nicholas Fuller.
Actions of trespass on case:
472:1/2 John Scott vs -----Dey. Discharged.
479:1/1 Francis Heath vs John Scott. Discharged.

[f159]

Portmoot court held at Guildhall on 10 November 1595 before William Metcalf mayor.

Actions of trespass on case:
415:13/16 *Scire facias* vs sureties Francis Collingwood & George Fones for Thos Bowle in suit of Ric Mead.
447:5/8+ *Hab. corpora* for Edm White vs Bart Steere next court.
Action of trespass:
452:5/7+ Response by Ric Gonn in suit of Ric Brown,and copy.
Action of debt:
455:4/6+ *Morat in lege* by Thos Turner in suit of Ric Cowper.
Action of ejectment:
466:3/6+ Second privilege day for Rob Banting in suit of Eth Doa.
Actions continuing: **460**:3/5+; **467**:3/6+; **469**:3/4.

[f159v]

Actions of trespass on case:
432:10/13+ *Sci. fa.* vs surety of Al Pickiver in suit of Jn Scott.

137 Actions **471** to **479** are omitted from d. 47.

472:2/2 Jn Scott requests day to declare through attorney Ric Wright vs --- Day, who draws bail from Wm Ball & Nic Taylor.

Actions of trespass:

440:9/12 *Scire facias* vs sureties of R Banting in suit of Bruce.

462:3/3 *Nihil dicit* by Wm Parsons in suit of Ralph Bradshawe and writ of inquiry granted into damages.

[f160]

Portmoot court held at Guildhall on 24 November 1595 before William Metcalf mayor.

(No other officers listed.)

Action of account:

429:6/9+ Royal writ of *procedendo* between Th & Mary Barton vs J Crost. (in d. 47 brought on behalf of defendant?)

Action of ejectment:

466:4/6+ Third privilege day for Rob Banting in suit of Eth Doae.

Actions of trespass:

440:10/12 *Alias sci. fa.* vs sureties of Rob Banting in suit of Magd Bruce.

452:6/7+ *Venire facias* for Ric Browne vs Ric Gonne next court.

460:4/5+ Peremptory day for Ben Norwood to respond to Dor Norwood next court.

Actions of debt:

455:5/6+ Peremptory day given Ric Cowper to replicate next court vs Thos Turner.

467:4/6+ Wm Rylie appoints Hen Redgate attorney vs Ric Coles and draws bail from Wm Wells & Rob Wynter; copy of declaration granted.

Action of assumpsit:

469:4/4 Continues between Ric Deane vs Fras Collingwood by assent. Discharged.

[f160v]

Actions of trespass on case:

415:14/16 *Alias sci. fa.* for sureties of Thos Bowle in suit of Ric Meade.

432:11/13+ *Alias sci. fa.* for sureties of Alice Pickiver in suit of Jn Scott.

447:6/8+ Names of jury between Edmund White pl. vs Bartholomew Steere def.:[138]

John Phillips,	Nicholas Taylor,	Richard Meade,
William Rayer,	William Flie,	John Dissell,
John Bruce,	William Hickes,	John Wilkinson,
John Bull,	Thomas Colgrove	& William Wells

sworn: We find for the plaintiff in damages 3s 4d and for costs of suit 2d.[139]

138 A few months later, in 1596, Bartholomew Steer was the leader of the agrarian revolt at Hampton Gay (see Walter & p. xli).

139 The rest of this entry is omitted from d. 47.

Nicholas Sherwyn says that being arrested he heard the party say in the sergeant's house that he the defendant had the saw and he delivered it home to White again. Saloman White says that coming from Mr Dormer's he saw the defendant carry a tenon-saw ('tenant saw') in his hand, who went into his father's house with the same. Edmund Stevens says that, being at work at Gosford with the defendant, he confessed that he had borrowed the saw, which the defendant and this deponent did then work withall, of Edmund White, for want of other tools of his own to use withall.

[f161]

Portmoot court held on 8 December 1595.

(No presiding officer listed.)

Actions of trespass on case:

415:15/16 Court adjudges that Ric Mead should recover vs Thos Bowle for damages 12d and for costs of suit 36s.

432:12/13+ Court adjudges that Jn Scott should recover vs Alice Pickiver for damages 6d and for costs 39s 7d.

Actions of trespass:

440:11/12 Court adjudges that Magd Bruce should recover vs Robt Banting for damages 20s and for court costs 36s 10d.

452:7/7+ *Hab. corpora* between Ric Brown vs Ric Gonn next court.

Actions of debt:

455:6/6+ Replication by Ric Cowper vs Thos Turner.

467:5/6+ Peremptory day for for Rc Coles to respond to Wm Riley.

Action continuing: **429**:7/9+.

[f161v][140]

Actions of trespass on case:

299:24/24+ *Sci. fa.* for surety of Jn Jervis in suit of W Ball (see *fl50v*).

447:7/8+ *Sci. fa.* vs surety of Barth Steere in suit of Edm White.

Action of account:

429:8/9+ Because Jn Crost does not appear when summoned three times in suit of Thos & Mary Barton, order granted for writ of inquiry into damages sustained in bringing the action.

Action of ejectment:

466:5/6+ Rob Banting responds to suit of Eth Doa, with copy.

Action of trespass:

480:1/2+ John Woodroff appoints Ric Wright attorney vs Robert Heath who bailed to Jn Taylor & Jn Heath; Woodroff declares and is granted a writ of *capias.*

Action of Dower:

481 To this court comes Elizabeth James, relict of Humphrey James, in person and requests the third part of one tenement with appurtenances lying and

[140] End of the Portmoot text in d. 47.

existing in the High Street of the borough aforesaid lately in the tenure of the said Humphrey and now in the tenure of a certain Thomas Paynter whereof the same Thomas deforces Elizabeth. And she asks for process against the same Thomas and it is allowed her. The sergeant-at-mace and official of this court is therefore ordered to summon the said Thomas Paynter to be here at the next court and the same day etc.
Actions continuing: **460**:5/5+; **470**:2/2+.

[f162]

Portmoot court held on 22 December 1595 before William Metcalf mayor.
Actions of trespass on case:
415:16/16 Ric Meade confesses himself satisfied with the sum of 38s. recovered vs Thos Bowle.
432:13/13+ Sergeant-at-mace produces an order in person in court for 40s. in suit of Jn Scott vs Alice Pickiver.
Actions of trespass:
440:12/12 Ric Wright attorney for Magd Bruce confesses satisfaction with the sum of 56s 10d recovered against Rob Bantinge.
480:2/2+ Copy of Jn Woodroff's declaration granted to Rob Heath.
Action of debt:
467:6/6+ Order for royal *writ of inquiry* into the damages for Wm Rilie sustained in the action against Ric Coles.

[f162v]

(Recognisances for Victuallers licensed in the borough.)
482[141]

Pledges, each in £5,	*for*	*Name, in £10.*
Richard Wright & John Heath		Michael Vaux, for himself
Thomas Blyth & John Heathe		Henry Redgat, for himself
Thomas Blithe & John Bruce		Maudlen Bruce +
Humphrey James & Nathan Sharp		Michael Mondye
Henry Redgat & Humphrey James		Thomas Blyth +
Humphrey James & Ralph Bradshaw		Margery Nursse +
Nicholas Tailor & Ralph Bradshawe		John Smyth, for himself
Ralph Bradshew & Nathan Sharp		Humphrey James +
Humphrey James & Nicholas Tailor		Thomas Paynter

141 No headings given here; but similar format & contents with headings given in victual licensing in B78/2 ff42, 42v, 72v, 132r&v, etc. . The '+' signs may refer to loans for the fees actually paid for the licences (compare with B78/2 ff18, 41v).

[f163]

Humphrey James & Thomas Paynter	Nicholas Tailor, for himself
John Heath & John Dissell	Alice Cave +
Thomas Paynter & Nicholas Tailor	Michael Glover +
John Heath & James Dissell	John Dissell +

[f163v]

Action of dower & conveyance:
427:5/5+ Edward Bulliphant requests in court that the claim to dower in right of his wife Anne, be renewed (see also **258** & *f153v*).
Action of account:
429:9/9+ Writ of *inquiry* into damages for Thos & wife Mary Barton sustained in action processed in this court in which the jury found for the plaintiffs to damages of £9.
Action of ejectment:
466:6/6+ *Ve. fa.* between Rob Banting def. vs Eth Doa pl.
Actions of trespass on case:
447:8/8+ *Alias sci. fa.* for Bart Steere in suit of Edm White.
484:1/2+ (John) Lock appoints Ric Wright attorney vs Robert Banting who draws bail from Thos Blyth & Jn Wilkieson; Lock requests day to declare next court and Banting is essoined by Hen Rudgate.
485 Because John Castell does not prosecute his process vs George Galloway, after three summonses in court,therefore he is in mercy.
Action of trespass:
483 Thomas Boddie appoints Ric Wright attorney vs William Harrys who is delivered bail from Thos Colgrove & Jn Yanes, and through Hen Rudgate his attorney is granted a copy.
Action unspecified:
486 John Taylor (in margin). Lowe pl. vs Edmund Hadwe (?).

[f164]

Actions of debt:
487:1/1 Robert Banting vs Ralph Bradshawe. Discharged.
488:1/1 John Newell vs William Wall. Discharged.
489:1/1 Robert Tassell vs Richard Coles. Discharged.
490:1/1 John Collyer vs Richard Coles. Discharged.
491:1/1 Thomas Haynes vs, John Coles. Discharged.
492:1/1 William Rayer vs Richard Coles. Discharged.
493:1/1 William Dunford vs Richard Coles. Discharged.
496:1/1 Alice Darling vs Robert Symon. Discharged.[142]
497:1/1 Richard Bushop vs Abraham Furnis. Discharged.

142 Alice Darling, servant to George Whitton, was mother of his illegitimate son and heir John. Her will is Ox. Arch. 18/1/l (1629).

501 Justinian Symons of Hordley vs John Willis & Edulphe Dingley in debt on demand for £5 by written bond.
502:1/1 Thomas Radborne & Joan his wife vs George Johnson in debt on demand for £3 by written bond. Discharged.
503 Thomas Janes & Elizabeth his wife vs Thomas Yveto for debt of 21s.
Action unspecified:
494 Thomas Boddy vs John Seelie (see **420**).
Actions of trespass:
495 Mayor & commonalty vs John Browne for his goods.
498 John Crosts vs Thomas Barton.
499:1/1 Thomas Osborne vs Robert Batson. Discharged.
500:1/1 Ralph Durbridge vs William Boreman. Discharged.

[f164v]

Actions of debt:
504:1/1 John Phillips vs John Gregory. Discharged.
505:1/1 Thomas Bradshaw vs Richard Coles. Discharged.
507 William Tanner vs Robert Wynter for sum of 20s.
510 John Rilie vs Richard Coles.
511 John Rilie vs Richard Coles for goods & chattels.
512 John Coles vs Thomas Selie.
513 John Browne vs Richard Coles.
514 John Goldsmyth vs Henry Walker.
Actions of trespass:
508 Gobbett vs John Heath.
509 John Heath vs Richard Coles.
Action of trespass on case:
484:2/2+ Jn Lock vs Rob. Banting.
Action of assumpsit:
506 Ralph Bradshaw vs Thomas Rew.

[f165 (Blank)*]*

[f165v]

(Recognisances for) Butchers (licensed in the borough.)[143]
515:1/2

Recognisance			*Fee*[144]
in £50	Michael Nursse	granted	12s.
in £50	John Coles	granted	12s.
in £50	Edward Barnes	granted	

143 The only heading given is 'Butchers'; these men are known butchers.
144 For comparable licence fees see B78/2, ff18,41v.

(Recognisances for Victuallers licensed in the borough.)[145]

515:2/2

Recognisance

£20	+Widow Nursse	granted
£20	+Widow Bruce	granted
£20	+Widow Mondi	granted
£20	Richard Meade	granted
£20	John Dissell	granted
£20	Thomas Blith	granted
£20	Michael Faux	granted
£20	Henry Rudgat	granted

Action of assumpsit of debt:

516 William Hix vs Edward Giles for sum of 20s.

Examination (criminal?).

517 25 February 1593. Thomas Grene of North Leigh ('Northly'), coper, sold a brown bay trotting mare, slit on top of the farther ear and half on the same, to Richard Carter of Oxford butcher in St. Peter Le Bailey ('in the bayley') aforesaid -- 31s 8d. (In margin:Thomas Francklen of the same county vouches T Grene.)

Action of trespass on case:

518 William Rathbone vs Richard Coles.

Action of debt:

519 John Dubber vs John Bull.

(End of text and paging.)

(On *f1r* are odd jottings on a few Portmoot actions: at the top of the page, and possibly dated 10 March (1596?), are three entries based on actions **501**, **502** & **503**; at the bottom of the page, and inverted, are two entries based on actions **296** and probably **117**.)

145 No heading given here; but all these persons are on the list **482**, except Widow Mondye replacing Michael Mondye, and Richard Meade.

APPENDIX 1

List of Officers at Portmoot Courts

This list gives the changes recorded in the officers attending these court meetings.
Ma = mayor; Cham = chamberlain(s); Con(s) = constables;
Tith = tithingmen; Ale-Ts = aletasters.

Portmoot Court 7 October 1588.

	Ma :Jn Pyman; No other officers listed.
21/10/'88	ditto ditto
9/12/'88	ditto; Cham: Thos Browne, Thos Prestman; Con: Ralph Bradshew; Tith: Jer White, Jn Wells, Jn Heth, Jn Dissell; Ale-T: Geo Fones, Nath Sharpe.
23/12/'88	as before plus Con:Humf James.
27/1/'89	as before except Cham:Hen Fletcher, Wm Metcalf.
24/3/'89	Cham. Hen Fletcher for Wm Metcalf.
13/10/'89	Ma: Jn Williams; Cham:as before; Cons: Jn Phillips & Jn Tailor; Tith: as before, with Hugh Hamon for Jn Wells; Ale-T: Jn Bruce sen for Geo Fones.

From Dec. '89 onwards variable numbers of supporting officers, with as few as 1 constable plus 2 tasters. Followed by full numbers in general from May 1590 onwards.

5 July 1590.	No supporting officers.
15 March 1591.	No supporting officers.
18 Oct. 1591.	Ma: Thos Browne; Chams: 2; Cons: 2; Tiths: 4.
20 Dec. 1591.	before Ma: Thos Browne & Wm Riley & Jn Pyman; Chams:2; Cons:2; Tiths:4; Ale-T: 1.

In this period variable numbers of supporting officers.

12 Feb. 1593.	No supporting officers listed.
26 Feb. 1593	ditto

Variable numbers of supporting officers.

11 June 1593.	Ma: Thos Browne; Cham: Jn Dubber, Ralph Bradshew; Cons:Fras Collingwood, Ric Meades; Tiths: Mich Nursse, Hugh Hamon, Thos Colgrave; Ale-Ts:Geo Fones, Jerome White.

17 Sept. 1593. No supporting officers listed.

1 Oct. '93.	Ma: John Williams.
15 Oct. '93.	Ma: Jn Williams; Chams:Ralph Bradshew, [blank]; Cons:Robt Banting, Ric Meades; Tiths:Thos Colgrave, Jn Bull, Geo Fones; Ale-Ts: [blank]

5 Nov '93.	Chams:Ric Wryt deputizing for Thos Duffild; No other supporting officers listed.
19 Nov. '93.	No supporting officers listed.
10 Dec. '93.	Cham: Jn Dubber.
21 Jan. 1594.	No supporting officers listed.
11 March '94.	ditto
22 April '94.	ditto
13 May '94.	ditto
27 May '94.	Chams:Ralph Bradshewe, Jn Dubber; Cons:Robt Banting, Ric Meades; Ale-Ts:Jer White, Geo Fones; Tith:Jn Heath, Jn Bull.
10 June '94.	No supporting officers listed.
9 Sept. '94.	ditto
23 Sept. '94.	ditto
21 Oct. '94.	Ma: Jn Williams; Chams: Ralph Bradshewe, Jn Dubber; Cons:Wm Rayer, Jn Dissell; Tiths: Wm Wells, Jn Janes; Ale-Ts: Jn Heath, Geo Fones.
2 Dec. '94.	No supporting officers listed.
16 Dec. '94.	ditto
13 Jan. 1595.	As for 21/10/94 with Tiths: Wm Wells, Jn Yanes, Jn Bruse, Jn Wilkinson.
3 Feb. 1595:	No supporting officers listed. As for: 17/3; 14/4; 28/4; 26/5; 16/6; 30/6; 14/7; 28/7; 1/9/'95. On 15 & 29 Sept. '95 neither presiding nor other officers were listed.
13 Oct. '95.	Ma:Wm Metcalf; other officers as for 13 Jan. 1595.
27 Oct. '95.	No supporting officers listed.
10 Nov. '95.	Cons: Jer White, Jn Heath; Tiths: Robt Bruce & Percival Pierson; Ale-Ts: Jn Bruce, Geo Fones.
24 Nov. '95.	No supporting officers listed.
8 Dec. '95.	No mayor listed.
22 Dec. '95.	Ma. :Wm Metcalf; Cham. :Ralph Bradshawe, Thos Bradshawe; Con. :Jer White, Jn Heath; Tith. :Wm Wells, Jn Yanes, Robt Bruce, Percival Pierson; Ale-Ts. :Jn Bruce, Geo Fones.

On five occasions, all in 1595, (14 & 28 July, 15 & 29 September, and 8 December) neither the mayor, nor another alderman, was recorded as the presiding JP at the Portmoot court. Presumably a JP did sit on those days, or at least an officer such as the town clerk or the sergeant-at-mace must have helped in conducting the proceedings. On 31 sittings, with 12 in the period March to October 1595, no officers other than mayor are listed. This record may reflect the lesser competence of Edulphe Dingley as town clerk after March 1594, perhaps in the recording as much as in ensuring attendances.

APPENDIX 2

Contents of WBM 77/1 including notes on Portmoot actions 1594-5

After two unnumbered folios there are 90 numbered folios in this book. A fair copy, in handwriting apparently matching that of one of Anthony Noble's hands, of the Portmoot courts 7 October 1588 to 17 September 1593 occupies *ff.1r-61r*. From there to *f.77v* the folios are blank. The rest of the volume is used turned top-to-bottom and working from the back towards the front of the book.

This latter record concerns Portmoot proceedings, but the occasional dates included are not Court days, and though some cases pre-date their appearances at Court others do not. Certain entries do not appear in B78/1 and for these full details are given here. Many cases correspond to actions in B78/1 but omitted from Bodl.d47 and for them their reference numbers are included.

These particular notes appear contemporaneous with the Courts and with the B78/1 records, and the handwriting here matches Edulphe Dingley's hand in that book.

Summary of Entries

ff. 90v & 90: (Blank)

f. 89v: 6 Dec. 1594 (Sat.), Eliz. 37.

383. John Kinge of Merton ('Marton') Oxon, husbandman qu. vs. Wm Haynes of Bladon, husbdmn., tresp.on case.

368.

Thos Barry of Chipping Norton vs. Wm Francis, trespass.

17 December 1594 (Tues.)

Ralph Townsend of Abingdon, Berks, qu. vs. Thos Higgins of Cowley, plaint of debt.

Robt Parran of Wootton, husbdmn. qu. vs. Thos Smyth of Long Combe, debt.

373, **374**, **377**, **390**.

Wm Metcalf qu. vs. Tymothe Hickes, tresp.on case.

Tymothie Hickes qu. vs. Wm Metcalf, tresp.on case.

George Howlbroke qu. vs. Thos Butcher, tresp.

392, **393**.

f. 89r: **394**, **397**, **399**, **398**, **369**, **400**, **401**, **402**, **403**, **404**, **405**, **406**.

Edmund Coulne qu. vs. Jn Hickes, tresp.

411, **412**.

Thos Browne qu. vs. Michael Vaux.

414.
Wm Harris & Queen vs. Fras Collingwood, debt *(Qui Tam).*
415, 416.
f. 88v: 1 May (1595), (Thurs.): **417, 418, 419, 420.**
13 May (1595) (Tues.): 421; 20 May (Tues.): **422, 423, 424, 425, 431**.
3 June (Tues.): **428, 429**.
15 June (Sunday): **430, 432, 434, 435, 436, 519, 437**.
12 August (Tues.): **443**.
2 September (Tues.): John Gregory qu. vs Wm Boreman, tresp.
f. 88r: **447**.
Jn Cowling qu. vs. Jn Hedges, debt.
448, 449, 450, 451, 452, 453, 454, 455.
6 October (Mon.): **456**; 7 Oct. (Tues.): **457**; 10 Oct. (Fri.): **458, 460**.
14 Oct. (Tues.): **461, 462, 469, 468, 463, 470**.
Ralph Bradshaw qu. vs. Wm Parsons, tresp.on case.
f. 87v: **465**.
Thos Norwood qu. vs. Benedict Norwood for goods & chattels, debt.
466.
George Whitton qu. vs. Robt Meades, tresp.
467, 471, 472, 473, 474, 475, 476, 477, 478, 479, 298, 480.
Wm Metcalf qu. vs. Jn Busbye, plt. debt.
Jn Phillips qu. vs. Ric Potter, plt. tresp.
f. 87r: 6 Dec. (1595) (Sat.):
Gabriel Wrett of county Worcester gent. qu. vs. Jn Coevill,
plt. debt both by his body and by his goods & chattels.
Edw Piddell qu. vs. Wm Busby, debt.
Jn Phillips qu. vs. Robt Sparrock, tresp.on case.
10 Dec. (1595) (Wed.): Robt Binckes qu. vs. Wm Fletcher, debt 40s.
485, 484, 483.
16 Dec. (1595) (Tues.): Edw Maul qu. vs. Thos Basely, debt for 36s 8d.
Michael Nurse qu. vs. Wm Fletcher, debt for 5s.

Of the 150 entries included in B78/1 but omitted in the Fair Copy in B77/1 with Bodl. d.47, 81 of them (all missing from d47) are referred to in these notes in the back pages (ff. 87r-89v) of B77/1. Also included here are 22 entries referring to plaints, perhaps not pursued, not mentioned in B78/1.

APPENDIX 3

Disposition of Portmoot Meetings in B78/1, B77/1 & MS. Bodl.d.47
In this concordance the page and folio numbers locate the bulk of each court's proceedings, but not always the start or the end. Within each court, entries are re-ordered to simplify presentation (see Editorial Note).

Court Date **1588-95**	Calendar p. No.	B78/1 *f.* Nos.	B77/1 *f.* Nos.
7/10/**1588**	1	2	1
21/10; 9/12	2	2v, 3	1v, 2
23/12; 13/1/**1589**	3	3v, 4	2v, 3
27/1; 3/3; 17/3	4	4v-5v	3v-4v
24/3; 7/4	5	6, 6v	5, 5v
21/4; 5/5;	5	(6a, 6av missing)	6-6v
5/5; 26/5	6	7	6v-7v
26/5; 9/6	7	7v-8v	7v-8v
23/6;	8	9, 9v	9, 9v
23/6; 14/7; 28/7	9	9v-10v	9v-10v
28/7; 11/8	10	10v-11v	10v-11v
11/8; 25/8	11	12, 12v	12, 12v
25/8; 8/9;	12	13-14v	12v, 13
8/9; 24/9	13	15-16v	13v, 14
24/9	14	16v-17v	14v
2/10	15	18-19v	15, 15v
13/10	16	20, 20v	16, 16v
13/10; 27/10	17	21-22v	16v, 17
10/11; 1/12	18	23-24	17v, 18
1/12; 15/12	19	24v-25v	18, 18v
12/1/**1590**; 9/2	20	26-28	19
2/3; 16/3	21	28v-30v	19v
30/3; 13/4	22	31-32	20, 20v
13/4; 27/4	23	32v-34	20v, 21
27/4; 11/5	24	34-35v	21v, 22
1/6; 15/6	25	36-37v	22v, 23
15/6; 6/7; 27/7	26	38-39	23, 23v
27/7; 10/8	27	39v, 40	24, 24v
10/8; 28/9	28	40v-41v	24v, 25
12/10; 26/10	29	42-43	25v, 26

Court Date **1588-95**	Calendar p.No.	B78/1 *f.* Nos.	B77/1 *f.* Nos.
26/10	30	44v	26v
9/11; 7/12	31	45v-46v	27,27v
20/12; 25/1/**1591**	32	47-48v	28, 28v
1/3	33	49,49v	29
15/3; 29/3	34	50-51	29v, 30
29/3	35	51v, 52	30
12/4; 17/5;	36	53-54	30v, 31
31/5; 14/6	37	55, 55v	31v, 32
28/6; 12/7	38	60; 60v	32v, 33
12/7; 26/7	39	61-62	33, 33v
26/7	40	62v-64v	34, 34v
9/8	41	64v-65v	35
23/8	42	66-67	35v
6/9	43	67v-68v	36v
20/9	44	69-70	37, 37v
20/9; 4/10	45	70v-72	38-40v
4/10; 18/10	46	72v, 73	40v,41
8/11; 22/11; 6/12	47	73v-74v	41v-42v
6/12; 20/12	48	74v, 75	42v, 43
10/1/**1592**	49	75v, 76	43v, 44
10/1; 24/1	50	76v-77v	44-45
21/2; 6/3; 3/4	51	77v-78v	45-46
17/4; 8/5; (22/5)	52	79-80	46,46v
5/6; 19/6	53	80v-81v	47, 47v
3/7; 17/7	54	82, 82v	48
31/7; 14/8	55	83-84v	48v, 49
28/8; 11/9	56	85, 85v	49v
9/10; 23/10	57	86v, 87	49v, 50
23/10; 6/11	58	87v, 88	50, 50v
6/11; 20/11;	59	88v-89v	50v, 51
20/11; 4/12	60	89v-91	51, 51v
4/12	61	91, 91v	52
4/12; 18/12	62	92-93	52, 52v
18/12; 8/1/**1593**	63	93v, 94	52v, 53
15/1; 29/1	64	94v-95v	53v, 54
29/1; 12/2	65	96, 96v	54, 54v
26/2; 12/3	66	97-98	55, 55v

Court Date **1588-95**	Calendar p. No.	B78/1 *f.* Nos.	B77/1 *f.* Nos.
12/3; 26/3	67	98v, 99	55v, 56
26/4	68	99v, 100	56v
28/5	69	100v, 101	57,57v
11/6	70	102,102v	57v, 58
11/6; 25/6	71	103,103v	58v, 59
9/7; 30/7	72	104,104v	59,59v
30/7; 13/8	73	105,105v	59v, 60
13/8; 27/8; 10/9	74	106-107	60,60v
10/9; 17/9	75	107-108	61
			MS.Bodl.d.47
1/10; 15/10	76	108-109v	3,3v
15/10	77	110-111	4,4v
5/11; 19/11	78	111v, 112	5,5v
19/11; 10/12	79	112-113	5v, 6
17/12	80	113v, 114	6v
7/1/**1594**	81	115,115v	7,7v
21/1	82	116,116v	8,8v
25/2; 11/3	83	117,117v	9,9v
11/3; 22/4	84	118,118v	9v, 10
13/5	85	119	10v, 11
27/5	86	119v-120v	11,11v
10/6; 24/6	87	121-122	12-13v
24/6; 15/7	88	122v, 123	14,14v
15/7	89	123v, 124	14v-16
15/7	90	125,125v	16-17
29/7	91	126v, 127	17, 17v
12/8	92	127v, 128	18, 18v
26/8	93	128v-129v	19, 19v
26/8; 9/9	94	130-131	20, 20v
9/9; 23/9	95	131v-132v	21, 21v
23/9; 7/10	96	132v-133v	21v, 22
7/10; 21/10	97	134,134v	22v-23v
21/10; 4/11	98	135-136v	23v, 24
4/11; 18/11	99	136v-138	24v, 25
18/11; 2/12	100	138v-139v	25v, 26
16/12	101	140-141	26v
16/12; 13/1/**1595**	102	141,141v	26v, 27
13/1	103	141v-142v	27v

Court Date **1588-95**	Calendar p. No.	B78/1 *f.* Nos.	MS.Bodl.d.47 *f.* Nos.
3/2; 17/2	104	143,143v	27v,28
17/2; 3/3	105	143v-144v	28,28v
17/3	106	145-146	28v,29
31/3	107	146,146v	29
31/3	108	147,147v	29v
31/3; 14/4	109	147v-148v	29v
14/4	110	148v,149	29v,30
28/4	111	149v,150	30v
26/5	112	150v,151	31
16/6	113	151v,152	31v
30/6; 14/7	114	152-153	32,32v
28/7	115	153,153v	32v,33
18/8; 1/9	116	154,154v	33,33v
15/9; 29/9	117	155,155v	33v,34
13/10	118	156-157	34,34v
27/10	119	157v,158	34v,35
27/10; 10/11	120	158-159	35v
10/11; 24/11	121	159v-160v	35v,36
8/12	122	160v-161v	36,36v
8/12; 22/12	123	161v,162	----
22/12	124	163v,164	----
22/12	125	164,164v	----
22/12	126	165v	----

INDEX OF PERSONS

Reference is made only to the first appearance in cases, which can then be followed in the text by case numbers in bold, e.g. **392**:1/6,2/6 etc.; there may be more than one entry for a name on the page.

References to pages in the introduction are in roman numerals. All numbers in the index refer to pages in this volume.

Standard abbreviations have been used for Christian names.

Abbreviations: ald., alderman; als., alias; alet., aletaster; bkr., baker; bro., brother; butch., butcher; carp., carpenter; chamb., chamberlain; chandl., chandler; chapm., chapman; clk., clerk; cloth., clothier; con., constable; counc., councillor; ct., court; d., died; dau., daughter; fam., family; fl., flourished; frmn., freeman; glov., glover; husb., husbandman; join., joiner; jun., junior; m., married; merc., mercer; sawy., sawyer; sen., senior; serg., sergeant-at-mace; shoem., shoemaker; sis., sister; s., son; tail., tailor; tan., tanner; tith., tithingman; twn-clk., town clerk; turn., turner; vctlr., victualler; wid., widow; w., wife; W., Woodstock; yeo., yeoman.

INDEX OF PLACES

Oxfordshire places are indexed without the county identification but other places are identified by the counties to which they belonged before 1974. In general, those places of litigants' provenance identified from sources other than the Portmoot texts are not included in this index. In the Introduction they are marked by asterisk, and most are mentioned on pages xxviii and xxxi.

INDEX OF SUBJECTS

Specific trades and occupations are grouped under the entry 'trades'; court and borough officers are grouped under 'officers'; references to other courts are collected under 'courts'; in the Portmoot the various plaints are grouped under 'actions', and the types of process under 'procedure' including a section on forms of writ.